I0146094

THE UNLIKELY SUCCESS

Two Stories From Men Who Have
Overcome (In)surmountable Odds
To Achieve Success On Their Own Terms

Written By:

James Wilson and Donel Poston

DEDICATION

THIS BOOK IS DEDICATED TO
ALL THOSE WHO HAVE FOUND
A WAY TO TRANSFORM PRISON
INTO SCHOOL AND PEN AND
PAPER
INTO TOOLS FOR MENTAL
FREEDOM.

"Those of us who nurture the lives
of those children who are not supposed to
exist, who are not supposed to grow up,
who are revolutionary in their very beings
are doing some of the most subversive
work in the world. If we do not know it,
the establishment does,"
- Alexis Pauline Gumbs

Introduction
Section

"Today's failures can be tomorrow's success."

Introduction

I am constantly reminded of a story one of my mentors told me about success. He was around 78 years old when he told me this. This is what he said:

> "There are 50 doors of success. 49 of them will
> be opened for you. But, the 50th door you must
> open for yourself."

I understood a few different things from this lesson he taught me: (1) There is more than one way to succeed, (2) people who are successful get help from others, and (3) there will be times you have to succeed alone (possibly because no one appreciates your success - and the plan to reach it - more than you do). I am aware that some (or many) will take offense at a former gang member, and prisoner, claiming that his life turned out as a "success story", and worthy to occupy the shelves with other books from authors whose own stories you may deem more worthy of your attention.

While I am certainly open to this criticism, I am more interested in, and inspired by, the following questions:

- What is the true definition of success for the millions of America's "failed" citizens who find themselves incarcerated for past criminal activity?
- Is redemption (and it's possibilities for success) truly possible?

In the hood (and in prison) "success" is as varied as it is in the world of law-abiding citizens. My mother was a law-abiding single parent woman, who worked most of her life. She raised seven children in the projects (the "ghetto"), which was overrun with drugs, gangs, and violence. Five of her children ran with a gang (one of them founded a gang), and six of us served time in jail or prison. Six of us are still alive, and only one of us (myself) is currently incarcerated. My mother is 74 years old, never saw a prison cell, worked most of her life, yet is poor and still living in the hood. Is this a success story?

While street, and prison life, is often glorified, and so many of us entered this "field" seeking a place at the "mythical top", the vast majority of us fail in this pursuit (the "top" being riches and hood fame). The rate of failure (in this regard) far exceeds the rate of "success".

What about those men and women who find a way, despite their past, "to snatch success out of the mouth of defeat," and make something out of the "nothingness" of their lives? That has to be worth something, right?

While I did not get rich, and only managed to gain some local "fame" (for terrorizing my own community), I have managed to:

1) Disavow gang membership.
2) Achieve sobriety.
3) Graduate from high school.
4) Read hundreds of books.
5) Write, and co-author, several books of my own.
6) Co-found five self-help groups for prisoners to rehabilitate themselves.
And, most importantly,
7) Stay alive.

Staying alive long enough to experience new things, including the desire and will to change, is a success in itself where I come from. Upon the death of her son, Tupac Shakur's late mother Afeni Shakur gave this seemingly simple advice to young people: "Just stay alive."

With life comes infinite likelihoods, including your own brand of success. What you will read about in this book is not new. This "unfortunate, but promising" concept was taught to us all of our lives. Remember Rudolph the Red Nose Reindeer, the Ugly Duckling, the Bad News Bears, and all the other underdogs that found their way to the top (whatever that meant for them).

Don't ever be counted out. It is said that most points in a World Series is scored with two strikes on the board. Step up to the plate, and take your swing. Who cares if the odds are against you?

By: James 'Ansar' Wilson

To The Reader

It is no coincidence (or mistake) that the numbers preceding each chapter increase in size as they progress in value.

Turning Points in History

Turning points (according to one historian) occur in history by one or more of the following reasons:

1. <u>Surprise</u> - Most people aren't prepared for what's going to happen.

2. <u>Conflict</u> - Not just physical conflict, but one of ideas. New ideas create new circumstances.

3. <u>Agency</u> - Things change because people take matters into their own hands.

4. <u>Crisis</u> - Opportunities arise out of difficult circumstances.

5. <u>Causes</u> - Events occur because of our actions, not from some remote control in outer space.

6. <u>Choices</u> - Decisions determine destiny.

Food For Thought

"A guy walks into a psychologist's office with a duck on his head and sits down, and the duck says, 'can you get this guy off my ass?'"

"When you're at the banquet of the gods, do not concern yourself with the food that's past you by; nor with the food you're yet to receive. Concentrate on the meal before you. When that ceases to matter, you are truly ready for the banquet of the gods."

"Life is interesting because of it's conflicts."

"James, you're never gonna walk away from gang banging until you find something else to be respected for.   - Charles Muhammad

"Those who have been hated have always held in their hands the things that other men love."

"Any dead fish can float downstream, but it takes a living fish to swim upstream."

"Kites rise by going against the wind, not with it."

"In order to lead the orchestra, the maestro must turn his back to the crowd."

"I grew up Black in America, a minority. In the streets I ran with a 'Blood' gang; the smaller group amongst rivals. I became a religious minority (Muslim) in a predominantly Christian nation. I know something about dealing with odds."

"It is not the critic who counts: not the man who points out how the strong man stumbles or where the doer of deeds could have done them better. The credit belongs to the man who is actually in the arena, whose face is marred by dust and sweat and blood, who strives valiantly, who errs, who comes up short again and again... who spends himself in a worthy cause; who, at the best, knows, in the end, the triumph of high achievement; and who at the worst, if he fails, at least fails while daring greatly."

                - Teddy Roosevelt

1

JAMES WILSON

Against All Odds

"There was no accident in your birth James." One of my mentors told me this after I expressed to him that it was my parent's choice to have me, and not mine. He then relayed the following story about the birth process to me:

> "At the time of conception there is about 500,000
> sperm cells emitted into the womb. One of them
> was you. All of these cells travel up the fallopian
> tube, racing to get to the finish line: the
> uterus. Many fall by the wayside. Others appear
> to sacrifice themselves along the way. The relative
> distance to the uterus for these cells is equivalent
> to the distance it would take a space shuttle
> to travel from Earth to the moon. You beat 1:500,000
> odds to get here at that long of a distance,
> and you think that was by accident?"

He went on to tell me that I was born "a winner", and that is how I had beat out all of the other cells, even without a fully formed brain. So, now that I have one, I shouldn't think, speak, and behave like a loser.

Recently I was watching PBS, and some guy was talking about the "hidden figures" (chances) of being born. He put it like this:

> "It was a one in 20,000 shot that your parents
> met, a one in 2,000 chance that these two unique
> people conceived a child when they chose to
> have sex, then a one in 400 quintillion chance
> that the right sperm met the egg (ovaries) of
> the woman."

There were other astronomical figures related to ancestry, and other related things, but I am sure you get the point. Like the late Tupac would say: "Against all odds."

Ancient Scriptures

On the subject of "pro choice birth", the Hindu's promoted the idea of reincarnation. Much of the time, we in the West quote this concept (in part) when we talk about "Karma". This word can not be separated from the full story, however. Karma is just the second part of a three part process.

The first part of the process is "Dharma". Dharma is the law of all creation. It is the "will" of the universe. It also preordains one's purpose. For instance, some people are born to be teachers, leaders, warriors, etc. If one does not fulfill their dharma, then the second condition (Karma) is applied. Karma (in a sense) is a debt against one's future transition. You "owe" the universe your dharma, so to speak, and you are forced to repay it through the third part of the process: Samsara. Samsara is the cycle of rebirth; the wheel of the dharma, in Buddhism.

In the Bible, "God" tells the prophet Jeremiah, "before you were in the womb, I knew you." Islam is not silent on this subject either. The prophet Muhammad is said to have been chosen 50,000 years before his birth. The Holy Quran states that "God" brought all of humanity from the loins of Adam at the beginning of creation and had them bear witness to the reality of "God".

Whatever the case, we are here. So, what are we gonna do? "You miss 100% of the shots you don't take," as it's said in basketball.

"Chances make champions."

Chapter One

Travailing In Birth

Originally from different parts of the deep South, my parents arrived in California some time after the Second World War. They were taking part in, what historians call, "The Great Migration". This was a period in American history when Black families were fleeing the racist and segregated South to find greener pastures, and safety. My father (Roosevelt Wilson) came from Arkansas, while my mother hailed from Louisiana. Coming from separate parts of the South, they nonetheless held similar interests, and met for the first time in Pasadena, California, around 1970.

Prior to meeting Roosevelt, my mother (Connie Piggee) had four children by two other men. Her first child was conceived when she was only 14 years old (Tyrone; 1961). Forced to leave school to manage her pregnancy while only an eighth grader made living at home with her mother (Johnnie Mae) almost unbearable. So, she left home to go it alone.

If I recall correctly, she moved in with a friend whom she described as a "bull dagger" (a lesbian). Although they were not sexually involved, my mother said that she was a trustworthy person who would watch her child as she ran the streets getting high on drugs, and partying. According to my mother, this came to an end when one of her girlfriends snuck out of the house to go to a party and died in a horrible car crash. This event woke my mother up, causing her to kick the drug habit, and stop running around with her friends so she could focus on raising her first born son.

Tyrone's father (Tony Ferdinand), at 22 years old, was eight years older than my mother. For a time they were "shacked up", and four years later a second son was born (Kenny; 1965). My mother decided to break up with Tony because (in her words) he was a "ladies man". One year later, the third son was coneived during a "one night stand" with a man named Robert Barnes (Damon; 1966). Without ever explaining why, my mother went back to Tony and a fourth child (Patrice) was soon born. My mother wasn't even 22 years old yet, and she already had four children.

Between my mother's fourth and fifth child (Jonathan; 1973), she claimed to have had several miscarriages, and at least seven abortions. My mother would explain later that this was "God's will" because "it was almost impossible to raise the seven kids who made it as it was being a poor single mother, living in the projects. The last two came in 1974 (myself), and 1979 (Jerome).

Apparently, my mother and father (Roosevelt) broke up for a short period (after she had already quit Tony for good) because Jonathan's last name on his birth certificate was "Thomas", not "Wilson" as mine and Jerome's was. In the end though, we all made it to become a family by the time my mother was 32 years old. Roosevelt would be the "father figure" all of my mother's kids laid claim to. He did not live with us, but he came around almost daily (usually after he left work). According to my mother, he was the supervisor at a company that made components for airplanes. Upon visits to his job, we paid little attention to this as we enjoyed stealing away to the dog pound next door to aggravate all of the dogs at the shelter.

My father lived with another woman named Mary Brooks, even though they had no children together. She was the sister of his best friend, Eugene. He had 14 years on my mother (he was born in 1933), and had children almost my mother's age from a previous marriage to a lady named Harper Wilson. Ironically, this woman became the manager of the housing project "The Community Arms" in Pasadena where my mother lives today.

One day, me, my brother Jonathan, and some of our "crew" stumbled across our father's "second" home (we never called it his first home) as youngsters while out stealing bikes on the other side of the city from where we lived. Both of his Cadillacs were parked in the stall of an apartment complex. My mother had pointed out Mary to us on several occasions, as Mary was privileged to his cars. This, while we had to catch city buses, especially when my mother had no car, or the one she had had broken down.

My mother told us that this was part of "his strategy" to keep her contained so no other man could discover her. He took us out of church because he felt that all preachers were pimps (like him), and preyed on the women of the community. Plus, he was an atheist. An issue that irked my maternal grandmother (Johnnie Mae), a Christian. He kept promising my mother that he'd leave Mary to come live with her and raise the youngest three kids. Something that never happened.

We lived in a low-income housing project called "The Kings' Manor". It was full of single parent mothers, drugs, and violence. This combination was only exacerbated when Crip and Blood gangs became popular in the late 70's, and crack cocaine hit the streets in the early 80's. The hood was set ablaze as drug dealers, crews, and gangs struggled for control over entire blocks, projects and cities. We grew up in a war zone. Life surrounded by death.

2

The Long Road Home

One day, a big fish was taking a small fish out in order to show him the ropes about hunting in the deep blue sea:

"See that line right there? At the bottom is
a sharp object called a hook. On the other end
of the line is a man. He is riding in something
called a boat. If you take the food on that
line you'll be snagged on a hook, and that man
will reel you onto his boat. He will hit you
with a stick, cut you open, and throw you into
an ice chest. Later, he'll take you to something
called a house. Once there, he will put you
into another cold place called a freezer. When
he gets hungry he will pull you out, let you
thaw out, and season you to taste. He has something
called a stove, and it produces fire. Next,
he will place you in a skillet on top of the
fire, and cook you. Then, he will eat you. In
his home is something called a bathroom which
has a thing called a toilet. One day, he will
sit on it and shit you out, and you will return
back to the sea, but you'll never be the same.
So, the short cut is the long way home. Don't
take the bait!"

A true story!

Some scientist doing an expirement (as they do) once bred a group of schooling fish. Throughout the breeding process the gene for "schooling" was bred out of them. Schooling is what gives these (usually smaller) fish the defense mechanism "survival by numbers" against larger mammals of the sea. By grouping, and swimming together (schooling), the chance that many of them will survive a feeding frenzy rises. When these "unschooled" fish were put in with a group of schooling fish, the latter group, against the better judgement of nature, began following the unschooled fish.

In another study, scientists put some Baracuta fish into a large aquarium. Down the middle they placed a clear partition. On the opposite side of the partition they placed the Baracuta's natural prey. Being able to see the food through the glass made the Barracutas run up against the partition in an attempt to get at them. After seeing that they couldn't penetrate the barrier they gave up trying. Eventually the scientists removed the partition, and both predator and prey were now swimming in the same aquarium peacefully. In the end, they all died in the midst of their own food.

"A fool will go thirsty in the midst of water."

Chapter Two

The Big Experiment

My mother had been on her own since she was a teenager, surviving by her wits, street knowledge, and internal will power. As a kid, our family was crammed into a four bedroom apartment in the Kings' Manor projects after the city paid families to move out of a residential complex directly across the street called "The Mortons". Later, The Mortons were "walled off" and upgraded, functioning like an oasis in a "desert" (the poorer surrounding neighborhoods, Kings' Manor being one). Naturally, it's occupants became middle class working families.

At the time, I had a White friend named Richard (we called him "Richie") who lived behind The Mortons' walls, just a short distance from my apartment in "the projects". Richie and I were classmates at Willard Elementary, the school we were both bused to. Willard was near the city of Rosemead, not too far from Cal Tech University (the college the characters from "The Big Bang Theory" worked at). Across the street from Willard was Wilson Junior High School.

Me, Richie, as well as the kids from the projects rode home together on the same school bus. The bus would pick us up, and drop us off, on Sunset and Hammond street; walking distance to the Mortons, and my front door. I had never asked Richie where he lived, finding out on my own while riding my bike.

I lived at 45 West Hammond Street. Jackie Robinson park and the back wall to the Mortons was the view from my front yard. One day, I saw Richie on a bike on the street that lead into the Mortons. Like kids do, our bikes merged together, and we rode throughout the Mortons enjoying ourselves. I wasn't unfamiliar with the area. Often, the other kids from the projects and I would invade back yards for bikes and other pricey things from inside it's walls.

After riding for a while, Richie stopped in front of a driveway. I could see a lady at the door of the house as she called to him. He beckoned me to follow, so I dashed into the house behind him. The lady didnt try to stop me, and I barely looked into her face that day. I was around eight years old at that time in 1982-83.

Their dwelling was in stark contrast to my own. they had two nice cars

12

in the driveway, and a well manicured lawn out front. I later learned that
I was (as was everyone) supposed to take my shoes off at the door prior to
entering their home. There were beads draping every doorway of the home, and
the living room was immaculate; almost appearing off limits. I remember a
huge fish tank full of colorful fish in that room that me and Richie would
peer through from opposite sides, examining it's contents.

Richie was an only child, so he had his own room. It was a kid's paradise.
He had his own T.V. with a gaming console set on top of it (probably an Atari).
He had his own smaller fish tank with bubble's percolating in it, and a group
of sea horses and other small fish. He also had a well organized set of Star
Wars action figures, and a remote controlled racing track.

I never brought anyone to Richie's home with me. It was my secret. When
I did go, his mother would feed us sandwiches, cookies, and punch. From my
point of view, his mother welcomed my presence. I could show up anytime, knock
on the door, and she'd let me in. "Richie, James is here!", she'd call. His
father (a pot-bellied, short, White man) rarely spoke to me. He mostly did
work in their garage, or retired to his room to watch television. Leaving
Richie's driveway I could see directly into Kings' Manor. There was no physical
partition between our communities. The barrier was in our minds. Once I crossed
Hammond Street, I was in another world.

During this time, P.C.P. was the popular drug in my community. The projects
were like a round-the-clock party. There were always fights, and police cars
zooming around in pursuit of someone running on foot. People would yell "Rollers!"
(slang for cops), and drug dealers would scatter like the roaches when the
lights are turned on (something I never saw in Richie's home).

Two of my brothers (Kenny and Damon) were teenage drug dealers at the
time. My mother had a zero tolerance for drugs in her home, so she would constantly
be arguing with, and chastising, them. Even kicking them out of the house
on many occasions. They were both constantly in and out of juvenile detention
facilities. I remember going with my mother to court appearances for them,
and to Juvenile Hall for visits. They eventually graduated to becoming crack
dealers (1884/85), finding themselves in and out of the county jail in Los
Angeles, then the same later with prison for selling cocaine.

Damon had taken a step forward, leaving Sherm (P.C.P.) for Primo's (weed
mixed with crack), then maturing into smoking "Coke" out of a pipe. This turned
him into a thief, and a scoundrel. To fund his habit he would steal from our

13

Daniel Webster Primary Schools
Pasadena Unified School District

Kindergarten Diploma

This certifies that James Wilson

has completed Kindergarten at

Daniel Webster Primary School

on this ███ day █████ 1981

Miss Murphy/Mrs. Flood
Teacher

Principal
Geralayne Fillhart

14

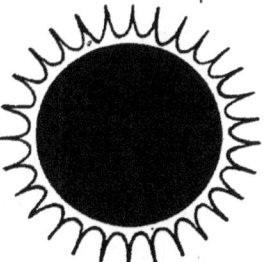

This is to certify that

James Wilson

has completed the required course of study at

Willard School and is therefore entitled to this

Diploma

Given at __8:45 a.m.__ this __18th__ day of __June__ 1984

PRINCIPAL

TEACHER

© VA704

COPYRIGHT, 1973, HAYES SCHOOL PUBLISHING CO., INC., WILKINSBURG, PA.

15

brothers, mother, and rob other drug dealers. It wasn't just our home though. The streets were full of "Damons". He earned the nickname "Sleprock" (bad fortune) for being a menace to the community.

Back then, many of the drug dealers smoked Primos, doing well for themselves in the dope game. The ones that had discipline could even become "ballers", or "high-rollers". A lot of them lost their footing, took to the pipe, and went down the drain. They hit rock bottom, literally.

Around 1984, my mother decided to get off of welfare and go back to school to get a job. The goal was to get all of us out of the projects. Crack had caught up with her own siblings. Many of our cousins were on it. Dozens of my friends had parents that succumbed to the drug, as well. My mother going back to school to better our situation had, for her, unintended consequences though.

While my mother was at night school, the house was fair game. My sister Patrice would play host to all of the local gang members and drug dealers. She was also pregnant with her first daughter. At the same time, Damon would be high on crack and trying to teach me how to masterbate so I could "fuck bitches" (as he put it). Shoot outs were taking place inside the projects, and at the park across the street. Now, the gang warfare was picking up (1984/85). It wasn't just about our "colors" (red and blue). It was now about the green: money.

The 1980's cemented community division all throughout America. Black and Brown neighborhoods went up in smoke - gun smoke and pipe smoke. It was an inferno. We had followed the "unschooled".

I can't tell you how many funerals our community attended. Death became a normal part of daily life. We were being "schooled" by a daily social curriculum of how to self-destruct. Just a decade-and-a-half prior (1965-75) our ancestors were in the street marching for civil rights, and Black liberation, and here we were throwing it all back. Our "gene" of self-love, protection, and preservation had been suppressed. We were feeding on each other now. No longer were our enemies outside of the community. We were our own worst enemies. We no longer "schooled" together. The game, instead, was to "skool" each other in all the wrong things.

Kids were dropping out of school to hustle, and get that fast money, in wholesale numbers. They saw it as a shortcut to fortune. While all this was going on, legislatures were making harsher laws based on the "new science"

16

of the "criminal" gene, and super-predator pseudo-science myths. These laws would empty our communities of potential leaders, fathers, mothers, and life coaches. Prison became the long way home, and drugs and gangs were the bait. We took it "hook, line, and sinker", while unbeknownst to us, Pasadena had one of the oldest Black middle class communities surrounding it (not too far from the Rose Bowl, the Supreme Court, "Old Town" Pasadena, and even some in The Mortons itself). We were going hungry in the midst of plenty.

We had not taken the baton from those before us. We had dropped it. While I lost touch with little Richie, I am sure he grew old right across the street from our living hell, secure in his paradise, a walk (or wall) away.

In the Book "Psychic Trauma", the author 'Sultan' (whom I met later at a Masjid in 2003) documented that the housing units we call "projects" began simply as that; a social experiment - a project! City planners got together with scientists to build "enclaves" to test out the theory of how many people could live in the smallest space, with limited resources, "before" they started fighting with eachother.

They had first tested their theory using mice in modeled living quarters. As expected, the mice (being cramped together and short on food) soon turned aggressive, and began fighting with eachother. The project was a "success". Up went low-income housing projects all across the United States. Down went life expectancy, quality of life, political aspirations, and school graduation rates. The "man" ate us up and shit us out. We haven't been the same since.

3

Not A Conspiracy

There was once a king who, after succeeding his father, his family ruled their country for over a hundred years. The king decided to celebrate his family's successful reign by throwing a great party. He invited all of his friends and supporters to join in this celebration, but amongst his friends were some of his enemies. they came to kill the king.

They offered him liquor, but he turned it down. He was not a man given to wine. They offered him drugs, but again he refused. His enemies (being wise and undeterred) decided to offer him some beautiful women, which he gratefully accepted.

He went into his chambers with them, and some offered him liquor, which he took. He drank to his heart's content. Others offered him the same drugs he had first rejected, and he gladly took them. Before you knew it, his Highness was high. At his lowest point, his enemies besieged him and his country, and it looked like he did it all to himself!

Remember: we are only as strong as our weaknesses. The enemy will attack where we lack!

What did our community lack? Awareness! Our light had dimmed. As it's said: "In the country of the blind, the man with one eye is King." We spent an entire generation teaching our people that "we shall overcome", but after some progress, we lost sight of the enemies of freedom, justice, and equality. "The greatest trick the devil has performed is to make people believe he doesn't exist." You can't protect yourself (or fight against) an enemy you can't see.

Heroine, P.C.P., and crack cocaine entered our community through the hands of memeber of the U.S. government. That is a conspiracy fact! They had a plan. In the 80's the U.S. government traded drugs, oil, and weapons to fund wars across the world. That is America's "G.O.D." (Guns, Oil, and Drugs).

There is an old saying: "Fatherlessness leaves holes that only demons can fill." Our forefathers, ancestors, and leaders were taken from us (imprisoned, assassinated, delegitimized), and their absence was filled with drugs, weapons, gangs, and division - demons. We must get our kingdom back. We must learn how to rule again by Good Orderly Direction!

"If you want to be light, you must withstand some burning."

Chapter Three

Out Of Control

Fed up with my shit, my mother kicked me out of her house when I was just 14 years old. By this time, we had been evicted from the projects and moved to another crime ridden part of the city of Pasadena (Parke Street). This was actually a street I was familiar with. My mother played Blackjack at a home on this street, and me and my brothers would come check on her when she stayed over night, gambling.

The house we eventually moved into had previously been occupied by my sister's baby-daddy, and his family. I was 12½ when we got there. Just prior to this, we had gone through a period of homelessness where we were sleeping inside my father's work truck. There were days we only had the food my mother brought home from working at school cafeterias. The truck was parked in my aunt's driveway. She refused to take us in, even though my mother had done her, and her kids, the same favor before. We were only allowed to shower and dress in the home. It was in the hood on Montana Street. There was no escaping.

For a while, we found a spot in Altadena, California, on Olive Street. Being from Pasadena, we had fights all the time at school, because all of the kids were Crips. It didn't work out. After a few more stops, we landed on Parke Street.

I found a girlfriend and tried to practice "fucking bitches", as my brother skooled me to do. My mother told me that I was "smelling my own nuts" (feeling myself). Then, I discovered the world of marijuana and started dreaming big. My sister and her friends from the local gang would get me high, and teach me gang signs. Soon, I was being skooled on the dope game by a female cousin, whose mother kept her in dope houses, chasing crack. She learned well, and she passed on the game to me. I scored sacks from my sister, and later from older homies on the block. I got caught, and sent to Juvenile Hall, and the rest is history.

They raided my mother's house to get me. She was confused and incensed, and I lied. My mom told me that, "God looks out for fools and babies." She told me that I wasn't slick, and she had seen better men in her days try, and fail, at what I was attempting. My father had prophesied: "James, you're gonna suffer the most out of all the kids." Obviously, I refused their counsel.

I pledged to the gang while in Juvenile Hall, and came home addicted to weed, drug dealing, and now I had a gang habit. Drugs bought me cars, motorcycles, guns, clothes; and brought me more trouble than it was all worth. Also, More than my mom could tolerate. "Stop what you are doing, and be a kid and let me raise you, or get out", she told me. I packed my belongings in bags with the help from a homie, and walked out the front door into a cruel, and heartless, world.

I posted up at my homie's house for a few days. They lived on Euclid Street, and had lived just behind us in the projects for years. I knew the entire family, and was welcomed to camp out. However, I was not down with the curfew policy that his mother enforced. The darkness ruled the streets, and I was a partner with the darkness.

I began sleeping in a Cadillac I had bought from an older drug dealer, then shower and dress at my homie's house, and faked going to school. I showed up at the Junior High School (which sat right across the street from the elementary school I had attended) just to flaunt my new clothes, pockets full of money, and new car. I thought I had "arrived".

Gang-banging brought more attention than selling drugs ever did. I could outmaneuver the cops, but the gang rivals operated by different schedules, and tactics. The Crips were a smaller, and more mobile, force. They were less recognizable, and usually went unseen. It was far more effective than an undercover cop. They could take you by surprise at any moment.

The "famine" hit around 1987-88. There was a dope drought due to huge drug seizures by the Feds, and consistent shifts in drug bosses and prices. The game increasingly became shady. With our neighborhoods' shrinking economies, people turned to "jacking" (robbing) drug dealers for cars, money, and jewelry. These crimes were mostly done in the neighborhood one belonged too, which only increased the inter-community conflict. There was overlapping gang, drug, and personal wars. It was within this environment that I tried to thrive.

Relying on all the game I picked up inside my sister's bedroom where the "hitters", movers, and shakers hung out, I hit the ground running. I had a vehicle, money, guns, and a supplier that had a surplus of inventory while others were hampered by the higher drug prices due to the relative drug shortages. One of the older guys I'd grown up with (who had killed one of the homies who had tried to rob him, and got off on self-defense) had a long sack (drug supply). He wasn't a tough guy, but with all of the guns floating around our neighborhoods, he didn't need to be to take a life. The most important thing was that he trusted me. He knew I took no sides in his dispute, like some had. He would take me to his spots (drug houses) across freeways, and let me sit in while he and his crew members cooked kilos of cocaine. This meant that I could get a healthy dose of "work" for a little bit of nothing.

I also had an older Crip drug connect who was a good friend of my older brother's, and related to some of my homies. He had a big sack too. He took a liking to me, and loved my mother, so he tried to shelter me. However, I wanted drugs, not nurturing. On top of these connections, I was dipping into the sacks of older "ballers" around my mother's house (I had scoped where they would hide their drugs all throughout Parke Street). I survived the famine with help, and treachery.

In the course of my trek, men were dying and getting snatched up by the Feds on drug trafficking charges. I fell into a depression, and started using Sherm. The weed, Sherm, and liquor was my attempt to medicate my pain, but it also made me careless, so I began catching one drug case after another. Then, I got caught up in a gang shooting, causing me to be flagged by the police.

My need to get high was bringing me lower by the day. Once, they even came to the school to arrest me for pulling a gun on someone in the restroom. The stakes were getting higher. Luckily, I had hidden the gun in a wall-encased fire extinguisher. I had gotten away with that one, but I could no longer play at being a kid. I was playing with the big boys, and I would be held to the same set of rules. I was out of my mother's house, and out of control.

I had grown up as a chubby kid. After a few trips to Juvenile Hall though, I began turning that fat into some muscle. It added to my feined adult persona. I also trimmed down around my waist. Usually a reserved and introverted child, the drugs and gang-banging acted to augment my "flaws" while, at the same time, putting me on center stage.

I fell right in to my chosen world, but I was falling out with the courts, and my probation officer (who was eager to show me that he was boss). I slipped, and fell into his hands, and eventually was in custody long enough to get better at being worse. I didn't get my "King dome" (mind) right.

4

No Hurt, No Big Shirt

The Honorable Elijah Muhammad told his followers a story about a donkey who fell down into a ditch. Every time people would pass by this donkey, they would throw stones at him. They threw so many stones that it created a pile, and one day that donkey was able to walk out of that ditch. "For every knock there is a boost," he said.

Another way of putting the moral to this story is: turn stumbling blocks into stepping stones. Here is a list of stumbling blocks:

- Racism
- Abuse
- Humiliation
- Low Self-Esteem
- Fear
- Anger
- Drugs
- Violence
- Gangs
- Prison
- Abandonment
- Insecurity
- Rejection
- Poverty

Obviously, the list could go on.

In the Book of Beginnings (The book of Genesis), "God" comes to this old man in his home country of Babylon. The man's name was Abraham. At the time, Abraham was 75 years old. "God" tells him to leave his country and travel to an unknown land (Canaan/Palestine). Once there, "God" promised to bless him enormously, so the man packed up and left.

"God" had promised him land, and a child, even though his wife (Sarah) was barren (infertile). On the way to Canaan he faced many difficulties (or, barriers) to "God's" promises. There was famine in the land. When he arrived in Egypt, his wife was kidnapped by the king. His nephew (Lot) was kidnapped next, and Abraham had to fight a war to get Lot back from the kings who had taken him. Did I mention already that he was old, and his wife was barren? Yeah, he had to go through some stuff to obtain "God's" promise (success).

This is kind of how life works. Nothing good comes easy. "In order to be something, you gotta go through something", as Shirley Murdock sang in her song "No Pain, No Gain". This was one of my mother's favorite songs in the mid-80's. She blasted it in the house while drinking hard liquor, and (most likely) to send a message to my deadbeat dad.

The root word for Abraham is 'Abar'. Abar means to "cross over" some dangerous passage, or course. Every man has his "Rubicon to cross," as it's been said. Life is a trial.

Check This "Build" Out

The Holy Quran says: "And we delivered Abraham and Lot and directed them to the land we blessed for the nations." Remember what we learned about Abraham. All 3 major religions trace their origins to Abraham (Judaism, Christianity, and Islam). These are the legacies, the success stories, of Abraham's descendants:

- His first son, Ishmael was the progenitor of a group of Arabs (Kedar) whom Muhammad descended from, and therefore ISLAM. Kedar means Black, as were the original Arabs.
- His second son, Isaac, fathered Jacob who became Israel. Israel had 12 sons, one called Judah, which Judaism sprung. (Genesis 29).
- Judah was the tribe from which Jesus came through, and therefore Christianity.

Further Insight

- Abraham's first name (Abram) contains ARAB if you remove the M and rearrange the last 4 letters. He had 3 wives and 1 was an Arab (Genesis 25) - Keturah
- The first part of his name ABR is synonomous with EBER, the tribe Abraham came from, and the name that creates children of Eb'r/Eber of the HEBRews. His first wife was a Hebrew named Sarah (Sarai). (Gen 10).
- The last part of his name HAM is the Biblical name for black people. Ham was the second son of Noah, and he fathered the Cushites (Ethiopians), Mizram (Egyptians), Canaanites (Now called Palestinians), and put (Lybians and some East Africans). - See Gen. 10:6-12 with footnotes. He also had an Egyptian wife named Hagar, who was a princess.

There is so much to a name!

"We didn't go from rags to riches, but rags to ditches."
- James Wilson

Chapter Four

The Long Tale Of A Short Story

One of the beauties of life is that if you live long enough, you can measure your growth; not just in how long you lived, but by how much you have actually learned. By depth, rather than length. With time comes more knowledge, and experience, the net result being more dimension and an enhanced perspective. I am in awe of life. This has not always been the case, however.

Honestly, I anticipated dying before I was 18 years old from either drugs, or gang-banging. Once 18 passed, the next "deadline" was 21. I am 46 at the time of this writing, so I count myself lucky.

My once dismal attitude about life, however, was not simply a subjective reality. Statistically, the most endangered age group for African Americans is between the ages of 16 and 25. I know this to be true because I lived this objective reality, growing up in the most dangerous area in America: the hood.

I know too many young people who did not make it out of their "teens and betweens", and not just from my neighborhood, but hoods all throughout California - America's war zones. I met most of these young people as prisoners of war in one, or more, of America's concentration camps: Juvenile Hall camps, Youth Authority, county jails, and prisons. My own entry into one of these juvenile facilities began at the age of 13, and once started, it never stopped.

Different hoods brought us to the same location(s). In captivity we got a chance to see, despite the color of our rags (gang affiliation, etc.), that we had much in common. However, commonality could not overcome centuries of one of America's more enduring legacies: Black self-hatred. Setting aside ancestry, the majority of us were poor, grew up in broken homes, did not value education, accepted violence (usually Black-on-Black violence) as a problem-solving method, suffered abuse of every kind, and could rattle off a list of our fallen "soldiers" (our dead homies). The roll-call of the living served as a predictor for life's outcome.

We were kids who knew more about deprivation, destruction, and death than we did concerning life, and all of it's possibilities. Worse than our survivors' guilt was our inordinate predilection for all things death; moral, social, mental, and physical. When I was 14 years old, my mother told me, "James, you have a death wish!" She had concluded that I wouldn't make it to see my 18th birthday.

In 1989, at the age of 14, I was committed by a court to a Juvenile Detention sentence. I stayed in custody until three months shy of my 18th birthday (1992). Once I paroled, I resumed "chasing a bullet" (as my mother would always put it). I was free for only two weeks before "violating" my parole for possession of a firearm, and was sent back to California Youth Authority (C.Y.A.).

One day, I called home and my mother told me that one of my friends was killed the night before. When I asked, "who?", her response was, "the kid you and your brother used to fight all the time." It turns out that it was a boy I knew named Jinx. He was 17 years old when he was murdered.

During the course of this, and other conversations from jail, she told me: "I am so happy you are in jail. Now I can rest, knowing that you are alive, and not dead in the streets." After I turned 18 in jail, my mother said: "Jail saved your life, James." Two years later, I was back out and chasing bullets once again. I lasted two months on the streets this time (1994). I was arrested again for gun possession at 19 years old.

As I was no longer a minor, now I was sent to the Los Angeles County Jail with the "big boys". I paroled five days shy of my 21st birthday. Less than 40 days later, I was back in county jail for chasing someone down with a gun, loaded with bullets with his name on it. My victim was only 17 years old (1996). Kids were having kids, and kids were killing kids where I was from.

Instead of being killed by 21, I was the one that did the killing. It was never lost on me, however, that, "today's killer could be tomorrow's homicide victim." My brother Jonathan was actually killed by Jinx's brother. A Black man's life story is too often a short story!

5

Just Dying To Live

In many poor communities, pregnancies and families are rarely planned.
This is in addition to the concept of "Accidental Birth": the impossibility
of choosing the family one is born into. "We choose our friends, not our family,"
as the saying goes.

To add some dimension to the story/theory, I want to offer some insight
on this subject from "The Sleeping Prophet", Edgar Cayce. On the subject of
reincarnation, he said:

> "...An infant attracted to a new body becomes
> a soul in the flesh when it draws it's first
> breath. Recognizing the growth opportunity implict
> in reincarnating, many souls want to enter the
> Earth plane, but may or may not be attracted
> to a particular family. Some souls may even
> be repelled by a given incarnation opportunity.
> When a soul incarnates and then is suddenly
> repelled, perhaps by a chance in circumstances,
> the soul withdraws and the child dies."

Basically, the child commits a form of pre-birth suicide if it elects not
to incarnate into a particular family.

The late African American scholar Bobby Wright wrote in "The Psychopathic
Racial Personality" that far more Black people are willing to take their own
lives now than at the height of slavery, when life seemed unworthy of living.
Mr. Wright also goes on to suggest that "suicide by other names" have just
as much validity as when a person takes his own physical life. The increased
reliance on dangerous drugs, gang-banging, and the apparent lack of will to
come together as a people to solve the crises that cripple our self-interest,
and survival, made the list for his "suicide by other names".

Mr. Wright saw racism as the root cause of Blacks' unwillingness to
live, and worked to have racism seen as a public health crisis that was ruining
the lives of Black Americans. He also believed that racism should be viewed
as a mental health issue. The man was obviously ahead of his time, as what
he was proclaiming in the 1980's has only recently become accepted in the
mainstream (in 2020-21, several states, after Black Lives Matter protests,
declared racism a public health crisis).

The famed pastor, and leader of "The Repairers of the Breach," William

Barber makes it clear that politicians are legislating death by the policies that they enact. These policies keep millions of poor White, Black, and Brown citizens locked into poverty due to a lack of livable wages, little to no health care access, homelessness, and student loan debts. Shorter life spans are even associated with lack of education, and the zip code you reside in.

Minister Louis Farrakhan, the leader of the Nation of Islam (N.O.I.), teaches that European powers are fulfilling the Biblical prophecy of "The Pale [White] Horse", whose rider brought death and hell, and was given the power to kill with the sword, hunger, and all forms of death and the beasts of the earth. William Cooper, in his book "Behold A Pale White Horse", unveils the plan of the United States government to destroy Black people with drugs, gangs, disease, and other policies of extermination (also called "population control"). Lindovist even discusses this drive to exterminate people of color in his book "The Dead Do Not Die".

If Edgar Cayce is to be believed, then millions of Black people choose to incarnate into families despite the odds against them, to fulfill their purposes on Earth. The fear of death "by a million cuts" is not a strong enough repellant. We choose life by all means necessary, even in the face of death.

"Everybody has a plan until they get punched in the face."
                                        - Mike Tyson

Chapter Five

The Battle Within

Before it was all over, I blew over six years of my teenage, and young adult years, in Juvenile Detention Facilities. Two girlfriends I had been with had also sought abortions rather than attempt a single parent existence. They knew that I was unwilling to be a "stay at home dad", to say the least. I was married to the game. Jail was my "home".

I maxed out my time (served my maximum sentence) at the Youth Training School (Y.T.S.) in Chino, California, five days before my 21st birthday, after doing my first stint in L.A. County Jail awaiting the parole board's decision. I knew I was headed back, so I didn't get my hopes up. Both my mother, and current girlfriend, would come visit me often; my girlfriend trying to leverage her pregnancy against my predilection for an early funeral. I lied and said I'd do better when I was released. Rightfully, neither of them believed me.

All was not lost though. During my second violation (at 17 years old) I converted to Islam, prior to going back to the C.Y.A. Reception Center in Norwalk, California. I was still under 18 during this stint, so I was in Juvenile Hall. Due to my size, all the staff thought that I was an adult and just hiding my age. Luckily, one of the counselors I knew from Mira Loma Camp in Lancaster where I served time at age 15 was now working at the Juvenile Hall I was sent too. We called him "Spike Lee" because he favored his look, and talked about Black history and politics when I was really not yet on that page. He hired me as a unit worker. This was in Silmar Juvenile Hall in the fall of 1992.

One day, a group of new arrivals came in from East Lake Juvenile Hall (located in East L.A.), and I noticed that one of my gang rivals was in the bunch. After staff gave them their orientation and bed rolls, they were sent to their rooms. I decided to follow my rival to his room, and I told him where I was from. I had met him in East Lake, but it was obvious that he didn't remember me. He shrugged his shoulders, so I attacked him violently. By the time I left the room, he was on the floor squirming in pain. During dinner, he showed up to the dayroom, swollen. The staff didn't recall if he'd arrived this way or not, so they called East Lake to discover the source, and the time, of his injuries. They sent him to the infirmary.

The next day, "Spike Lee" came to my room early in the morning before work, and said, "I am disappointed in you. Come with me." I followed him through the staff office to the side of the unit that was reserved for inmates in lock up (the hole). At this point, he told me to step into a room. I complied, and he shut and locked the door.

The window I had in this room was reverse tinted, so I couldn't see out of the window but others could see inside. Moments later, several counselors, and my victim, appeared before the glass. I heard, "is that him?" The dude apparently shook his head in the affirmative, then was lead away. He had snitched me out. After the line up, I was read my rights, and told that the incident was being referred to the courts for possible new charges. Pictures were taken of my hands, then I was taken to a permanent cell, given bedding, and told I'd be there until a court decided my fate. About an hour later my door opened. It was "Spike Lee". He tossed two books onto my bed and said, "read these", before closing the door behind him.

The two books were "The Autobiography of Malcolm X", and "Nigger" by Dick Gregory. At this time, I wasn't much of a reader. On my first C.Y.A. term I had read all of the Donald Goines street novels, and then the Bible; that was it. During that term and on my unit in Fred C. Nelles School for Boys (1990-92) had been two Black counselors: Bo Jay and Kalifonte. Bo Jay was a member of the Nation of Islam, and "Kal" was a former Black Panther. They would bring books in for us to read. It is the first time I saw "Message to the Black Man" by Elijah Muhammad, or learned about "The Panthers". Kal would bring in photo albums full of pictures of Black men with big afros, raising their fist and striking militant poses.

None of that appealed to me at that time. This was around the time of the L.A. Rebellion ("Riots") in the spring of 1992. I was only interested in gang-banging and would say, "I aint with none of that Black shit." It is what I would tell "Spike Lee" years earlier when he worked in the youth camp I was housed at. Years later I would read about Kal in the book "A Taste of Power", by Elaine Brown. Kal was once a member of the street gang "The Slauson Boys" (a precursor to the Bloods and Crips). The gang, under the leadership of Bunchie Carter, transitioned into the ranks of the Black Panther Party for self-defense in 1969. While in prison, Bunchie Carter (like Eldridge Cleaver) was a minister in the Nation of Islam. According to Colton Simpson, in his book "Inside the Crips" and other sources (e.g., "F.B.I. War Against Tupac and Other Black Leaders", John Potash), Bunchie also helped write "Constitutions"

for prison organizations ran by street gangs (trying to politicize then as they entered prison in the 60's).

Kal's street name was 'Bird'. He wore a beret to work, and both he and Bo Jay tried to school us youngsters. We would have none of it, however. The closest Bo Jay got to reaching the brothers was a group running around "the cottage" (housing unit) saying they were a part of the "Nigga's of Islam". After the L.A. "Riots", some gang members caught the "peace treaty" wave and became pro-Black.

After "Spike Lee" left, I opened the "Nigger" book and read it. It took a few days, and it reminded me of much of my own growing up poor. Although I wasn't running from K.K.K. members in the Deep South, I was running from the cops within my own community for things both deserved, and undeserved. I related to the poverty his family endured. It was the first time I understood what Martin Luther King Jr., and the Civil Rights' Movement, was all about. A pin drop of light had seeped into an ocean of darkness.

The Malcolm X book sat me up. I read it, and it made me angry at White people. I became disillusioned with Christianity, and the process by which my ancestors were "force converted" into that religion. I decided to go to the small church service held in the hole to try some of this stuff out for myself. From age 14-15 I had read the Bible, and the European depictions of those like Jesus, angels, and "God" were all White people - European people in the heart of the Middle East, a land of people of color. I never once questioned this in my head. I had no academic references to do so.

My grandmother (Johnny Mae) was a "standard" Black Christian who talked about Jesus saving us from Hell, but she couldn't get off P.C.P, Night Train, and cocaine. Jesus could only save us after we died. In the American "world", the county check and White power structure was "God". Church was a joke, and a fashion show. Later, my mom would become "Born Again" and our relationship would deteriorate further.

I went to the service with the intent of finding out if what Malcolm X said was true. There was all White women there that day. They passed out pamphlets with pictures of White Jesus on the front. I pounced. "Is this a real picture of Jesus?", I asked. Startled by my question, everyone (wards of the state included) turned and looked at me. Neither knew where I was going with my inquiry. There were Black, White, and Latino wards sitting around the circle in the small dayroom. I am sure, subconsciously, all of them thought

34

that this White man "Jesus" was going to save them from court, and give them a second chance, as I had often prayed.

The lady closest to me reached over as if to console me. "Oh, Jesus is the son of God," She started. I interrupted: "No, is Jesus White?". The next lady took her turn. "God has no color," she said. I shot back, "was Jesus a Hebrew?" Someone said, "yes," so I continued: "And weren't the Hebrews Black?" I knew my comment hit the mark because they laughed with cheshire smiles. "Yeah, they were dark in complexion," they conceded, "kind of like him." She pointed to a Latino. "But, he wasn't White like the man on this booklet?", I pressed. They said that he wasn't, and that they'd talk with their church about changing the picture. I never went back, and after the courts didn't pick up new charges against me I was transferred back into the Youth Authority system. Still gang-banging, but now open to reading "Black shit".

Later, I would meet a brother from san Diego ("C.K. Bill"; R.I.P.) at the reception center, who was into Reggae music, didn't eat pork, and told me that he was a Muslim. He was a Piru (Blood), and 17 years old like myself at the time (1992). He would often sing Bob Marley songs to me and interpret the lyrics so I'd understand the historical and political significance of what Mr. Marley was saying. It caught my attention when the doors were closed, but during program time it was all about "banging".

When I went up north to Preston C.Y.A., I met two more Muslims. One a Crip (Barbie) from "Four Duce" and the other (Poppa) from "Black Stone", a Blood. They saw that I had a lot of influence with other gang members and approached me about doing Sutra (security) for them while they prayed. I had never seen someone pray as Malcolm had described in his book, so I agreed. I watched with amazement as these young men spoke in a foreign language. On occasion, I would pull up as they studied their Qurans, and as they would be studying the Arabic alphabet. I listened.

When the kid from Black Peace Stone left, he called me to his locker: "Sleprock, I want to give you a gift for securing me and the brothers during Salat [prayer]". He gave me a big green Quran that was wrapped inside of a colorful rug. It was a prayer rug. I accepted it, and began to read it on my free time. It had answers to many of the questions I had from reading the Bible years earlier. It didn't promote Jesus as "God". It talked about a universal God that had sent prophets and messengers to all people. It reprimanded people for trying to make one God into three parts (the trinity) and said that all humans are from one creator, and God could choose anyone, not just Jews or

35

Christians, for his message. It made sense. I decided to become Muslim.

It was 1993, in the same month my mother told me that Jinx had been killed. Life and death choices were being made, and played out in real time. When I was out, it was the first time that me and Jinx were on good terms. Prior to reconciling, I had put a gun to his head in the projects. One of the older homies caught up with me later, and told me, "you have been in jail for years. Since then, Jinx has been out here holding it down for the little homies. Y'all are stronger together." I went to his house in the projects, and apologized. We went up to his room and got high on Chronic. Less than a week later (September 1992) I was back in custody. By early 1993, he was dead.

A few months later I met a brother from Oakland. He was a Muslim as well, and he was really immersed in Black history and culture. His name was "Black". Somewhat older than I was, he started lacing me up and sharing books with me, like "African Origin of Civilization" by Cheik Anta Diop, and "Visions for Black Men" by Naim Akbar (an Afri-centric psychologist). There was now a raging battle in my head between banging and Blackness, but I kept reading, and even started writing my own lessons and literature to circulate to other brothers.

One day, a White counselor approached my bunk. I had stayed inside that day rather than go out for recreation. I was in Pine Grove Fire Camp. She wanted to know what I was doing, and I told her I was reading "Malcolm X Speaks", another book that Black had lent me. She offered her take on Malcolm X and his message. I didn't have the vocabulary at the time to dialogue with her in any substantive way, so I said, "I will write you what I think." And I did. I took it to the staff booth and handed it to her, then went back to my bunk and watched as she read my words. Her head was shaking left to right. By this time, other wards had come into the dorm. I told my buddy 'Radar' (from Oak Park) what I had done, and we sat on the bunk giggling as she read my letter over, and over, again. The next day, the senior counselor caught me outside and pulled me over.

He was a chubby Black man who wore a lot of gold, and had a jeri-curl. His last name was 'Roe'. He told me, "pull your pants up." I was sagging, as was customary for gang members. He went on to tell me that the views I expressed to his staff were not acceptable at "his" camp. He let it be known that he was the "head nigga in charge", and that he had been watching me since

36

I had rolled up to his camp, and he didn't like my style. I just listened.
He reminded me of my father, Roosevelt, who wore gold and a jeri-curl. Mr.
Roe drove a Cadillac too, and talked about being "from the hood" to all the
youngsters. I never paid him much attention until this day. "You got one time
to fuck up here, and you're gone," he told me. Never one to delay fucking
up, I was soon sent to "Chad" in Stockton, California, for extortion (as it
was claimed). Me and Radar got kicked out together.

At Chad, I met another brother from Oakland named 'Askari X', a Bay
Area rapper. He had gotten a hold of some of my writings that I was sharing
with brothers and reached out to me. I was on the lock-up row, and once I
completed my time their, he convinced the cottage staff to move me into the
cell next to his. At that time ('93-'94), he was writing songs for his upcoming
album, "Message to the Black Man". We became cool, and he understood what
my leadership among the Bloods could do for strengthening the Black alliance
in our unit.

At that time, I wasn't fully into a Black united front. After all, I
was in the lock-up cells for fighting with a Crip. Nevertheless, he began
to teach me about the Nation of Islam, and everything Malcolm X got wrong.
He belonged to a sect of the N.O.I. called "The Ansar El Muhammads". I got
in with him and earned my "X"*, and title: Ansar El Muhammad, so-called Awaan
Ahmad (both meaning "helper" and "praise-worthy", as well as "helper of Muhammad").
I also called myself, "I am Muhammad". I was about 18 when I joined N.O.I.
(many years later I would come under the N.O.I., as lead by the honorable
minister Louis Farrakhan).

I became the minster of communication and information for the Ansar
El Muhammads in C.Y.A. My job was to disseminate lessons, and answer the
questions of others in the ranks throughout the Youth Authority system. I
would also have to contact the "Royal House" (headquarters) to report on our
progress. Perfect strangers were changing my mind-state, gradually.

I paroled in 1994, shortly after my brother Jonathan was accidentally
shot by John Kennedy, who became the mayor of Pasadena. He survived, and took
the money he received from the resulting lawsuit to fund a new gang, drugs

---

*The "X" represents the name taken from Blacks, and the name to be given in
the future.

BLOODS & CRIPS
1992
PEACE TREATY
APRIL 28TH

and guns. I wanted no part of the streets at this point. I stayed home reading and entertaining my new girlfriend, who would become pregnant.

I was living with my mom, now a Born Again Christian. She took offense that I did not eat pork anymore, and prayed to some "heathen God" (as her pastor explained it to her). His name was "Brother Hampton", and he had "saved" my mother from drinking and gambling; the evil remnants left by my father. The "straw that broke the camels back" for me came when "Brother Hampton" showed up to visit. Like her own mother (Johnny Mae), my mom had an emotional connection to Christianity that was handed down from their Southern roots. They had no knowledge of Biblical scholarship, and I had been studying for about two years by that time. My mother would tell me: "My pastor will eat you up with the Bible." Not intending to be anybody's dinner, I told her: "I am no pork chop, and I accept the beef!"

One day, I entered the house to find them studying at the kitchen table. "This is my son, James; the one who just got out of jail," my mother introduced me. I walked over and shook his hand. He formally introduced himself, and my mother wasted no time: "And, I have told him that he can't mess with you and the Bible." He snickered. My father had taught me that these preachers were pimps. He had my mother wrapped up in him, not the Bible.

Mr. Hampton started off with the common Christian spiel of, "God sent Jesus to die for our sins," and all that. We ended up debating the authenticity of the savior doctrine, the veracity of Biblical scriptures, and Jesus' divinity, amongst other things. I took him on a journey throughout history, and all the cultures that predated Christianity which had "saviors" born from virgins, and that had sacrificed their lives to save humanity; particularly stories from Babylon and Egypt. I explained to him how it was actually "demons" at the council of Nicea (300 years after Jesus' death) where divinity was attached to Jesus and Sunday. A day to worship a Pagan "sun god" was affixed to the resurrection day, the day of the rising sun. I showed him dozens of contradictions in the Bible, especially places where Jesus never claimed to be God: "The sender is not equal to Him [the Father] who sent him." My mother jumped up and said, "boy, show this man some respect!" Mr. Hampton was happy she had thrown in the towel, but I could see that my mother was reluctantly impressed. Her son knew his stuff!

I didn't last at her house. The "Holy War' was on, so I moved out. She still lived on Parke Street, and at the time the faction on Parke Street was

39

at war with other factions of the hood (read my other book "Evidence of Long, Lost Letters" to learn about that). Blood was running in the streets.

Many of my old hood mentors were alive, and admired my neutral stance in the conflict. They did try to bring me back into the fold, though, by offering me "a new gang, and a new name". I respectfully declined. My brother's effort to found his own gang brought additional conflict into the hood. Men were dropping like flies everyday. The funeral parlors surrounding us were busy, and profiting.

Later, after returning to custody, my mother would come (as I said before, with my pregnant girlfriend) to visit me in the L.A. County Jail. One day, she told me, "if your life-style was as good as your talk, you probably could have converted me to Muslim." She could never come to call it "Islam", but I would never forget that opportunity I missed when I decided to go back into the streets, and act the fool. "When all you have is a hammer," it is said, "you treat everything like a nail." That was my plan: destroy everything, including good relationships. I felt that the whole world was against me. I was my own worst enemy.

6

Discovering New Worlds

There was once a frog who was born and raised inside of a well. The well is all he knew. He swam around it thinking it was the whole world. Then, one day another frog stumbled upon him, and asked, "do you live here?" The frog replied, "yes, this is all mine."

The frog who was a stranger was puzzled at the limitation the other frog had accepted for himself. "Follow me," he said. He took the "well frog" to a pond. The well frog couldn't believe his eyes. This was certainly much bigger than his "world".

The "stranger" frog told him that there was more, so they hopped along to a river. "Wow!", the well frog exclaimed.."I had never imagined anything like this." The stranger frog beckoned him further down until they came upon an ocean. This blew the well frog's mind. This time he said nothing. He jumped in, and never turned back.

The mentor I met in Ironwood State Prison (1996-2002), Abdul Malik, told me that progress (change) takes time. He would always use numbers, or analogies involving nature, to make his point. Using the natural metamorphosis of both the tadpole to frog, and caterpillar to butterfly, he explained the growth process of a boy to a man:

> "Ansar, just as the embryo is inside the sperm, the frog is inside of the egg. It is there in a crude state, even though you can't see it. It is the same with the butterfly; it is there inside of that ugly looking caterpillar. That is how growth takes place. It starts off in the worst condition. That is how "God" found us in America. We were mentally, and spiritually, dead. His coming to find the Honorable Elijah Muhammad was the first crackling of light, and life, in our spiritual resurrection as a people.

> That is how you will grow, Ansar: in stages. People will condemn the process, because sperm is despicable looking. So is the larvae of a frog and the caterpillar. No one likes the look and smell of their own shit, but from it, "God" makes fertilizer.

Right now, you are like a mental "child";
you break everything in the house because you
don't know it's value. If you stay on your path,
however, one day you'll grow into a valuable
man. Have you ever smelled a dead body? It stinks,
huh? That's you right now, because you're still
mentally dead. You have no pulse (love or compassion),
and you don't respond to light (truth). That's
a sign of death, but there's life inside of
death, just as there's a man inside of the child.
Can you bear the process, Ansar? Growth is an
ugly process."

Abdul would grill me like this for hours sometimes.

How do we get the small,scared boy,out

out of the big strong man?

"Those ignorant to history are condemned to repeat it."

Chapter Six

Down, But Not Out

Less than two months after maxing out at C.Y.A. I was extradited to the West Valley County Jail, near Upland. I was being charged with murder, and the Pasadena and Fontana police departments got together to track me down. It was February 1996, and I was 21 years old.

The case settled with a plea. It turned out that the detectives had coerced one of my associates to lie, and make up some wild story that I had confessed to the homicide to him. Court documents showed that the detectives also tried planting informants in the jail to intercept all of my phone, and social, communications. This was a different level of the game for me. They were playing for keeps.

My attorney on the case, a Mr. Duncan, reminded me of the drunk, but highly adept, lawyer in the movie "A Time to Kill". He just looked intoxicated all the time, but he was smart and could smell a rat. He advised me not to take the seven year "deal" the prosecutor offered. He told me that it would be a 'strike' (one of the three allowed in California before receiving an automatic life-sentence), and would come back to haunt me in the future:

"James, it began as a high-profile gang execution. For months they were calling for a capital conviction. Now, they are handing you this sweet deal. It's bullshit, take it to the box."

My mother and older brother Tyrone showed up to court. I told my lawyer to ask my mom if I should take the deal. She sent back a piece of paper that simply said, "have faith." I took the deal. My rationale was that I had just ran off six years, so what's another seven?

While in prison I continued to study. I joined study groups lead by N.O.I. members, pro-Black educators, and ran a few myself. I was heavily involved with gang politics, however, and stayed in the hole for fights and getting behavioral reports. I ended up doing the entire seven years instead of the 85% of it that California offered for those who are not disciplinary problems. I was learning a lot, but I wasn't unlearning old patterns of behavior. I still wanted a reputation for being a bad guy.

All of the O.G.'s on the yard liked me. I stood on my own, and fought

Members of the Black Panther
Party for Self Defense

my own battles, including those of some of my homies. The young Bloods from other cities despised me because I wanted the P.D.L.'s to exercise alone, and study books. They thought I was trying to separate the Bloods. Capitalizing on their envy, and shortsightedness, I created distance from the convoluted, and excessive gang and prison politics that come from rolling too deep. I wasn't having their problems, and by then I had developed a reliable enough reputation not to be taken for granted. My motivations, by now, weren't hating Crips. It was about anyone who posed a threat; Crip or Blood. Every Crip wasn't an enemy, and every Blood was not a friend. I even had "crossed the line", and chosen a few Crips as cellmates.

I had quit drinking alcohol, gambling, and eating meat. I read, exercised, and turned to studying a little bit about the law. I knew I had an open case in Pasadena for assault with a deadly weapon, and this time I wanted to have an understanding of the law as I sat in court. My mind told me to prepare (in the end, it would result in a second strike).

I went to the law library and persuaded two older brothers to mentor me. "If you are serious, you'll come here every day after work, and look up cases," they told me. I showed up. They taught me how to shepardize (look up cases) related to any particulars of my case. They wanted me to gain a basic knowledge of the U.S. Constitutional, and penal, law. I took it all in. Little did I know that these "basics" would help me grow as a self-represented defendant for a future capital murder case. I also learned about the Title 15, California Codes and Regulations for the Department of Corrections (basically, the rule book for California inmates).

I had a few older homies from my hood on the yard with me. One of them gave me a plan:

> "Sleprock, I got a challenge for you. I want
> you to go around and see how many of these O.G.
> Bloods and Crips will allow you to interview
> them about the origins of their hood, where
> it's located, who their rivals are, and if they
> see any possibilities of Bloods and Crips coming
> together."

I took the challenge. I put together a folder with the above questions, and went around interviewing people. My older homie called this "reconnaissance work", and said it would help me in the future. At first, I thought they'd

47

be suspicious of my intent. Surprisingly, they respected my efforts as a youngster who was interested in learning from the old heads.

I learned about Tookie and Raymond Washington, the founders of the Crips, from men who claimed to have known them from the 70's. They told me that gangs as we know them were designed to protect our communities, not destroy them. When Black families started migrating from the South to California, the White community didn't want Blacks in their spaces (Los Angeles, for example). White gangs would raid Black neighborhoods, so young Blacks got together and formed their own (i.e., The Slauson Boys, Gladiators, and Brims). I was shocked that these men were intamitely involved in these origin stories, yet had accepted the current Black-on-Black warfare spawned by Crips and Bloods. Some of these men had been Christians, and in prison before I was born.

I also found a few other religious mentors. Most surprising for me was that I found out that the "Black Peace Stone" Blood gang from L.A. was founded by Black Stone Rangers from Chicago, and that the "Black Stone" phrase had it's roots in Islam. More specifically, the Black Stone encased on the house of worship, the "Kaaba", in Mecca, Arabia; built thousands of years ago by Prophet Abraham and his first son, Ishmael. According to tradition, the Black Stone fell out of Heaven to mark the location "God" wanted them to build this sacred house, so Abraham installed it as a memorial to the divine instruction.

Many of the Black Stone Rangers took to Islam in the 60's and 70's, and derived the meaning of the Black Stone from Islamic history. Hence, "Black Stone" Rangers. I took all this as almost a mandate to continue on my path. If that got my attention though, the next insight blew my mind.

The Bloods used the Swahili word 'Damu' (Blood) to refer to themselves. I was told that this word derives it's meaning from the Biblical and Quranic first man (Adam), whose name in Hebrew means "Red Clay"; or, blood from the earth (Adamu'ah is said to be the root word for Adam). In Arabic, the root word for Adam means "dark clay", or Black. "How did all this stuff get so perverted?", I thought. Here, we were desecrating the heritage of our ancestors, and religious forebearers. This could not be a good thing for future generations.

Further enhancing my knowledge, I also learned how the Chicago leader of the Black Panther Party (Fred Hampton) sought to forge a union with the Black Stone Rangers. The F.B.I., however, had built a counter-intelligence program to stay apprised of Black liberation movements (especially the Black Panthers), and found a way to break up this prospective union. This happened in 1969, shortly before the local police killed Fred Hampton and Mark Clark in their beds as they slept. An informant in the Black Panthers had given the police the layout of the house. This story is portrayed in the movie "Judas and The Black Messiah". It is also covered in the book "Agents of Repression."

I was seeing some framework, and basis, for unity among the gangs. I paroled in December 2002, and took my chances in Los Angeles as an intern. The program was called 'Amity', and had recently started in L.A. a few months before I paroled. I had participated in the start-up program at Ironwood State Prison in 2001 under former prisoners like Carlee Anthony, a former Crip from San Diego. He was a Muslim, and recruited me to help him encourage people to participate and make the program a success.

Amity's L.A. branch was on 38th and Grand Street. Not too far from U.S.C. and the Colliseum. There were gangs all around this area too. I was allowed to check into a computer class down the street that was upstairs from a Mexican market. I paid one dollar to learn Microsoft Windows. On the same floor was a social advocacy group called 'ACORN'.* I went over, and stuck my nose around their office and found it full of attractive women, and some rough looking guys. It turned out that the Black man who oversaw operations there was a former prisoner. Inside of his office was a large poster of George Jackson and Che Guevara.

We talked about prison and progress, and he eventually asked me if I wanted to earn some money by doing telephonic outreach for the group. I assented. I also did some protest work with them over cuts to 'AFIC' (Assistance for Instants and Children). It was my first experience with joining a protest. I was 27 years old.

I went to several Los Angeles Mosques, including the Nation of Islam's temple when it was on Western and Vermont. The assistant minister of the mosque Charles Muhammad was from Pasadena, and had visited Ironwood State Prison prior to my release. I had told him that once I paroled I'd come by, so I did. It turned out that the annual "Savior's Day" event was coming up (February 26, 2003), so I volunteered to go to the Slauson Swapmeet in the heart of Gangland in a suit and bowtie to sell "Final Call" newspapers, and promote the keynote address of Minister Farrakhan. While running around the parking lot over the weekend, I ran into a few of my homies from Pasadena and some guys I'd served time with in both C.Y.A., and prison. They couldn't believe their eyes. They congratulated me.

---

*ACORN - Association of Community Organizing Right Now

I also went and visited the mosque in Chino, California, to meet the Imam of the Ahmadiyya branch of Islam. This man had stayed in touch with me during my entire prison term. I celebrated the Eid (an event commemorating Ramadan) with their community, and got to meet Sultan Latif, the author of "Psychic Trauma". He had flown in from New York to promote his latest book "African and Indian Prophecies". We sat and ate together, and took some pictures (see: Appendix).

The Nation of Islam was also hosting a "Ten Thousand Man March" to end gang violence, so I got some brothers together from the program, and we went in support. We also did some intervention work with F.A.M.E. (First African American Methodist Episcopal) church when Cecil Murray was it's pastor. This took me into Watts, "The Jungles" (the territory of the Black Stones), and several of the hoods of men I interviewed in prison. I was welcomed by all, despite my gang affiliation. I was trying to put into action what I had learned in prison.

I had also enrolled in L.A. City College for a short stint. My goal was to get my drug and alcohol counselling degree. Soon, I met up with John Kennedy, and he introduced me to a Black man who ran a small business in Pasadena, and he offered to hire me. In the meantime, I had met a female at the college, and the rest is history. Being back in Pasadena, I fell back in with old friends, and family. Before long, I was back in jail for violating parole by allegedly "associating with a gang member"; someone who had not been involved with gangs since he was a teenager. The same guy whose house I stayed at when my mother kicked me out at 14. We had grown up together, and were like family. The parole commissioner wasn't having it, however, She remanded me to prison for eight months. I returned home at the end of 2003.

For the first time since 1985, all of my mother's seven children were home together. We had been victims of the "revolving door". When some of us were free, the others were incarcerated. We planned on taking a family photo to celebrate this milestone. Unfortunately, the photo was never to be. Jonathan was arrested a day after my release.

The next time we were "almost" all out of jail at the same time was in 2004. My sister was scheduled to get married in March of that year. All of us were present except Damon this time, who was in on a parole violation. Kenny had long since stopped going to jail after his first term in 1985. Tragically, when he paroled from prison in 1987, Damon was arrested as Kenny was on the way home on the Greyhound bus. The same year (1987) I entered the Dope game. The cycle continued. We couldn't choose our family, and the friends we did choose were not much better. All of our families were "broken".

A few days before my sister's wedding, the police raided her house looking for me for allegedly kidnapping and shooting a street vendor (who was also a Muslim). I went on the run until the wedding. Later, I went to my parole officer to clear up the misunderstanding. He walked me over to speak with the detectives at the Pasadena Police Department, and when I refused to talk about a crime I didn't commit, I was arrested for another parole violation (gang association) for speaking with the leader of a rival gang.

Ironically, the reason I was speaking with the "rival gang leader" was an attempt to end the feud between the gangs in our city. The detectives, while investigating me for the crime, happened to see us talking in front of my sister's house. Even though a preliminary investigation exonerated me, the violation stood.

About a week into the parole violation, my nephew Deangelo (Milkman) was killed in a botched jewelery store robbery. He had hooked up with some youngsters he had been in C.Y.A. with to commit the heist. The group consisted of both Crips and Bloods, and he had brought them to me so I could meet them. I advised him against his plan, but after I was arrested he went forward with it anyway. He was the only person killed.

The tragedy for our family wasn't over, either. Less than two weeks after Milkman's death, my brother Jonathan was murdered by a childhood rival. Once I knew they were beefing, I told Jonathan not to fight this guy because the guy knew that he had no chance to win. He was a shooter, not a fighter. Everybody knew that he didn't want to fight my brother with his hands. Not following that advice, Jonathan accosted him and, like the coward he was, he brought out a gun and started shooting.

Maybe jail had saved not just my life, but the lives of many others. Had I been out when Jonathan was shot, reacting out of love and emotion, it's easy to imagine myself hurting a lot of people just to flush out the assailant who was on the run. As Askari X told me: "What the devil uses against us [e.g., prison], 'God' can use for us." As it was, I had to bite the bullet, considering my circumstances and things beyond my control.

During World War II, a story is told about General MacArthur. He and his men came under fire in the Philippines and he told his men to retreat.

"We are the men of General MacArthur," they said, "we never retreat." Not one to be outdone, the General responded: "Well, we won't retreat then. We will just advance in a different direction." I was being forced to advance in a different direction.

It Will Be Greater Later

There is a story in the Holy Quran about Moses that doesn't appear in the Bible. The story provides some insight as to how Moses found an Ethiopian wife (as the book of Numbers in the Old Testament says). The Quran has Moses travelling with his young companion (probably Joshua) to a junction of two seas, or rivers. These two rivers are said to be those of the White and Blue Niles - where Upper Egypt meets Ethiopia in East Africa.

Some Islamic scholars interpret the "two rivers" metaphorically, and say that it represents where material (or earthly) knowledge meets the higher spiritual knowledge. Moses, although a prophet, still had something to learn. Therefore, God sent Moses a teacher to show him things that he didn't yet understand about life: that everything, despite their physical appearances, are headed toward a good end. This moral is the same as the Bible states after Joseph's brothers sold him into bondage in Egypt. After forgiving his brothers for this horrible betrayal, Joseph tells them, "you meant it for evil; God meant it for good."

The story of Moses is in chapter 18 of the Quran, and reads as the following:

"And when Moses said to his servants: I will not cease until I reach the junction of the two rivers, otherwise I will go on for years.

So when they reached the junction of the two rivers, they forgot their fish, and it took its way into the river, being free.

But when they had gone further, he said to his servant: 'Bring to us our morning meal, certainly we have found fatigue in this our journey.'

He said: sawest thou when we took refuge on the rock, I forgot the fish, and none but the devil made me forget to speak of it, and it took its way into the river; what a wonder!

He said: this is what we sought for. So they returned retracing their footsteps.

Then they found one of our servants whom we granted mercy from us, and whom we had taught knowledge from ourselves.

Moses said to him: may I follow thee that

thou mayest teach me of the good thou has been
taught?

He said: thou canst not have patience with
me. And how canst thou have patience in that
whereof thou has not a comprehensive knowledge?

He said: if Allah please, thou wilt find
me patient, nor shall I disobey thee in aught.

He said: if thou wouldst follow me, question
me not about aught until I myself speak to thee
about it.

Long story short, the wise teacher commits a series of acts that Moses questions,
and condemns (he kills a young boy, destroys someone's boat, and at the end
of the story builds up a wall that has a hidden treasure beneath it, "even
though the occupants of the town denies them hospitality").

Every time Moses objects to one of his actions the wise man, whose name
is Kadeer (Green, in Arabic), reminds Moses, "didn't I tell you that you would
not be able to have patience with me?" In the end, he decides to part company
with Moses, but not before explaining why he had taken those particular actions.
Kadeer explains that the boy he killed was a bad kid, and his parents were
righteous, and "we" (an expression of the divine will) wished that he be removed
and his parents be given a righteous son. As for the boat, there was a king
seizing all boats on the sea, so in order to save the occupants' lives Kadeer
scuttled it. As to the story ending on a good note, the wall was erected because
beneath it was a treasure that belonged to some orphans, and God wished that
they should grow up and attain their inheritance.

In the hadiths (the sayings of Prophet Muhammad) this experience came
upon Moses because Moses had answered "yes" to being asked if he was the wisest
man on Earth. God wanted to teach Moses a lesson. As Socrates said: "A wise
man knows nothing."

A similar occurrence happened with Peter, one of the disciples of Jesus.
Being a Jew, he did not believe that God would permit Gentiles (non-Jews)
into his covenant, so God sent Peter a vision. In his vision were all kinds
of animals that Jews considered unclean, and so would not eat. A voice commanded
Peter to eat.

"No Lord, I have never eaten unclean food," Peter replied. Eventually,
the voice told Peter that these "foods" were no longer unclean. That these

animals (food) were symbolic of the Gentile people with whom God had "grafted into the vine", and were no longer prohibited from God's covenant. Peter got the message. Jews and Gentiles were now members of God's family.

In the N.O.I. there is a lesson book called the "Supreme Wisdom". It is a series of questions put to the honorable Elijah Muhammad three years after meeting his teacher Master Fard Muhammad (1930-33). The book contains Elijah's answers to those questions. Almost 40 years after that book was published (1973), Elijah Muhammad was asked if his answers to those questions would have been the same. He responded:

> "No. I was only 3½ years old [spiritually] when
> I answered those questions. Today my answers
> would have been different."

Supreme wisdom to a spiritual "baby" isn't the same as to an "adult". Times change, and with it, so does our level of understanding. We go from "milk drinkers" (basics) to "meat eaters" (complex).

The minister Louis Farrakhan relays a story about his own account of travelling with a wise man (Elijah Muhammad). When Minister Malcolm X was suspended from the N.O.I., Minister Farrakhan assumed the role Malcolm X once occupied. Following Malcolm X's diatribe for popularizing White people as "devils", Farrakhan tried the same approach. One day, the honorable Elijah Muhammad called him and said, "don't throw trash in a well I intend to take a drink from," then followed it with, "As-Salaam-Alaikum," and hung up the phone.

Trash is the residue of something after the true value has been taken from it, Farrakhan reflected. Once the message had achieved it's goal, it was no longer necessary to continue with it in the [same] fashion as Malcolm X. Later, the minister would say, "when you're travelling with a wise man you must not get stuck in the past tense, or you'll become ineffective in the present tense." Throwing trash in a well only contaminates it.

Attaining knowledge requires time (patience), discipline, and the humility to learn from others. The Holy Quran tells us to, "seek assistance from God through patience and prayer. This is a hard except for the humble ones."

When we ask God to assist us, often this assistance will come through a human being. God works through people. These people come into our lives to give us the knowledge we need to assist ourselves. We have to be patient with teachers, including our parents, who were given to us as guides for our

growth and development. We must be humble, and willing to accept "the things we don't know."

The word 'patient' is also related to someone who seeks medical assistance from a doctor - a patient. The original word for doctor (Docēre in French) is teacher. Every time we gain understanding from life experience, or from a person, a kind of healing is taking place. The reason we suffer so much is due to our ignorance. It is the most prevelant disease, and (sadly) many of us find a perverse sense of pride within it. The Holy Quran says: "Above every man of knowledge is someone with higher knowledge."

Gaining higher levels of knowledge is not for the faint of heart. In Islam we say, "when you ask God for patience, he sends you a trial." The patience required to gain higher knowledge is met with hard trials, and difficulties. Everything of value has a difficulty factor imposed on it. You have to dig for gold, drill for diamonds, and dive for pearls!

The deeper you want to go, the more pressure exists. The same applies to the higher you want to go. "If you wanna be light, then you must bear the burning." As Shakespeare said: "Uneasy lies the head of the man who [wants to] wear the crown."

"Setbacks are setups for comebacks."

Chapter Seven

The Unlikely Success

In January of 2005, I paroled from Corcoran State Prison. It was the prison Jonathan had served his last parole violation in, and I landed on the yard he last stayed on. His name was even etched into a table on the yard - John Byrd, PJG, CK/BK.

This was inscribed on a table near the workout area where the Bloods assembled. No one had scratched it out, and obviously no one had even attempted to stop him from scratching it into the stainless steel table when he wrote it. A few homies still on the yard told me that they had warned him to slow down and watch himself before he was released. In light of what happened, they offered me the same advice.

Some of these guys were under "constitution" (prison political Blood structures, like the United Blood Nation), and it was rumored that high ranking members of this group had put a "hit" out on Jonathan for founding a break-away gang from P.D.L. (i.e., Projeck Gangsters). Instead of claiming to just be a "Crip Killer" (CK), Jonathan also promoted "Blood Killer" (BK). He even had large tattoos on his body expressing these views.[*]

I hit the streets under a cloud of suspicion. "What is Sleprock gonna do to avenge John Byrd's death?", I heard being asked. My family, parole officer, and fiance at the time told me that the cops were just waiting for me to do anything so they could pick me back up. One day, my sister Patrice called me and said that Detective Broghamer had knocked on her door, desiring to speak with me. He had left his card, but I didn't call. I never had, nor wanted, those kind of relationships with law enforcement, and I'm sure he understood that. What could he possibly want? I heard that Detective Broghamer had driven in the ambulance with Jonathan the day he was shot.

I showed up to the court house to support my family after the assailant had been caught, and was coming to court that day. I arrived with Big Sleprock (Damon). As we were parking in the lot adjacent to the court house, I noticed a minivan driving up. Imagine my surprise when I saw the assailant's baby's mother and his young son getting out of that van. They paused when they noticed

---

[*]More of this is in my book "Evidence of Long, Lost Letters".

us. His son looked just like him. We kept walking.

The word in the street was that I was intimidating the informant in the case, and trying to stop him from testifying on the assailant so he could get off, and I could hold court on him in the streets instead. I learned shortly that this was why the detective was looking for me. Somehow, he found out that I was at the court house, so he came over from the police department just across the street:

> "James, I am sorry about what happened to your
> brother. I know you guys were tight. But, I can't
> have you interfering with this case."

He then motioned me away from other bystanders, and whispered:

> "James, I know you. It's just a matter of time
> before the shit hits the fan. I hear it was the
> U.B.N.'s [the aforementioned United Blood Nation]
> that had Jonathan killed. Now, I know I can't
> stop you, but this guy's family is terrified
> of you. James, kill anyone you want to. Just
> don't kill the wrong people."

I told him that I was there to support my mother, who was talking to the District Attorney on the bench about "letting God deal with it" at that time.

She didn't want to testify at a possible trial. It was my mother's opinion that Jonathan's death had brought many people to Christ. "James, at the funeral, so many people accepted Christ into their lives," she'd say. In my opinion, they were all there to ensure that John Byrd was truly dead, and thanking "God" for it.

I walked over and introduced myself to the assailant's baby's mother, and son. I went into my pocket and gave the kid all of the change I had on me. He took it, and we all went into the court house. I sat next to him as his father, the assailant, came out in handcuffs with the few bailiffs escorting him.

He sat by his attorney, but couldn't take his eyes off of his son sitting next to his worth nightmare. I saw the dread on his face, and leaned over to tell the kid, "there is daddy." We both laughed. The assailant didn't.

The case ended in a settlement. There was to be no trial. On sentencing day, I spoke for my family. The court room was packed with both side's family members and a heavy police presence. They expected that my family would run into the well[*] of the court room and give the assailant street justice. I had other plans.

I grabbed his son and walked into the well. We stood side-by-side, his son and I. The (now convicted) man's legacy was in my hands, and he was fuming. I put my hand on the boy's head, and began speaking.

I did not seek to condemn my brother's killer for his crime. After all, I had sat just where he was sitting in many court rooms. I explained that by the time he was to be released his son would be a teenager, possibly in a gang, and fair game in the streets. I exhorted him to change his life, and come home as a father; something Jonathan would never be again because he was dead.

I thanked the judge and the D.A., then turned to the full room of cops, finishing with, "and I'd like to thank all of his bodyguards." The court erupted into laughter, including the judge and D.A. I put my hand on his son's shoulder and led him out of the well into the corridor with everyone else following in tandem. I felt that I had killed him with kindness.

Instead of falling back into old patterns in the hood, I hooked up with some older homies and started working towards bringing some unity and healing to the community. I wasn't a fool though. I knew that I was surrounded by enemies, and I did everything I could to "stick and move".

I forged a preliminary cease-fire with the young gang members from P.D.L., Projecks, and Squiggley Lane Bloods. I tried to impose the old-skool view that "Bloods don't kill Bloods". We had several meetings that went well, and I got a few of them to hang out together when a week prior they were shooting at, and fighting, one another.

Soon, I had a "little bird" whispering in my ear:

> "James, some dudes from the U.B.N. are calling
> home from prison. They don't approve of what
> you're doing."

I didn't work for them though. Nor had I swore any allegiance to a "prison bound" group. I was trying to use my influence to free the next generation

---

[*] The well is the part of the court room where the attorneys and defendants sit.

from a war that started before they were even born.

I reached out to Hard Rock (leader of a break-away group from P.D.L.), and some reputable P.D.L.'s like Bo-gart and Wee Lo (R.I.P.). I spoke with Bam from P-Nine (a break-away group from P.D.L.), and several others. We held a peace picnic at Robinson Park. It was a front page story in the Pasadena Star newspaper.

Unsurprisingly, some guys were violating the cease-fire "at night, while smiling in my face during the day." A move that endangered lives, including my own. This was also undermining my credibility with all sides that convened at meetings, even secret meetings we were conducting at private places in order to shield our objectives from would-be saboteurs. Little did I know, many of the guys at these meetings were active informants for the Pasadena Police.

Now I understand why people would come to me asking for guns. They were weapon-checking me for the cops. I always denied having any guns, and reminded them that we should be focused on the forging of a peace treaty. Some of them would later testify against me at a preliminary hearing, or provide information about my whereabouts to cops. Given the insincerity of the more clandestine individuals amongst the group, it's not surprising that the peace treaty never fully coalesced.

I started taking a few youngsters out to Los Angeles with me to participate in "Stop the Violence" rallies, and "Stop Police Violence" protests happening in the spring and summer of 2005. I also took some younger homies to hear Minister Farrakhan speak via satellite, but I was still on the radar with the Fruit of Islam (military men in the N.O.I.) for the trumped up case that got me violated, because the victim was Muslim. We became surrounded at the Greek Theater in Los Angeles. I saw the play, so I got up and walked over to speak with the captain of the N.O.I. mosque (Captain Allen) right on the spot. He told me that, "it was out of the abundance of caution." We heard the minister's address, and split.

Surprisingly, despite the circumstances the youngsters enjoyed the message, so I took them to see the minister in person when he spoke at Compton College in the summer of 2005. To be fair to future events, we were all still "straddling the fence" between our old lives, and new. After all, street life gave us all the "respect" that society had always denied us. I had not walked away, as Charlee Muhammad predicted years earlier.

63

Before it was all over, the cops used an old tactic to have me arrested - "gang association". This was despite the supervisor of parole (Ms. Linda Wilhelm) modifying my parole conditions so that I could do gang intervention work. This arrangement was brokered by my cousin (Ricky Pickens Jr.) who, it turns out, was instructed by the chief of police to keep an eye on me.

The goal, once again, was to hold me down while they investigated me for a homicide and dozens of other crimes, including carjacking and sexual assault. The commissioner saw their move, however, and told them that he was, "not holding him in custody for your homicide investigation." He gave me time served, and I was set to be released the next morning. Never ones to allow themselves to be (even officially) outmaneuvered, the "police machine" went straight to work flexing their power.

At Receiving and Release I learned that I had a "new" parole officer (the one I had previously spoke up for me at the board hearing). I was given a "new violation", and sat in jail until the news broke: Pasadena Gang Leader Charged with Murder and Terrorizing Community! It was all over the television news, and newspapers. Before it was all over, I would live in the L.A. County Jail for the next (nearly) 10 years of my life fighting a capital murder case, and possible death sentence.

My turning point came when I met the man (a Buddhist master) who would nudge my mind, and focus, on a new trajectory. His name was Daniel "Nagy" Buckley. He worked inside the jail as a chaplain (read my book "Nagy Notes" for more about this experience), and would gift me with seven years of his tutelage, and "higher learning" training. Throughout these years of mentoring, and his example, I read hundreds of books, adopted meditation into my spiritual practice, and met my current mentor (and spiritual brother), Rabbi Brian Z. Mayer.

I walked away from the gang after dropping my gang name, and distancing myself from those I knew had it in for me anyway. It was an open secret that I was a targeted man. Luckily, all of my years prior to this fissure with the gang had equipped me to stand strong, and walk to the beat of my own drum. I had never been a follower, or so dependent on the gang that I couldn't roll solo anyway.

I took my chance at representing myself in court after seven years in custody. Not only did my studying the law pay off, but so did the patience (amongst other things) that I had naturally, and learned at the feet of my friend, and mentor, Nagy (as well as the time it all bought both me, and my case). I was there long enough for the truth to come out about the detectives on my (and other people's) case, including Detective Broghamer. They had engaged in witness tampering, falsifying documents, paying unregistered informants (including juveniles), perjuring themselves on the witness stand, and suppressing evidence. All things I had told my former attorney, but was told that, "it's not what you say, it's what you can prove in court."

Finally, after 9½ years fighting, the case was settled. With 29 charges against me being dismissed, I walked away with my life. I learned upon leaving the court room after sentencing that the detectives (Broghamer and Okamoto) expressed anger with the district attorney. They, like so many others, simply wanted me dead.

I returned to a California prison in 2014 as a non-affiliate. I hit the main-line (general population) and people couldn't believe that I was no longer in a gang, and no longer going by my nickname "Lil' Sleprock II". I had succeeded, against all odds, to stay alive, change my life, and write my story; despite circumstances where so many others perished, failed along the way, and were unable to tell their own.

No longer was my "Dharma" to engage in self-destructive acts against other people. My world view had changed as a result of my experiences, and walking with "masters" that had shaped my life, even when I had no absolute knowledge of where it would all take me in the end. I had been a student all my life, even taking notes from the older homies in my sister's room, and from/in the streets as a kid.

Prison had become, not a cage, but a classroom. A training ground for the liberation of my mind and spirit. I had come to the junction of the two rivers: what had started out bad, ended good. I was finally being respected for other things than my street reputation. I had successfully walked away

Hinduism

 The Aum

Judaism

 Star of David

Islam

 Star and Crescent

Christianity

 The Cross

Buddhism

 Wheel of Dharma

Sikhism

The Khanda

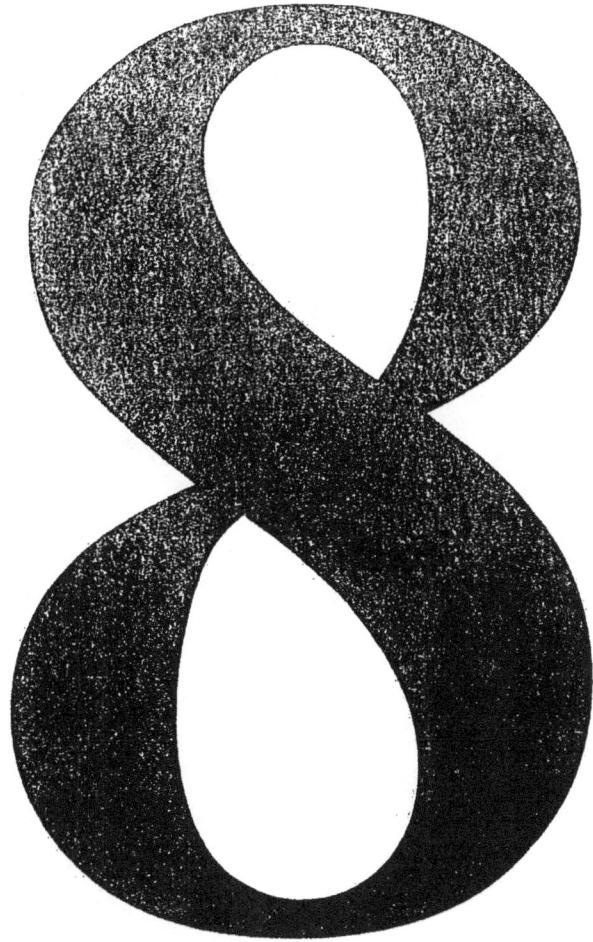

A Jail Bird Isn't a Bird Brain

Not long before deciding to represent myself in court, my "second chair"[*]
came to visit me. The goal was to get me to settle the case with a deal for,
"Life Without the Possibility of Parole; to save my life." I refused.

In his attempt to convince me though, he told me a story:

> "There was a kid in Greece who doubted that the
> Oracle of Delphi could actually predict the future,
> so the boy devised a scheme to trick the Oracle.
> He arrived with a bird in his hand, and behind
> his back. He asked the Oracle, "is the bird I
> have in my hand dead or alive?' If the Oracle
> said alive, he would crush the bird; if the Oracle
> said it was dead, the kid would present the bird
> as alive. Both ruses would prove that the Oracle
> could not predict the future. However, the Oracle,
> being much smarter than the kid said: 'Little
> boy, the power of life and death is in your hands.'

Not missing my opportunity, I shot back with a "bird story" of my own:

> "I will tell you a story about a bird. There
> was once a bird that was always reluctant to
> fly south with the rest of it's flock. When winter
> came he delayed, and his wings froze, so he was
> grounded. While freezing to death in front of
> a barn, a horse backed out and took a shit on
> him. Quite naturally, the bird was upset. However,
> as he sat in the poop, he felt it's warmth begin
> to thaw out his wings, and he felt life returning
> to his being. He cheered up, and started singing,
> but his singing caught the ear of a wolf passing
> by. The wolf came over and removed the shit off
> of the bird, and ate him. Not everyone who shits
> on you is an enemy, and everyone who takes shit
> off of you is not a friend."

---

[*] In death penalty cases you have two attorneys. The second one is referred
to as "the second chair".

He seemed to get my message: I didn't need him to get me out of shit! Not long after this, I officially went pro-per (a self-represented defendant) and learned that my wings, even during the winter of my discontent, could fly well!

There is a story about a snail that, one bitter cold morning in January, started to climb the frozen trunk of a cherry tree. As he slowly moved upward, a beetle stuck it's head out of a crack in the tree, and said, "hey buddy, you're wasting your time. There aren't any cherries up there." Not missing a beat, the snail kept right on going. "There will be when I get there," he said.

Everything we strive for will eventually come into sight. Can't stop, won't stop!

"Turn your mess into a message."

- Rick James

Chapter Eight

There are things that I understand now better than I did when I first
learned them. We are given the meaning of things that correspond with our
capacity to comprehend them. The more we grow, the more we know. I find myself
(now in my mid 40's) reciting things that I ignored when my mother first told
them to me as a child. I wrote about some of those experiences in a previous
book ("Evidence of Long, Lost Letters"), and today they form much of who I
have become.

My mother (Connie Piggee) stressed upon all of her children the need
for us to be leaders, and it shows in most of our lives. Tyrome (the eldest)
never joined a gang. He was, instead, a leader in sports, the community,
and even had his own body guard service. Kenny is an entrepreneur as well,
and owns a barber shop in Pasadena, California, called "Back At Home". Damon
became a street vendor, selling clothing. Jonathan founded a gang. Jerome
distinguishes himself by having witnessed all of the hood madness, and missing
it all by a mile. He also sold clothing, and other accessories. My sister
(Patrice) set up a beauty shop in her home, where she would tend to the hair-
styling of the girls, and women, of our community. I even became a street
vendor myself in 2005, selling clothing, watches, and other accessories.

You will see from the additional bio-sketch included that I have tried
my hand at many different things in my life. I became a Muslim at 17 years
old while being a full-fledged gang member in C.Y.A. Islam and gang-banging
had also taught me something about being a leader. Growing up a Blood in my
times (when we were far outnumbered by our rivals - The Crips), we had to
preach unity, structure, and leadership.

Many of our older homies in the prison functioned with political revolutionary
groups in the 1980's (B.G.F., Black Panthers, Nation of Islam, etc.), and
impressed a degree of militancy upon us as we came into the ranks. We were
made to be warriors, but mostly for the wrong cause. What makes you a "good"
gangster, however, can also make you a good man, a good leader, a good father,
a good teacher, etc. The principles we were taught: unity, loyalty, dependability,
trust, and determination (among others) are universal. Families and militaries
are both built upon these. So are nations.

We had our own origin stories, one being that we were the bastards of the Black Panther Party (see documentary by the same name), and due to the police (local and FBI) our ambitions were fractured. The Black Panthers began in 1966, followed by the Crips in 1971, and the Bloods in, or around, 1973. One year before my birth.

The word "Blood" ('young blood', etc.) signifying family and brotherhood had preceded gangs. Putting an ideology to it, older folks used eponyms to describe their gangs' origin. Crips came to stand for "California Revolutionary Inner Party Service", Brim stood for "Black Revolutionary Independent Movement", and Blood for "Black Liberation Organized to Overcome Discrimination". They were attempting to infuse street life with higher meaning, and purpose, instead of it being the lost cause that it is today.

Parental, street, and book lessons have all converged to improve the man I constantly strive to become. I am a work in progress. Freedom from sin and ignorance is a constant struggle. Many of the things you read from my lessons in the book have different meanings to me today. I wrote about this transition in another book, "Degree's of Freedom". My growth and understanding have both evolved, and I have friends now from all walks of life.

I credit the philosophy of N.O.I.'s teaching for this: good homes, wealth, and to have friendships in all walks of life. We were encouraged to read books like, "How to Win Friends and Influence People" by Dale Carnegie, "Think and Grow Rich" by Napoleon Hill, and "The Greatest Salesman" by Ogg Mandigo. It wasn't about hating White people, it was about loving Black people like we loved everyone else. This is the message that developed within me over the decades.

Above all, I have developed into a helper (Ansar), not a hinderer. Crime, Gang-banging, and racism will not be the bookend to my story. My mother, the Nation of Islam, and my street life all taught me how to do for myself, be entrepreneurial, and develop as a leader. My experiences gave me something to look forward to after overcoming self-hatred, and the limitations imposed on me from growing up Black in a country that hated me for no more than the color of my skin; a more deadly form of gang-banging: nation-banging (a form of nationalism that tends to prize "Whiteness", and conflate it with patriotism).

Today, I am better as a result of all of my experiences. I have grown into the ability to say, like the Greek philosopher Diodenes did: "I am a citizen of the world."

By: James 'Ansar' Wilson

"When lions write their own history, the hunter is not a hero."

Late Note

The Pasadena Police and District Attorney's Office had me court ordered into the segregated housing unit (High Power) in Los Angeles County Jail in 2006, a year into my arrest. I would spend the next eight years of my life housed in a single cell inside the jail. Then, upon arriving to prison in 2014, a detective called the Reception Center, providing false information about my stay in the Los Angeles County Jail, so the prison single-celled me, as well (see my book "Evidence of Long, Lost Letters" about this topic).

Seeking to isolate me and circumscribe my efforts had only served to carve out a space for me where I could operate without the interruptions, and hassles, of having a cell-mate inside a living area about as big as a standard bathroom. I had space and time to create. I transformed this attempted limitation (and desired road-block) into everything I needed to grow, and transform:

- A workout area (for health).
- A classroom (for study).
- A monastary (for meditation).
- A Mosque (for spiritual growth).
- An office (for work).

I transformed a stumbling block into a stepping stone.

There is an old story about two men inside of a prison cell, both looking out of a window. One man was looking down and could only see the ground, the other man was looking up to behold the stars. I am happy that I discovered that I am like the latter man. Where others see problems, I imagine possibilities.

James 'Ansar' Wilson

State of California

High School Equivalency Certificate

This is to certify that

JAMES F WILSON

has met the standards established by the California State Board of Education for successful completion of the tests of General Educational Development and is therefore entitled to this High School Equivalency Certificate.

Tom Torlakson
State Superintendent of Public Instruction

Michael W. Kirst
President of the
California State Board of Education

72

A LETTER TO MY VICTIM(S)

Read during my sentencing
hearing in August, 2014.

A Letter To My Victims

August, 2014

What is done in the dark comes to the light only to afford us an opportunity to clearly confront better our misdeeds. Not surprisingly, I stand before you and the world both guilty, and convicted, not only in court, but in my heart. I come before you repentant.

With legal formalities now set aside, unveiling another one of my 'hiding' places, I write this letter fully contrite, exposed, and painfully begging for your unearned forgiveness. I make this plea to any human being I have ever injured, in any way, throughout my entire life. I am sorry.

I am a 39-year old childless man, so I can not possibly fathom the depth of pain experienced when one is lost, or harmed. Undeniably, I cannot imagine. And my willingness to accept guilt, and the consequences of my actions, only tells the beginning of this process, and not it's ending. I have a lot of work to do. Continuing to prove, and improve, myself will be a life-time journey, and battle. Further, any forgiveness granted me from my victims will prove to be the most valuable asset in my 'armory' to confront these uphill battles. For they are legion.

Going forward I will seek help, further my education, and work to stay in the light more than anything! I accept my challenges. Thank you for listening these words, and I wish you well in your own lifes' journey.

James

MEMO

ATTORNEY WORK PRODUCT

CASE NAME: People vs. James Wilson

DATE: January 25, 2013

ATTORNEY: Pro per

INVESTIGATOR: Robert Royce

CONFIDENTIAL ATTORNEY WORK PRODUCT

On January 25, 2013, I spoke with attorney Michael Kraut. Mr. Kraut is the attorney who started the internal affairs criminal investigation on officer Okomoto and officer Gomez.

Mr. Kraut referred me to a website where I located a copy of the letter he sent to the Pasadena Police Department which began the investigation. He told me he had countless hours of research into officers of Pasadena Police Department and their conduct with criminal cases. He states officer Okomoto is currently off duty on suspension and Officer Gomez is still working for the Pasadena Police Department.

Mr. Kraut says officer Okomoto is about to be indicted on numerous criminal charges and therefore will have to claim the Fifth Amendment and will be unable to testify in your case. This may be the reason why the district attorney is trying to rush your case to trial as soon as possible.

Mr. Kraut says there's too much information for him to discuss verbally and recommended that we obtain a copy of the trial transcripts and all transcript hearings held in the case of People vs. Edward Damas Case # GA 079201. Mr. Kraut said the officers made numerous statements during hearings in which they admitted to their unlawful activity. This case was heard in Department E in Pasadena Superior Court[1].

---

[1] Due to the volume of the material involved and the expense involved, you will need to have a court order approved which directs the court reporter to prepare the trial transcripts and hearing transcripts at no cost to you because of your indigent status.

People vs. James Wilson   75   Re: Michael Kraut

PO Box 86923 Los Angeles, CA 90086

Mr. Kraut also filed a very lengthy motion in the above titled case. He states the motion lists in detail dates, times and places of corrupt acts by the officers. Furthermore, attached to the motion are declarations from citizens who had factual information about the officer's conduct[2].

Mr. Kraut suggested you send a letter to the DA's office asking them to supply you with all Brady information concerning the officers involved.

Mr. Kraut has documented and recorded information regarding Detective Broghamer's unlawful and unethical behavior during the course of his investigations.

Detective Broghamer is caught on tape attempting to the use intimidation to solicit an in custody inmate to become an informant and if he does not become an informant the word will be put out in the jail that this person is a child molester and will be green-lighted. Mr. Kraut told me there is a lot more information about this detective that he possesses.

Mr. Kraut is willing to accept a subpoena from you to appear in court with copies of all documents and recordings that he has and will assist in any way possible only during the court hearing to help you get possession of all the documents on the officers. Mr. Kraut told me that ethical and legal guidelines prevent him from sharing the information with you without first being ordered to do so by the trial judge.

END OF MEMO

CONFIDENTIAL
ATTORNEY WORK PRODUCT

---

[2] This motion will also require that you obtain a court order directing the court clerk in Pasadena to waive any fees associated with the reproduction of these documents because you aren't indigent defendant.

People vs. James Wilson   Re: Michael Kraut

PO Box 86923 Los Angeles, CA 90086

Amy E. Jacks

Attorney at Law
315 E. 8th St. #801
Los Angeles, CA 90014
amyejacks@sbcglobal.net

(213) 489-9025   (213) 489-9027 fax

October 17, 2014

B Yard Facility Sergeant's Office
North Kern State Prison
P.O. Box 567
Delano, CA 93216-0567

B Yard Facility Counselor's Center
CC-I Assigned Counselor for James Wilson (CDC # AU5200, B6-221)
North Kern State Prison
P.O. Box 567
Delano, CA 93216-0567

Re: *Inmate James Floyd Wilson (CDC # AU5200)*

Dear sir/mam:

I was trial counsel for inmate James Wilson and have represented him since 2006. As part of my representation, I have reviewed Mr. Wilson's CDC Central File and additional documents regarding an unsustained allegation that Mr. Wilson committed an in-custody sexual assault while serving a prison term at Ironwood State Prison.

Mr. Wilson recently wrote me regarding concerns he had about his current custody classification. He asked me to contact you in an effort to clear up any misconceptions about his conduct while in local custody in Los Angeles.

During the pendency of his case, Mr. Wilson was placed in a single man cell within the "High Power" Unit at Los Angeles County Jail ("LACJ") at the request of the Los Angeles County District Attorney and the Pasadena Police Department. I believe that this request was made due to the nature of the criminal allegations against him. Mr. Wilson was not single celled because of his conduct within the LACJ. Mr. Wilson was housed in the LACJ for approximately nine (9) years and, during that time, was not involved in any cell assaults of any kind.

Mr. Wilson and I were aware that the LACJ classified Mr. Wilson as a "keep away" from other inmates. The individuals designated as "keep aways" were either co-defendants on Mr. Wilson's case or alleged victims of non-custodial crimes, including sexual assault, charged against Mr. Wilson. Ultimately, Mr. Wilson was not convicted of any of the alleged sexual assaults.

Previously, while serving a prison term at Ironwood State Prison, Mr. Wilson was accused of sexually assaulting another inmate. That inmate has provided inconsistent stories regarding the alleged assault. The accusation was not sustained.

Mr. Wilson accepted responsibility for the crimes for which he is now incarcerated. He has committed himself to conforming his behavior to the rules of the institution in which he is housed. He is hopeful that any discussion regarding these unsubstantiated allegations of sexual assault will be limited to that which is necessary to insure the safety and security of the institution.

I am happy to address any questions or concerns you have about the content of this letter. And, Mr. Wilson and I appreciate your anticipated professionalism.

Sincerely,

Amy E. Jacks

cc: James Wilson (CDC # AU5200, B6-221)
       P.O. Box 4999-NKSP
       Delano, CA 93126
       Legal Mail. Please Open in Inmate's Presence

Overview

The lengthy record of the informants/witnesses in
my case. Many of them committing crimes while set
to testify, in witness protection programs, and also
receiving witness protection funds/reward money.

JACKIE LACEY • District Attorney
SHARON J. MATSUMOTO • Chief Deputy District Attorney
JOSEPH P. ESPOSITO • Assistant District Attorney

DAVID E. DEMERJIAN • Director

May 3, 2013

Robert P. Royce
Criminal Defense Investigator
P.O. Box 86923
Los Angeles, CA 90086

HAND DELIVERED

Re: People v. Wilson, GA064251

Dear Mr. Royce,

Pursuant to my discovery obligations and Mr. Wilson's request, I have checked the criminal history for material civilian witnesses. Please forward to Mr. Wilson. Enclosed herein please find all discoverable moral turpitude information for each witness. I have included all felony convictions, as well as all arrests and/or convictions (felony or misdemeanor) involving moral turpitude. Where the arrest resulted in a court filing, I have enclosed the court case numbers. Where the arrest did not result in further action by the court, I have included the arrest date and the arresting agency.

John Doe 1:
1) 2/9/00 arrest for PC 594 (LASD Temple Station);
2) 2/5/04 misd conviction for VC 20001(a) (San Bernardino Sheriff) (Court case FRE006678);
3) 7/28/04 misd conviction for PC 496(a) (Salinas Sheriff) (Court Case King City MK076531(b);
4) 8/1/04 arrest for PC 459 (LASD Altadena Station) (Pasadena case 4PA42329);
5) 10/8/04 arrest for PC 459 (Pasadena PD) (Court Case 4PA04703);
6) 3/16/05 misd conviction for PC 148(a) (LASD La Crescenta Station) (Pasadena Case 5PA45925);
7) 5/13/05 misd conviction for PC 243(e)(1) (Pasadena PD) (Pasadena case 5PA46174);
8) 5/28/05 arrest for PC 273.5(a) (Pasadena PD) (5PA02509);
9) 8/12/05 arrest for PC 243(e)(1) (Glendale PD);
10) 11/10/05 arrest for PC 243(e)(1) (Pasadena PD) (5PA05285);
11) 5/26/06 arrest for PC 261.5 (Pasadena PD) (5PA05980);
12) 10/6/06 arrest for PC 261.5 (Pasadena PD)

80

13) 12/22/08 misd conviction for PC 12020(a)(4) (LASD Altadena Station) (case 7PS63514);
14) 12/15/07 arrest for PC 459 (San Bernardino Sheriff);
15) 5/27/08 arrest for PC 459 (San Bernardino Sheriff) (Rancho Cucamonga Court MSB708595);
16) 8/25/10 misd conviction for PC 484 (Rancho Cucamonga case MWV804111);
17) 9/23/08 arrest for PC 666 (Pasadena PD);
18) 11/3/08 arrest for PC 459 (Pasadena PD) (case 8PS04403);
19) 3/12/09 arrest for H&S 11379(a) (Pasadena PD) (case GA076186);
20) 7/1/09 felony conviction for PC 273.5(a) (GA076895);
21) 9/13/09 arrest for PC 148(a) (Pomona PD);
22) 8/30/10 misd conviction for PC 484 (Pomona PD) (case 9PK08222);
23) 12/14/07 arrest for PC 459 (Colton PD)
24) 12/7/08 arrest for PC 12020(a)(4) (Pasadena case 7PS63514)

John Doe 2:
1) 6/16/04 arrest for PC 12025(b)(3) (Pasadena PD);
2) 5/5/05 arrest for PC 487(d) (Pasadena PD);
3) 8/16/07 misdemeanor conviction for PC 12025(a)(2) (Fontana Case MSB704197);
4) 10/5/07 felony conviction for PC 476 (Fontana Case FVA701194);
5) 12/13/08 arrest for PC 243.4(e) (San Bernardino Sherriff) (case MSB900286);
6) 10/1/09 arrest for PC 243(e)(1) (San Bernardino Court Case MSB905893);
7) 11/12/09 felony conviction for H&S 11359 (San Bernardino Case FSB904724);
8) 12/1/09 felony conviction for PC 476 (Tehachapi Court Case AB5525);
9) 2002 arrest for PC 245(a)(1) (Juvenile Case No. GJ17669020402);

John Doe 3:
1) 2/2/02 arrest for PC 484(a) (Pasadena PD);
2) 2/18/05 arrest for PC 459 (LAPD) (case GJ16877);
3) 12/25/05 arrest for PC 211 (Pasadena PD);
4) 4/12/06 arrest for PC 211 (Pasadena PD);
5) 5/30/06 arrest fpr PC 422.7(a) (Pasadena PD);
6) 3/4/10 felony conviction for PC 12021(c) (LA Case BA367866);
7) 9/14/10 felony conviction for PC 12021(a)(1) (LA Case BA375903);
8) 9/15/11 felony conviction for PC 211 (LA Case BA388916);
9) 12/28/05 arrest for PC 487(c) (Pasadena PD) (case 5PA06059);
10) 4/14/06 misd. Conviction for PC 484(a) and 148(a) (also arrested for PC 245) (Case 6PS01427);
11) 8/23/12 felony conviction for PC 137(a) (Case BA389538);

John Doe 4:
1) 2/27/06 misd conviction for PC 484(a) (Alhambra PD) (court case 6AH00100);
2) 11/6/06 felony conviction for PC 243(c)(2) and misd conviction for PC 148(a) (case GA067421);
3) 9/27/07 felony conviction for PC 211 (case BA318025);
4) 11/14/11 felony conviction for H&S 11377(a) (BA375355).

Richard Moten:
1) 10/18/97 arrest for PC 148(a), 496, and VC 10851 (San Jose Sheriff);
2) 5/15/00 arrest for PC 459, 148, 422, 496, and VC 10851 (Milpitas PD, Santa Clara County) (San Jose Case No. CC072091);
3) 12/1/00 felony conviction for PC 245(a)(1) and misd convictions for PC 136.1(a), 148(a), 2800.2(a), and 10851(a) (same Santa Clara County Case CC072091)
4) 6/14/12 felony conviction for VC 10851 and PC 496d(a) (Stockton case SF118083B).

Ricky Pickens:
1) 9/9/02 arrest for PC 273.5(a) (Pasadena PD) (Case 2PA03406);
2) 5/21/96 misd conviction for PC 273.5(a) (LASD) (case 6PA11409)

Kevin Neal:
1) 5/18/03 arrest for PC 484(a) (LASD Altadena Station);
2) 6/7/04 arrest for PC 245(a)(2) (Pasadena PD);
3) 11/17/09 arrest for PC 273.5(a) (Pasadena PD) (Case 9PS04507);

Rodney Fletcher:
1) 3/10/94 arrest for PC 459 (Pasadena PD);
2) 3/28/96 arrest for PC 211 (Pasadena PD) (case J307321);
3) 6/22/96 arrest for PC 487h(a) (Pasadena PD) (case J307789);
4) 8/26/96 arrest for PC 487H(a) (Pasadena PD) (case J308168);
4) 6/7/99 felony conviction for PC 245(a)(1) (Solano County F283848);
5) 4/5/02 arrest for PC 487(a) (Pasadena PD);
6) 7/9/02 felony conviction for PC 487(a) (case GA049309);
7) 12/22/03 arrest for H&S 11352 (Pasadena PD) (case 3PA05085);
8) 8/8/05 arrest for PC 12021.1(a) (Pasadena PD);

Kenneth Fitts:
1) 10/1/03 arrest for PC 69 (Pasadena PD);
2) 5/6/06 arrest for PC 211 (Pasadena PD);
3) 2/22/10 felony conviction for PC 664/187, 626.9(d), 487(c) (case GA069219);
4) 6/7/12 felony conviction for PC 4502(a) (Corcoran case 12CM7269)

Muriel Clark:
1) 4/28/77 arrest for PC 459 and 496 (Pasadena PD);
2) 8/7/81 felony conviction for PC 470 (LA case A561059);
3) 2/25/92 misd conviction for PC 487 (San Bernardino Sheriff) (San Bernardino Case FWV26752B);
4) 10/6/93 felony conviction for PC 459 (Ontario Case FWV01149);
5) 1/25/95 felony conviction for PC 459 (Ontario Case FWV03384);
6) 6/1/94 felony conviction for PC 459 (FWV03912);
7) 12/18/94 arrest for PC 470A and 496 (San Bernardino Sheriff) (case MWV017558);
8) 12/18/94 arrest for PC 459 (San Bernardino Sheriff) (case FWV03886);
9) 7/24/96 felony conviction for PC 470 (San Bernardino Case FWV010368).

Predon Walk:
1)   10/18/01 arrest for PC 496(a) (Los Alamitos PD);
2)   11/1/02 arrest for 10 885 US—Desertion (CAPR LA Barry Nidorf Juv);
3)   8/1/03 arrest for PC 211 (LAPD Metro);
4)   10/3/09 arrest for PC 487(d) (Pasadena PD);
5)   5/28/10 arrest for H&S 11351.5 (Pasadena PD);
6)   11/3/10 arrest for PC 647.6 (Pasadena PD) (case 0PS04982).

Kristin Joyner:
1)   10/8/85 arrest for PC 211 (LAPD);
2)   8/10/90 arrest for H&S 11351 (Pasadena PD);
3)   9/18/90 arrest for PC 148.9(a) (Pasadena PD) (case GA005047);
4)   6/9/93 arrest for H&S 11351.5 (Pasadena PD) (case GA015763);
5)   12/28/93 misd conviction for PC 245(a)(1) (Lancaster court case 93M10148);
6)   6/22/99 misd conviction for PC 148.9 (Pomona case 9PM03808);
7)   12/8/00 felony conviction for PC 32 (Riverside case RIF090003);
8)   4/2/03 felony conviction for PC 459 and 530.5(a) (case GA052238);

Manuel Carranza:
1)   11/28/05 arrest for PC 626.10(b) (Pasadena PD);
2)   6/16/07 arrest for H&S 11359 (Pasadena PD) (GA070046).

In addition, I have bates stamped and enclosed a copy of your PC 969b package, as well as FI cards in our possession for James Wilson, Frank Mitchell, John Doe 3, John Doe 2, and Rodney Fletcher. Although I believe these were already provided in the discovery, I have bates stamped these documents pages 4689 through 4736 and provided them herein out of an abundance of caution.

Thank you for your time and work on this case. If you need any additional information or clarification on the discovery, please contact me at 213-974-3809.

Sincerely,

Habib Balian
Deputy District Attorney
Los Angeles County

I acknowledge receipt of the above-referenced items on behalf of Mr. Wilson:

Date:_____   Signature:_____

LOS ANGELES COUNTY DISTRICT ATTORNEY'S OFFICE

STEVE COOLEY • District Attorney
JOHN K. SPILLANE • Chief Deputy District Attorney

CURTIS A. HAZELL
Assistant District Attorney

February 20, 2009

Amy Jacks, Esq.
315 East 8th Street, #801
Los Angeles, California 90041

Dear Ms. Jacks:

In re   *People v. James Floyd Wilson, Rodney Davon Fletcher, and Damon Lamont Barnes;* Case No. GA064251

The Special Circumstances Committee met and discussed the appropriate penalty in your client's case. The District Attorney's Office will seek the death penalty for your client, James Floyd Wilson.

Should new information arise which you believe might affect this penalty decision, please feel free to forward it in writing to me.

Very truly yours,

STEVE COOLEY
District Attorney

By *Curt Hazell*

CURTIS A. HAZELL, Chairman
Special Circumstances Committee

jw

84

LOS ANGELES COUNTY DISTRICT ATTORNEY'S OFFICE

STEVE COOLEY • District Attorney
JOHN K. SPILLANE • Chief Deputy District Attorney

CURTIS A. HAZELL
Assistant District Attorney

March 5, 2008

Amy Jacks, Esq.
315 East 8th Street, #801
Los Angeles, California 90041

Dear Ms. Jacks:

In re   *People v. James Floyd Wilson, Rodney Davon Fletcher, and Damon Lamont Barnes*
         Case No. GA064251

Charges have been filed against your client, James Floyd Wilson, in the above-referenced case alleging murder with the special circumstances of lying in wait, active participant in furthering the activities of a criminal street gang, and intentional killing of a witness to a crime. This case will be considered by the Special Circumstances Committee on Wednesday, April 23, 2008.

The Committee will consider whether the District Attorney's Office seeks the death penalty against your client. If you wish, you may provide the Committee, in writing, any mitigating evidence you believe would be helpful to the Committee in making its decision. Any information you provide will not be privileged.

Please ensure that the material you submit is received by me at least two days before the Committee is scheduled to meet.

Very truly yours,

STEVE COOLEY
District Attorney

By ~~Curt Hazell~~

CURTIS A. HAZELL, Chairman
Special Circumstances Committee

jw

c: DDA Vivian Moreno
      DDA Garrett Worchell

Called 3/9/08
Msg. memo
from DA
Called 3/31/08
again

18-201 Clara Shortridge Foltz Criminal Justice Center
210 West Temple Street
Los Angeles, CA 90012
(213) 974-5959

85

LOS ANGELES COUNTY DISTRICT ATTORNEY'S OFFICE

JACKIE LACEY • District Attorney
SHARON J. MATSUMOTO • Chief Deputy District Attorney

JOSEPH P. ESPOSITO
Assistant District Attorney

June 14, 2013

HAND DELIVERED

Mr. James Floyd Wilson

Dear Mr. Wilson:

In re *People v. James Floyd Wilson*, Case No. GA064251

After further review of the facts of this case, this office has decided to no longer seek the death penalty should you be found guilty of first-degree murder and the special circumstance found to be true.

Accordingly, I invite you to waive in advance the penalty trial which would normally follow a conviction of first-degree murder with any special circumstance found true. Of course, waiver of the penalty trial will not preclude you from presenting any matter to the trial judge as otherwise provided by law.

Please respond to this letter within ten (10) calendar days of the above date. Address your reply to Gary Hearnsberger, Head Deputy District Attorney, 210 West Temple Street, Room 17-1140, Los Angeles, California 90012.

In the event you are willing to waive the penalty trial, please execute and date the enclosed Waiver and Agreement form, and return the original and two copies to Mr. Hearnsberger who will then file the original with the court.

If you have any questions about this procedure, please contact Mr. Hearnsberger at (213) 974-3800.

Very truly yours,

JACKIE LACEY
District Attorney

By

JOSEPH P. ESPOSITO, Chairman
Special Circumstances Committee

cc

Enclosure

18-201 Clara Shortridge Foltz Criminal Justice Center
210 West Temple Street
Los Angeles, CA 90012
(213) 974-5959

PICTURE SECTION

"One conscious man is more of
a threat to the devil than ten
thousand ignorant worshippers."

- Prophet Muhammad

SLED-PULL
SHOT-PUTT
BENCH PRESS
200 lbs- RUN

A.A.U.- NORTH AMERICAN CHAMPIONSHIP RECORD HOLDER
SINGLE LIFT - BENCH PRESS
RAW OPEN - AGE GROUP CATAGORY:

212 ½ kg   or 468 ¼ lbs
110 kg   or 242 lbs

Brother Tyrone

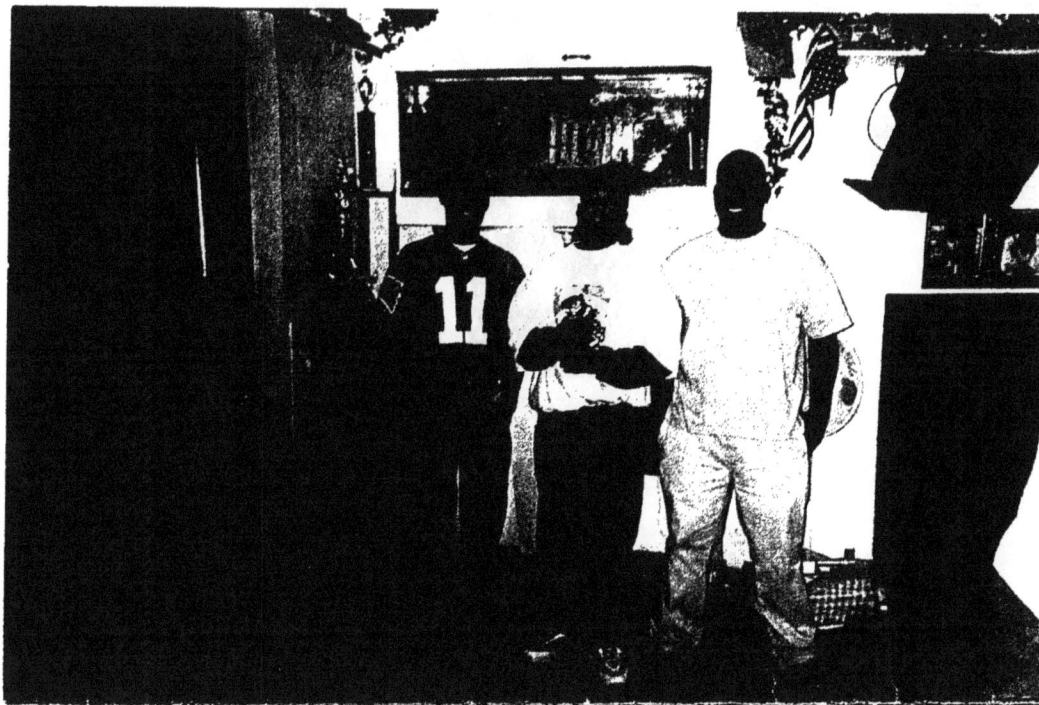

Kenny, James, & Carlee(Monk,SanDiego)

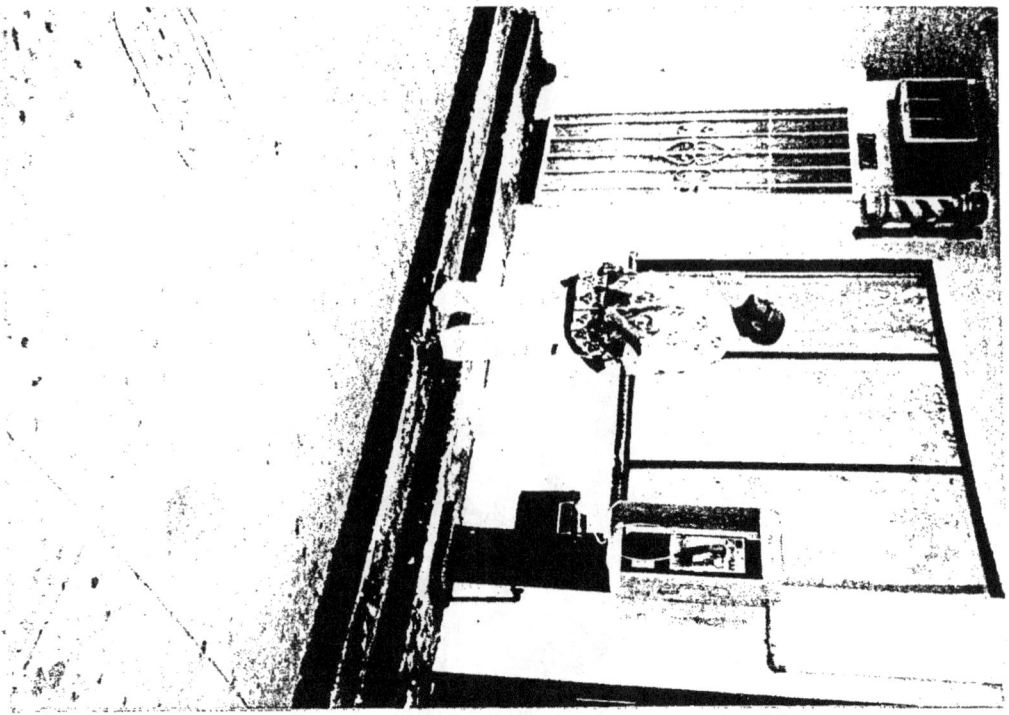

Damon in front of Kenney's old barber shop;Damon's former business card

Big D's

Name Brand Fashion • We Deliver

- enyce
- Phat Farm
- G-Unit

* Sean John
* Akademiks
* Roca Wear & More

(626) 786-3238 • 174*413682*16

Jerome

Patrice &
Family member's

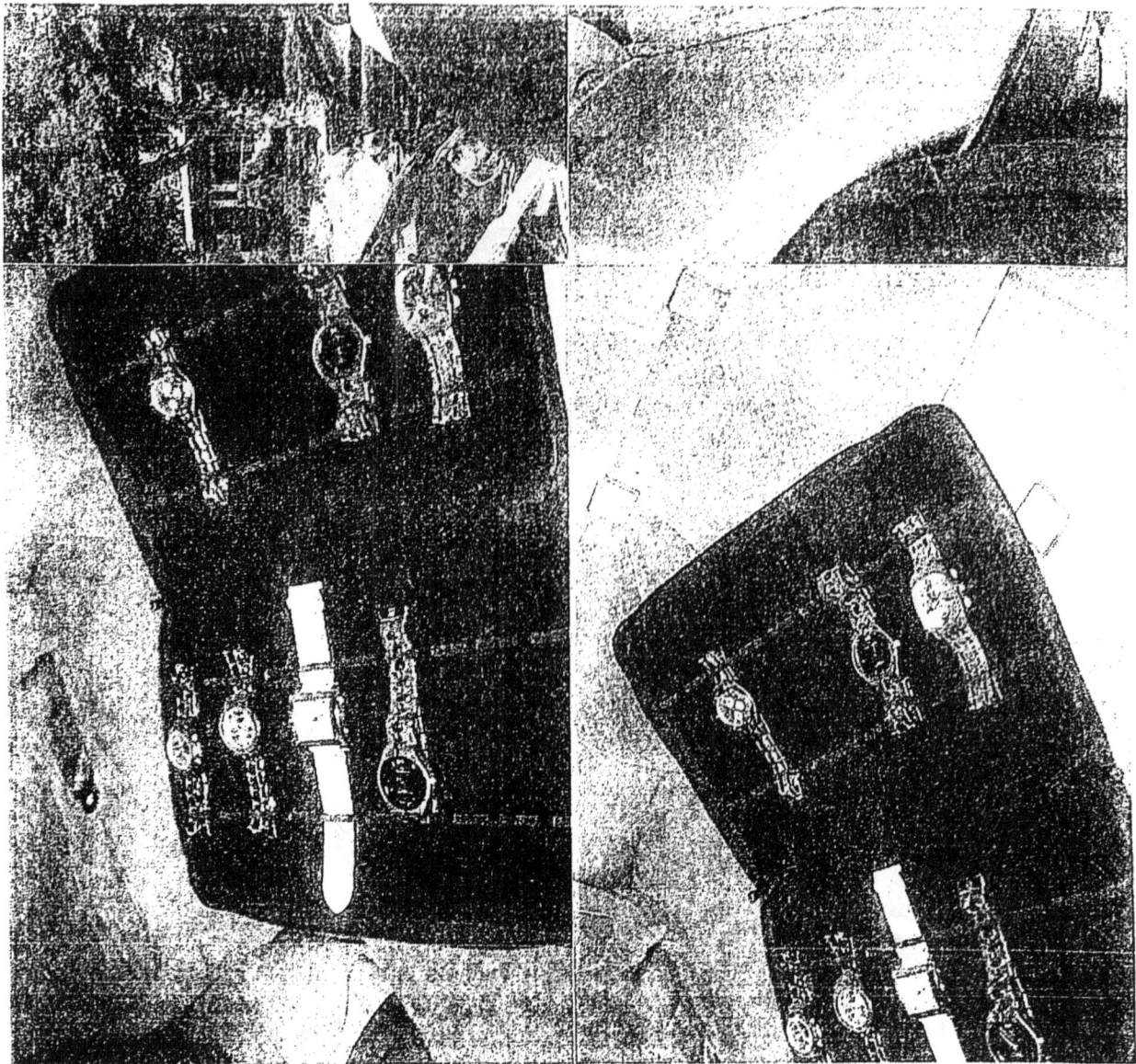

TRAFFIC STOP BY GOMEZ

WATCHES WERE IN A VEHICLE DRIVEN BY JAMES WILSON
PASSENGER: FRANK MITCHELL
PHOTOS OF WATCHES TAKEN BY OFFICER K. GOMEZ ON
4/29/05

03827

<u>Appendix</u>
<u>From a Byrds Eye View</u>

A short book by James Wilson about his late brother Jonathan Thomas, the history of Pasadena gangs, community divisions, and possible hope

From A Byrds-Eye View

The Philosophy And Teachings of John Byrd
1973-2004

Brother Jonathan, Gang founder

Community Division

The Crips began coming to Pasadena in the early to mid-70s. During this period the Bloods were a small minority. Even some of the P.D.L.'s early O.G.s had Crip backgrounds. The precursor for Crips in Pasadena was called "Alley Cats". The progeny for Blood was O.G.B. - "Original Ghetto Boys".

In the late '70s and early '80s, as the Alley Cats morphed into two separate factions: Raymond Avenue Crips and West Side Crips, the Ghetto Boys became what was known as Pasadena Devil Lane. During these "formative years" - late '70s, early '80s - these two factions basically co-existed in much of the same territory, settling much of their disputes with "fights". At one time the Kings Mannor's were occupied by both "Bloods and Crips". The Washington Westside Crips (cliqued w/ R.A.C.) were above "Pepper Street" and everything below Pepper Street were mostly P.D.L.s in Kings Mannors. What brought these ideological conflicts into open warfare and gun battles was the '80s "crack epidemic" and the ensuing "turf wars" for gang "fiefdoms" between high'rollin' O.G. Bloods / their affiliates and Crips and their associates. The drug explosion brought unprecedented amounts of cash and along with it unlimited conflicts and guns and violence to match the pursuit for territorial control into Pasadena's northwest community. This was the Doc-Holiday and Elrader Browning (Ray-Ray) era in Pasadena. It began in the late '70s to early mid/late '80s. Doc-Holiday was a known B.G.F. and purported to be one of its founders. He was also from L.A. and had a family background associated w/ Crips. He paroled to Pasadena after serving a prison term for murder in the mid-60s to mid-70s. This is when he and "Ray-Ray" hooked up. Ray-Ray and his family were linked w/ the Bloods in Pasadena. Ray-Ray was also a B.G.F.

Allegedly Ray was trying to force drug dealers to sell drugs for him or pay him tribute. This drug and turf dispute was only aggravated by the "gang" factor. These elements and their motivations turned King Mannors into a war zone. Much of these gun battles took place directly in front of my house: Hammond Street and Robinson Park. Hammond Street was the "hottest spot" of the King Mannors w/ its adjacency to the "park". There were groups that refused to cooperate w/ Ray-Rays factions, and this caused more violence. Some gangsters would "rob" Ray's "dealers" and shootouts would occur directly in front of my house. Ray-Rays workers invaded our house searching for my brother, who had robbed one of Ray's "workers". My brother Damon had his hands involved with some of these robberies in the projects. My brother worked for another faction of drug/gang crews under a man named Sam Brunston (AKA Lunchmeat). Lunchmeat was an O.G. P.D.L. who ran a drug enterprise comprised of several of his family members and other ranking P.D.L.s. Lunchmeat's group gradually dissolved after his death in 1985. Ray-Ray's group declined after his arrest in 87-88. However, the community divsions and strife they sponsored left Pasadena and P.D.L. a deeply torn and volatile gang w/ a loose and deteriorating leadership and rivers of blood running between people. It was during this period (85-6) that Squiggley Lane came into existence through a man named Franklin Thompson (A.K.A. Hard Rock). He was also a high profile drug dealer and gang member.

Gang History: P.D.L.

P.D.L. was born "with two faces" from it's inception. One facing east, the other west. The founders of P.D.L. created both a west and east side. The west has always been the more numerous and dominant section. The most notable east siders are/were "Rosco" and "Master Blaster" (A.K.A. Bucky). P.D.L. also had one eye to L.A. and the other to Pasadena as we'll soon discover. Several clique-related factions began to emerge after the mid-80s. The most prominent being "King Mannor Projects", the epicenter of drug and gang activity. This area was one of Lunchmeat's Fiefdoms and also a disputed area for Ray-Ray and his workers. This "project" idea was merely a correlation w/ the housing complex called a "project" like similar low-income apartments:

The Pueblos   Imperial Courts (P.J. Watts)   Jordan Downs
                         Nickerson Gardens

There is a "study" which deals w/ the concept which went into the building idea of "projects". It began as a research project to solve the demographic problem w/ "integration". The goal was to find a small area which could house the city's most poor people in the largest amounts. The researchers used test/lab mice to corroborate their research. They called their experimental group site "enclaves" after this research "project" experiment. This info is in a book called Psychic Trauma by Sultan Latif.

So, the King Mannor adopts the above name sake: the project's, housing project. This era precedes "P.J.G." of the mid-90s - founded by my brother, Johnathan (A.K.A. John Byrd). One idea of the early project idea was "K.M.G." - Kings Mannor Gangsters. It was never Project Gangsters until '97. Most Bloods wouldn't use the term "projects" to describe their gang because of it's close link w/ Crip gangs: P.J. Watts Crips, or Project Watts Crips. Bloods would just say: "I live in the projects" or "from the projects", but it was never a distinct gang in Pasadena under the project banner until John Byrd created it. His idea showed no deference to any Blood progeny or perogative. During the mid-to-late 80s the Kings Mannor (projects) drug and gang scene was dominated by a man named "Herald Blaylock". He was viewed as a <u>big homie</u> in P.D.L. and King Mannors. His life and times are seen as P.D.L.'s "golden age" when <u>street level</u> P.D.L.s finally gained control of the drug and gang scene. Even non-affiliated project residence were in the game. By this time the Crips had been run out of King Mannors and lost much of their neighboring territory around northwest Pasadena. Lunchmeat died ('85) and much of his influence and crew died w/ him. Ray-Ray's dominion had dwindled by the time he was arrested (87-88). P.D.L. was left to it's own reins w/ a "loose" leadership. This vacuum left the drug scene open to young and mid-age gang bangers w/ not only a talent and thirst for making money, but a high propensity for violence and the urge to protect their new territorial gains procured mostly by their predecessors. But they had inherited a deeply wounded and fractured territory. S.L.G., Dog Family and Snake Pits (community arms) became 3 of P.D.L.'s largest cliques or extended "sects" - all w/ their own "sectarian" leadership. All of these cliques existed within the traditional boundaries of the larger P.D.L. gang. A map will be drawn up to show their particular and general fiefdoms. This will show that P.D.L. was never a monolithic gang which enjoy a leadership hierarchy that only existed, slightly, in prison. Historical tension existed between P.D.L.s and S.L.G.s, not due to territory per se, but Squiggley's claim of being "their own gang". P.D.L. had long since exerted their right to control and author the destiny of the "Bloods" in Pasadena's northwest sector. The compromise between P.D.L. and S.L.G. was a jail/prison disposition: S.L.G.'s street "independence" would dissolve if any of their members went to jail. They would become nominal "P.D.L.s" while incarcerated. This compromise would later be ignored by John Byrd.

This slight protectorate status had a lot to do w/ P.D.L.'s own rigorous acceptance in prison: L.A. were (1) reluctant to accept them as "Valley Bloods" and (2) the conflict over "Devil" vs. "Denver" Lane was an issue.

The first generation of Pasadena Devil Lanes had to fight in L.A.C.J.'s "Blood Module" to be independently accepted by other "city Bloods". The P.D.L.s were a minority within a minority of the Bloods themselves who were always outnumbered by the Crips. the P.D.L.'s success w/ fighting for their own identity in jails/prisons not only gave them respectability throughout the jail and amongst the Bloods, but it also brought them into closer proximity w/ L.A.'s influence: The <u>"Denver"</u> Lane association and the latter day adoption of this word in substitute for "Devil" became a gradual intrusion into the original Pasadena concept. Although several people resisted this transition, honestly,

99

it was too late. But, P.D.L.'s respectability in the jail also levied it a similar perogative: to designate authority and title over Pasadena Bloods (all Blood cliques, including S.L.G.). This quasi "P.D.L.-S.L.G." union would be broken in '96-97' after Hard Rock paroled in '95. Even Hard Rock had to submit to P.D.L.'s dominance during his near-decade stretch in prison (86-95?). S.L.G. was through playing a back seat to P.D.L. But this independence would not come easy. It was signed in blood, more division, and several life sentences.

Some of P.D.L.'s other notable cliques are:

- Low end (Summit St.)
- Tip Top (Sumitt St.)
- Fair Oaks Street Bloods

These exist today.

Other cliques have "died off/out":

Second Circle Gangsters (the 2nd circle is a cul-de-sac in the "Dead-End" Street on Pepper which runs through King Mannors). the 1st "circle" was on Clairmont Street; before that, dead-end was made a "through street". These were basically K.M.G.s who lived or hung out in the 'Mannors' or on Pepper Street.

The Dog Family was decimated in their war between the P-Nine "brakaway" conflict ('90-'93).

K.M.G. gave way to the more hard line idea of "projects" or w/ the demographic change in the King Mannors. The K.M.G. concept was "absorbed" or faded out and only exist among 2nd generation P.D.L.s ('86-'89?).

But P.D.L. leveraged so much influence in Pasadena that even one southsider gang who shared territory w/ P.D.L.s wore "red rags" instead of the traditional blue rags for southern Mexican gangs. While cliques existed in Pasadena, they were always intended to be subsumed and subject to P.D.L. Independence was never an option. This "dominance doctrine" would first be challenged by a group of P.D.L. defectors calling themselves "P-Nine". Prior to that ('87-'88) P.D.L.'s expanded to Altadena calling themselves: ADL - Altadena Denver Langs. One of the troubles w/ having a large gang was that:

(1) You couldn't manage and supervise your total rank and file
(2) There was always divided loyaltys and interest; and
(3) It was extremely difficult to erect a single leadership which could speak to the multiple levels of interest and divisions.

Kings Manor built in 70's
PDL claim location as the projects or KMG

Community arm's apartment Housing built early 80s
PDL claim location as the "Snake Pit"

OGB

Ray Ray Browning ERA

79-82 Transition Period

82

Low incarceration period (UBN-influences)

1st Generation) PDL (Devil)

Lunch meat HRA

83-84

Devil Lanes fight in jail for recognition

Drug/Tuff Wars Esca-lates

PDL (Denver) 2nd Generation

High Incarceration Period 2nd Generation

Low Period

Violent Gang Infusion w/drug war

85

Mid Period

Projects Hey Day (85-89)

SLG Formed Lunch-meat Killed

SLG Founder Incarcerated 85-86

High Period

Eviction Period from Kings Mannors

87-88 K.M.G Era 2nd

Browning Era continues

HB killed by Dillenger

3rd Generation H. B. ERA in projects 86-90

P-Nine Go to war 90-93 Dillenger Killed

90-91 P-Nine Forms

Rockin Reg Killed by SLG setup

Several Arrest 86-87

Arrest 89

Sent to camp CYA 90-92

Paroled 9/92 RTC 9/92

CK Killed over Rockin Reg incident

PDL/Dog Family & P-Nine Go to war 90-93

Low Period in Projects 91-92

PDL & SLG Relations

SLG & P Nine form union

RTC 9/92-9/94 RTC 11/94

Several PDL' & P-nines members killed (91-93)

J-Dog killed by PDL

T-Krazy killed by SLG J-Dog

93

LA Riots Peace Treaty

Paroled 12/95

Several PDL & SLG Are murdered

PDL & SLG WAR ENSUE

PonyTail killed by SLG 95-6

PDL continues to fracture 94

RTC 2/96

PJG founded by John Byrd 96-7

7yrs incar-cerated RTC 5/03 Pa-roled 2/04 RTC 1/05

PDL,PJG SLG Conflict continues to present 97-12

John Byrd Killed 4/04

Juvenile Arrest Record

Adult Arrest Record

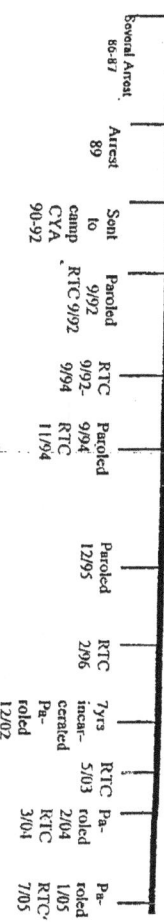

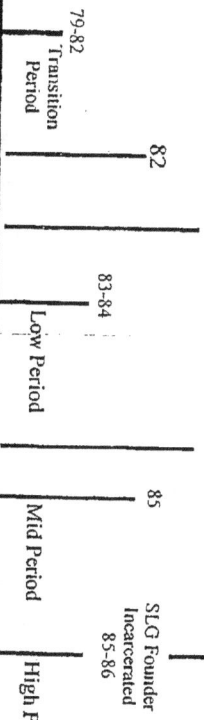

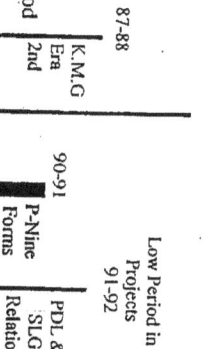

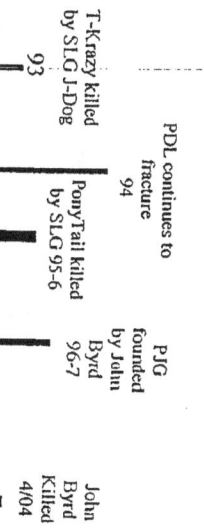

Paroled 12/95 RTC 2/96 Pa-roled 12/02 RTC 5/03 Pa-roled 2/04 RTC 1/05 Pa-roled 3/04 RTC 7/05

1980's TRANSITION PERIOD

HOMICIDE RATES ——► LOW ——— MIDDLE ———HIGHS

1990's: INTERNAL CONFLICTS   & BREAK-AWAYS PERIOD

THE 90's MARKED INDEPENDENCE ERA OF GROUPS FROM PDL

101

Prison History

P.D.L.'s history has been "storied". Since the infiltration of the "Denver" concept into P.D.L. during the 1st generation of P.D.L.s, the gang has experienced several indentations. It was the 1st generation of P.D.L.s, after their prison sentences in the early '80s, who brought "home" the fresh idea of "Denver Lane". This idea, with some difficulty, began to take root and influence among the "low" second generation P.D.L. until it gradually infused most of the "new born" latter day P.D.L.s. Everything else is "history", as it is said. One aspect of this history is written in the mire of prison gang structures. A man by the name of "Peabody", a well-known L.A. Denver Lane Blood was given a life sentence in the late '70s (early '80s). While in prison he formed a "Blood union" or an umbrella group to unify the small population of Bloods slowly filtering into a "sea of Crips" who had come into the prison system and replaced the older group structures (i.e. black Panthers, Black Muslims, and Black Guerilla Family). This umbrella group was and is known as: U.B.N. (United Blood Nation). This consolidation effort was a means to: (1) unify the less numerous Bloods, (2) provide them w/ discipline and (3) ward off the larger Crip gangs and their growing prison groups: C.C.O.s (Consolidated Crip Organization) and Blue Notes.

Around this same time (late '70s early '80s) one of P.D.L.'s founders - Jerry Smallwood - was given a life sentence and he became a formidable member of "Peabody's" U.B.N. Group. Through this Devil/Denver Lane camaraderie a special door of entitlement over P.D.L.'s and D.L.s members merged. Many of the P.D.L.s and D.L.s come under the "U.B.N." when they enter prison. It isn't mandatory but it's influence is highly persuasive. This prison organization absorbs most of the local gangs' independence and rights over divided interest. They basically lose their individual sovereignty to a single "nation" idea. Many "west side" Bloods from L.A. join the UBN ranks. Also, other Bloods in general. A second umbrella group call themselves: Blood Line, and their purported goals and operation is the same: to unify Bloods in prison and indoctrinate them.

These so-called "unity doctrines" would later proliferate into more divisions amongst the Bloods and pit them against each other and make them just as hostile towards each other as the Crips. The idea that "Bloods didn't fight or kill other Bloods" was coming to an end.

The Prison-Gang Factor

Prisoners brought home more than "prison politics", it also shoveled out more sophisticated and pedigreed and seasoned gang members. The escalating war between Bloods and Crips in jails and prisons flooded into the streets w/ a heightened intensity. This new "unity drive" co-mingled w/ the crucible created by the gang-drug epidemic simultaneously taking place in the communities on the "outs". The results: more violence, homicides, and their corollary: prisons. The prison explosion set off an incarceration frenzy. So many young men went to prison during this period ('85-'91) that it became cliche that prison was the place "boys became men". Prison and multiple levels of incarceration also came to be accepted as a "rites of passage" ceremony. The black community became a "feeder" to the system and a breeding ground for hostility, division, and conflict. Many kids grew up "aspiring to go to jail" to emulate the most prevalent model of "manhood" they saw around them: ex-cons. The period was only "upset" with the introduction of gangster rap music (N. W.A., etc.) and gang movies like "Colors" and prison gang movies like "American Me" and later, South Central and Boys In the Hood. Prison, like drugs, gangs, and violence, became a culture; an influence which dominated the lives of generations. With the fall of the "prisoners conscious" movement (B.G.F.s, Black Muslims, etc.) and the introduction of crack into the black community gave rise to the more violent and territorial oriented warfare throughout California gangs. the formative years of the prison Blood Groups (UBN/B.L.) corresponded w/ the time Stanley "Tookie" Williams and his "brain child", the Crips, were on the rise in jails and communities throughout California. In 1985-6 the gangs would employ another instrument into their means of destruction: The Drive By (with semi-automatic weapons). Drive-by shooting distributes indiscriminate violence into the community, taking dozens of innocent lives, many of them kids.

Break Away Groups

By the making of the 3rd generation of P.D.L.s ('89-'90), P.D.L. was more at war with itself than anyone else. Many of the older Crips did not have the turnaround success as the O.G. Bloods. The P.D.L.s were sweeping the youth into its rank and file while most of the Crips' new recruits came from their younger brothers, cousins, and their peers. Their recruitment pool was very small. Pasadena was becoming known as a "Blood City". This one "rejected stone" would now provide a sizable number of the Bloods' population and force throughout the juvenile and prison systems. P.D.L.s are one of the largest Blood gangs in California, and one of the most populous single blood gangs in jails throughout California. However, these numbers haven't always worked to it's advantage. These numbers have served only to provide the basis for

103

more in-fighting and divisions. The first all-out conflict took place in the early-to-mid '90s between several P.D.L. "areas". Parke Street was a known fiefdom of Lunchmeat and also enjoyed some of Ray-Ray's associates. Lunchmeat was actually killed on Parke Street in 1985. This is the location my mother moved us to after we were "evicted" from the Kings Mannor. The cycle of social degeneration continued:same drama, new scene. Parke Street is where ideas learned in the projects gained their "flesh" and practice.

This is where I:

- Wore my first gang colors
- Called myself a P.D.L.
- Sold drugs
- "Shot" a firearm
- Fought w/ Crips
- Went to jail
- Got tattoos and ran away from home, had a girlfriend

Although my "gang life" was born on Parke Street, it was always understood that I was "conceived" in the projects - Kings Mannors. In 1990 a P.D.L. member named Reginald Thompson (A.K.A. Dillenger) murdered Herald Blaylock (H.B.) over a "female drug dispute". Dillenger hung out on Parke Str. w/ several well-known P.D.L.s like"

- Alonzo Hamilton (A.K.A. Bam)
- Lorenzo Newborne (Sunday Shoes)
- Ronals McKenzie (Trick Shot)
- Robert Leagans
- Felton Leagans
- Herb McClain

H.B. was a recognized big homie in the "projects". He had the drugs, the status, the influence. Many other older P.D.L.s were incarcerated. The ones who were out respected H.B. and insisted that the P.D.L.s on Parke Street turn him over for, and to, "street justice". The P.D.L.s on Parke Street refused. The war was on. P-Nine was born. The P.D.L.s firebombed the hangout spot on Parke Street. The occupants were the family member of Bam and Sunday Shoes, including their grandmother. this was in 1992. The P.D.L. clique which took up this beef were "The Dog Family" and some of the "Denver Family" boys. All the Dog Family members have "dog" in their names, like: Pook Dogg and Walt Dogg (founders of D.F.) and Dre Dogg, etc. Same w/ the Denver Family: Denver Den, Denver Kev, Denver Denver Ed, Denver Bam, etc. The "Denvers" were not a clique, but they were amongst those second generation P.D.L.s which were responsible vehicles for driving home the "Denver Land" concept into the "dying" 1st generations, Devil Lanes. They basically ran the Hood as the driving force of the new birthed P.D.L. of the mid-to-late '80s ('86-'89). Many of the east side P.D.L.s joined the fray against the P-Nines, too. Several members of the "Squiggleys" (S.L.G.s) allied w/ the P-Nines, and a "S"-Nine faction was born and with it a group of S.L.G.s now willing to take up arms against the larger P.D.L. group. The first leg of their independence was being put down. P.D.L. was just beginning to walk into the war that would divide it forever. As "all" P.D.L.s were not at war w/ P-Nine, not all S.L.G.s united w/ P-Nine. It was a "sectional war" that laid the foundation for a subsequent "gang war" between P.D.L. and S.L.G. The first death to occur between "S.L.G. and P.D.L.s" was in 1989. A P.D.L. named Rockin' Reg was allegedly "set up" by a S.L.G., Chris King (A.K.A. C.K.). This incident was silently passed over as a "conspiracy theory", but the theory morphed into a hardened belief when, in 1992, "CK" was allegedly killed by a gorup of P.D.L.s - in a darkened alley? the winds of war was on the rise. In 1993, on Parke Street, a young and upcoming P.D.L. (T. Krazy) was shot and killed by J. Dog, a S.L.G. The momentum was building. The gauntlet was finally down when Pony Tails, T-Krazy's Roll-Dog, killed Jay-Dog. About a year later, after Pony Tails paroled from Y.T.S., he was killed by S.L.G.s in 1996, or '96. Pony Tail was a solid P.D.L. member and his death ended any illusion of unity between P.D.L. and S.L.G. There was no turning back. Maps were written, boundaries drawn, and the next episodes were written in scarlet. Squiggley's founder, Hard Rock, had been out of prison about a year. He had long since been ready to assume total leadership of his brainchild (S.L.G.) w/o P.D.L.'s influence. In 1997, his right-hand man, Damon Thomas (A.K.A. Damon Lane) was gunned down by P.D.L.s, and since then the death-toll has alternated. A once respected P.D.L. (8-Ball) was shot during the above incident because he had the audacity to assocate w/ a S.L.G. This is the position I placed myself in when I paroled and decided to be a unifier instead of a divider. We'll have to pull up the above case (Scott vs. Adams). It is within the above hostile climate ('96-'97) that Johnathan formed his idea of P.J.G. - Project Gangsters. His intentions was a totally independent gang from P.D.L.

- They wore black instead of red.
- They were CK/BK instead of simply "CK"
- Their numbers were 754 instead of P.D.L.'s "2X's" or S.L.G.'s "52" (5-Deuce).

Due to their relative proximity w/ P.D.L. and many of their members coming from the "mother gang" of P.D.L. or their familial relationship w/ P.D.L.s their relationship with S.L.G. soured. Johnathan did not remain free enough to lever his complate severance idea and w/ some P.J.G.s, the line between Project P.D.L. and P.J.G got blurred. Johnathan and a few of his members remained P.J.G. "no cuts".

A Page Out Of P-Nine's Book

John Byrd had been "conceived" in the projects, too. but his "birth" was on Parke Street. John Byrd had developed a dislike for the "way" P.D.L. was ran; it's lack of leadership, it's failures to respond to it's fallen, it's lack of unity. He expressed these sentiments to me many times. Johnathan never seen himself as a gang member until the early '90s ('93-'94). Even while in camp ('88) he was not "banging". He was just a P.D.L. "affiliate". When P-Nine was formed, it created multi-ethnic and gang alliances. Mexicans joined and so did Crips and several S.L.G.s and P.D.L. defectors. This is where John Byrd took a page out of the P-Nine's book. He took that "page" and wrote it into his first learning and experience: the projects. His idea was as original as it was revolutionary. Johnathan came to birth during the high period conflict between P.D.L. and P-Nine. He never took a side 'cuz we grew up on both sides of this war. The project was a neutral approach to the conflict between two warring but "family" factions. But to make the message clear, Johnathan wasn't just CK - BK, but: <u>anybody killer</u>. Although, to my knowledge, no Crips ever joined the "P.J.G." it was obvious Byrd took a page from a former Crip gang's book: Hoovers.

Hoover's, now known as Hoover criminals, were once Hoover Crips. They distinguish themselves by using the same proposition as J-Byrd adopted: CK/BK - anybody killer. John Byrd understood that over the years P.D.L. had become it's own worst enemy: P.D.L.s killed more P.D.L.s than all of their rivals put together. In practice P.D.L. to John Byrd was already CK/BK. He felt no need to explain his philosophy. The P.D.L.s could not lecture him about "Blood love". They were their own damn threat. They had no ground on which to negotiate with him from. In the late '90s when Byrd went to prison, he aroused animosity from P.D.L.s for two reasons: (1) he did not respect their sovereignty or entitlement over Pasadena Bloods; he did not "go P.D.L." in jail and (2) he wore his infamous CK - BK tattoos in prison w/ pride. This infuriated reputable P.D.L./UBN affiliates, which gave rise to the theory that his assasswination was ordered by ranking P.D.L. members in the UBN. John Byrd went against the historical grain, and embarrassed P.D.L. and their leadership. One of his tattoos provided a footnote w/ a one word commentary to this position. Johnathan tattooed "misunderstood" across his stomach.

"We were born to be leaders, James."
- John Byrd

Philosophy and Teachings of John-Byrd

- Be loyal to your family and friends
- Protect the weak and those outnumbered
- Think for yourself and fight for what you believe
- Make your own decisions in spite of consequences
- Never give up your freedom to speak as an individual
- Choose your own friends and enemies
- Be a leader, not a follower. You can be a leader without a "gang"
- Don't fear change, know when to step up your game
- Choose death over cowardice
- The brave can forgive their enemies and forge peace

The black rag , for John Byrd, symbolized independence from conforming to traditionally established concepts and beliefs. The black rag represented the freedom and right to seek and choose one's own destiny; the black flag was a symbol of liberation from old norms after John-Byrd embraced Islam (late '90's) and began to study black history. The black flag held the potential for the unity of black people regardless of the color of one's rag. The black rag represented family, not simply a gang.

"James, Allah preserved us because He has a mission, a purpose, for us."
- John Byrd (1998)

"Is it so bad to be misunderstood?
Pythagoras was misunderstood, and Socrates,
and Jesus, and Luther, and Copernicus, and Galileo,
and Newton, and every pure and wise spirit that ever
took flesh. To be great is to be misunderstood."
- Ralph Waldo Emerson
Teacher, Philosopher, Abolitionist

"If a man does not keep pace with his companions, perhaps
it is because he hears a different drummer. Let him step to
the music he hears, however measured or far away."
- Henry David Thoreau
Philosopher, Naturalist, Abolitionist

Late Note

Less than a year after forming his new gang, John Byrd was sent to prison, where I had already been for almost two years. We exchanged letters throughout his incarceration. In one of his letters (dated: November 18, 1998), he wrote in his post script (actual P.S. below) the following:

> P.S.　　You know what time it is:
>
>　　　　　West Side Pasadena A.K.
>　　　　　Projeck　　　　　　B.K.
>　　　　　Gangstas　　　　　 C.K.
>
> Say Bro, I forgot to let you know how
> the PDL's were talking about doing a
> brotha. But you know I can handle myself.
> A coward dies many deaths, but a soldier
> only dies once.
>
>　　　　　John Muthafuck'n Byrd

Note: the letter in it's entirety was seized from my home during a search warrant by Pasadena Police, and became part of the discovery provided to me by the prosecution.

LOOKING BACK AND FORWARD
A Brief Bio-Sketch

"The mythical Sankofa bird of West Africa has
two heads: one facing forward, the other
backwards. Why? The further you look back,
the more you can see ahead. Our future is
rooted in our history."

ACCEPTING THE CHALLENGE
A JOURNEY OF SELF DISCOVERY

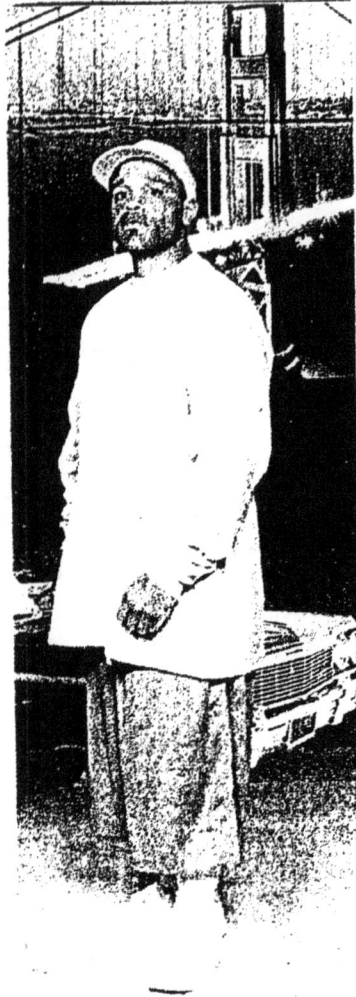

BY: JAMES WILSON

Co-Organizer of 2019

PLEDGE OF PEACE

"From the Projects to Prison"
Back Story

I was born in Pasadena, California. I lived with 6 other siblings in a public housing project called the Kings Mannors. By the early 80's it was over ran with drugs, gangs, and violence. My mother was a single parent, high school dropout, who survived off her wits and public assistance for many years. But she was unable to supervise our entire family adequately, so most of us fell into stealing, gangs, drugs use and sales. It wasn't long before my history with crime and violence would take me into juvenile detention centers, camps, and Youth Authorities where I learned new ways to be a worse person.

I went in a superficial gangmember and emerged years later as a sophisticated gang banger with a reputation and leadership status in the gang. I had built an image, which needed to be fed with what it craved: more senseless violence and criminal behavior. This would keep me under some form of criminal justice supervision for all of my teenage years and extend through various prison terms, the first for murder, until I was 30 years old and facing the death penalty. While destroying other peoples lives and my community I was bringing myself to an end.

"Can't Mix Good with the Bad"
<u>Prison Life</u>

While on my first term (96-2002) I found myself in every conceivable form of trouble. But, there were some older lifers there who were telling me that I was good at other things. They would say, "Youngster, you are smart. You have a lot of influence. Why don't you do something else with your life?" They would give me books to read and try to advise me. But I still couldn't break from the negative thinking I'd developed, much of it written in undisclosed pain and domestic abuse. The external adult monster was really a badly hurt inner child.

I left from prison at age 28. I tried to give myself a fresh start. It didn't last. I found myself returned to custody for gang association and parole violations.

While in custody my brother, John Bryd, was murdered in an internal gang dispute which broke my hopes in trying to do good.

When I paroled in 2005 my mother said; "James, you are a leader. God wants you to use your gifts for good." With her and other peoples advice I tried to mend the gang rift in my city and even entered the Social Justice Protest Movement. But, it became obvious that I was surrounded by internal demons within and old gang rivals without. Plus, I hadn't properly mourned the death of my brother, neither had I forgiven the gang for his death. I went on a rampage which landed me back in custody on a capital case indictment and at total odds with my former gang. It would be totally impossible to work for good while harboring ill-will and maintaining old relationships in the streets. But, the light was about to penetrate into my hard dark skull. It would come in the most difficult period of my life.

At Deaths Door
Light shines In

I spent 9 years in L.A county Jail fighting not to go to death row. While there I had loss my fiancé, family and friends. But, I had met a Buddhist chaplain, Daniel "Nagy" Buckley and Rabbi (Brian Mayer) who took personal interest in me, he told me: "James, even in prison you'll have a life. You have a good mind. Use it." Nagy would bring me dozens of books and visit me weekly. Little did I know he'd ask deputies in the jail how I was doing. For a few years

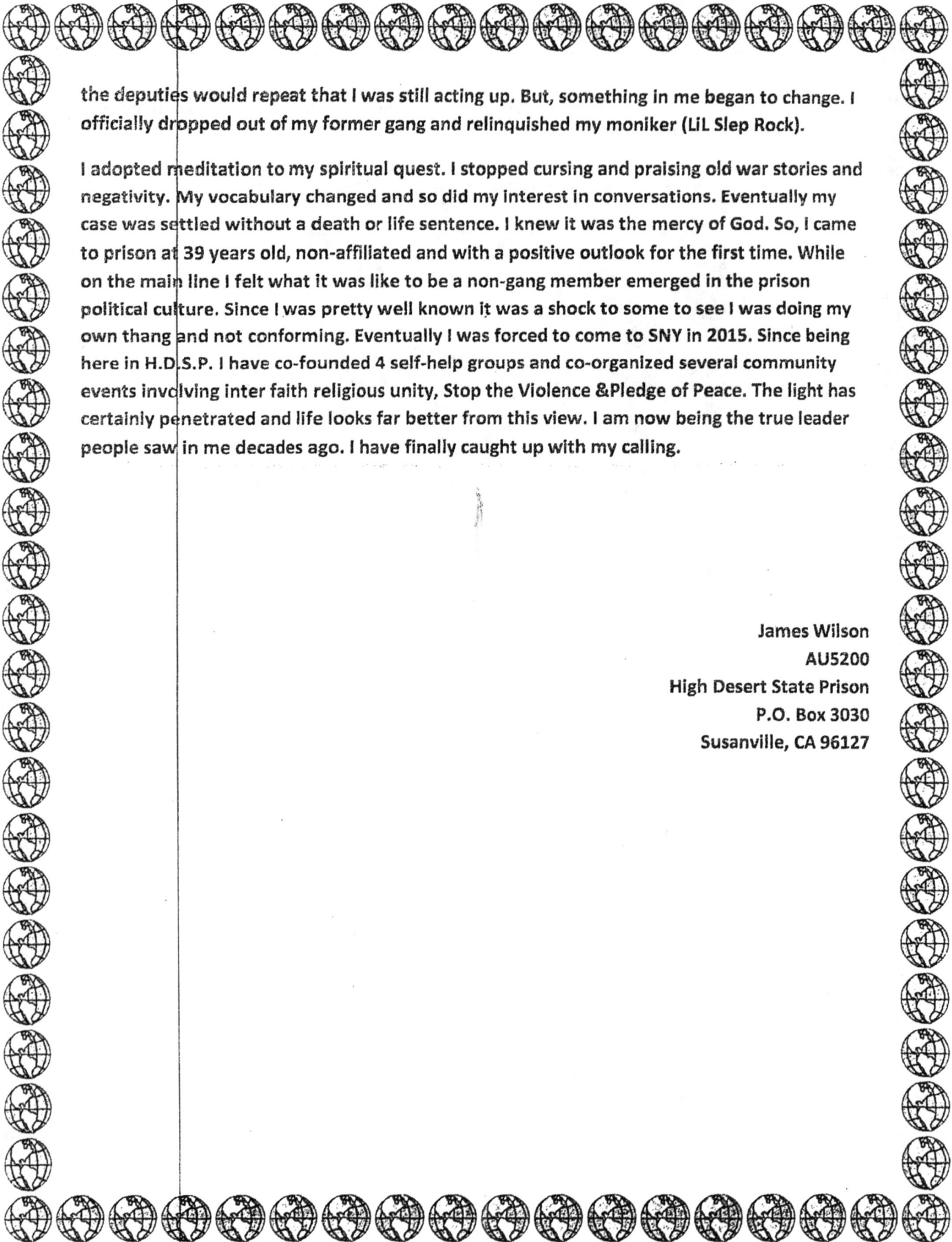

the deputies would repeat that I was still acting up. But, something in me began to change. I officially dropped out of my former gang and relinquished my moniker (LiL Slep Rock).

I adopted meditation to my spiritual quest. I stopped cursing and praising old war stories and negativity. My vocabulary changed and so did my interest in conversations. Eventually my case was settled without a death or life sentence. I knew it was the mercy of God. So, I came to prison at 39 years old, non-affiliated and with a positive outlook for the first time. While on the main line I felt what it was like to be a non-gang member emerged in the prison political culture. Since I was pretty well known it was a shock to some to see I was doing my own thang and not conforming. Eventually I was forced to come to SNY in 2015. Since being here in H.D.S.P. I have co-founded 4 self-help groups and co-organized several community events involving inter faith religious unity, Stop the Violence &Pledge of Peace. The light has certainly penetrated and life looks far better from this view. I am now being the true leader people saw in me decades ago. I have finally caught up with my calling.

James Wilson
AU5200
High Desert State Prison
P.O. Box 3030
Susanville, CA 96127

Doing gang intervention work in Los Angeles, California in the area
where black and mexican gangs are at war.

At the Mosque in the city of Chino, California with Muslims from around the world.

At the Ten Thousand Men March in
Los Angeles, California, in 2003

Stop the Killing Rally in
Los Angeles California.

"Don't Delay Destiny"
Rear View to My Future Work

Between 29 and 30 years old I had tried to use my influence for good on the streets. But, I was still heavy into gang life, selling drugs and committing other crimes. It would take almost another decade before I was ready to confront my pain, my wrong and completely devote my life to be a positive leader with no gang affiliation and criminal behavior.

"In a country that imprisons man falsely, the place for a righteous man is then in prison"-**Henry David Thoreau**

Backstory

There is an old saying; "Do not look for Africa's Leaders in school. But look for them from in prison".

This quote had its origin in a time when African countries had been invaded by foreigners' and all of the men were being arrested and imprisoned.

But this is not unique to just Africa, you will find that that large scale men, were imprisoned in parts of Asia, Europe, Latin America, and now the crisis of mass incarceration in north America. So many men have been locked up that it is predictable that, "the Leaders of the future will come out of prison".

"If you want to know what a nation is like, Visit it's prisons"-Nelson Mandela

(Former South African Prisoner)

"Regimes may come and go, but Prison's go on forever, although change occurs within its walls. When a revolution succeeds, the gates of the prison are opened and the prisoners, victims of the regime that has just fallen, go free, literally on their heels, the gates close on new prisoners, victims of the new regime that has just been set up.

Humanity is still waiting for the revolution that will not exchange prisoners but will do away

with prisons."-Menachen Begin

(Former Prisoner in Russia)

SOCIAL HISTORY SUMMARY AND RAP SHEET OF JAMES WILSON

Confidential: Attorney Work Product
To: Defense Team
From: Angela Mason, LCSW
Re: Witnesses to be interviewed to complete the social life history of James Wilson

James Wilson, Terminal Annex, P.O. Box 86164, Los Angeles, Ca 90086-0164

**Interviewed

Mitigation Witness List

Last Name	First Name	Address Phone No.	Relationship to Defendant
Anthony	Karlee	Blythe or San Diego	Ran drug program
Avonia Samuels	Markie	Arizona	Hope Wilson's son, prosecuted for molesting Ronisha McKenzie, also molested Johnnie Reddix
Barnes	Damon	Incarcerated at Twin Towers	Brother DOB 10/17/66 Product of one night stand between Connie Piggee and Robert Cleon Barnes
Barnes	Mimi	May live in Pasadena	Damon's wife
Barnes	Dimitri		Damon's daughter
Brooks	Mary	Pasadena	Former Girlfriend of Roosevelt Wilson, has No children with him
Capuano	Gary		Retired cop, knowledgeable on King's Manor
**Carter	Derrick	Compton, 90220	Parole Agent, former guard at Ironwood Prison
Clark	Leroy	Deceased	Boyfriend of Connie Piggee. They had three children: Didi (Muriel), Tony and Terry.
Clark	Didi "Muriel"		Maternal Aunt May testify against James History of cocaine and pill use
Clark	Terry	Lancaster	Maternal Uncle Drug addict
**Clark	Toni	Palmdale, CA 93550	Maternal Aunt History of crack abuse
**Clifford	Gary	Glendale, CA 91204	Ex-Cop (King's Manor area), professor, former

People vs. James Wilson
Witnesses to be interviewed

			mayor of Glendora, Senior VP of Ivy Hill DOB: 8/14/59
**Cunegin	Yolanda	Arcadia, CA 91006	Aunt, ordained minister Former wife of Tyrone Ferdinand DOB: 2/14/58
**Dillard	Annette Reddix	Lancaster	Maternal Aunt DOB: August 16, 1963
**Evans	Mother Dorothy	Refuge Christian Center	Church Pastor, presided over brother Jonathan's funeral
**Ferdinand	Tony	Yucca Valley, CA 92284	Had three children with Connie Piggee: Tyrone, Kenny and Patrice Ferdinand DOB: 9/24/39
**Ferdinand	Kenny	Pasadena, CA 91104	Half Brother DOB: 8/14/65 Son of Tony Ferdinand and Connie Piggee
**Ferdinand	Manuel	Manuel Ferdinand Pasadena, CA 91103	Step brother Second oldest son of Tony Ferdinand
**Ferdinand, North	Patrice	Lancaster, CA 93535	Half Sister Daughter of Tony Ferdinand and Connie Piggee
**Ferdinand	Tyrone	Pasadena, CA 91116	Half Brother Son of Tony Ferdinand and Connie Piggee
Ferdinand	Tyra		Adopted daughter of Yolanda Cunegin
Harrison	Mr.	Pasadena	Dean at Wilson Junior High, lives across the street from John Kennedy's mother
**Haggerty	Aaron	Pasadena, CA 91103	Children of Dorothy Piggee: Cousin
Haggerty	Darin	Pasadena, CA 91103	
"	Erik	Emilino and Mentor, Pasadena	Cousin
"	Derek		Cousin

People vs. Wilson
Mitigation Witness List
Angela Mason, LCSW

124

"	April	Resides behind Dorothy Piggee	Cousin
Hampton	Pastor George		Helped "save" Connie in 1994 when she quit drinking
Harris	Mr.		Former middle school teacher
Haynes	Connie		Daughter of Patrice Ferdinand/North DOB: 10/29/85
Haynes	Darrell	Crack addict, incarcerated for murder	Father of Connie and Rosalind Haynes (Patrice's children)
Haynes	Rosalind	Lancaster	Daughter of Patrice Ferdinand/North DOB: 8/30/86
Howl	Captain	Ironwood Prison Blythe, CA	
Hudson	Mrs.		Former teacher lived next door to Aunt Dorothy Piggee
Kennedy	John	Pasadena	Brother, Tyrone's best friend, James' mentor and friend
**Kajiwara	Ginny	Alta Dena, CA 91001	James former elementary school teacher
Law	Rick		Police commander who grew up in King's Manor
McKenzie	Ronald	Recently released from prison	Father of Ronisha McKenzie, (Patrice's daughter)
*McKenzie	Ronisha	Lancaster, CA	Daughter of Patricia and Ronald McKenzie. DOB: 2/8/89
**Moses	Regina	Alta Dena, CA 91001	Principal Willard Elementary
Meyer	Derek Veronica	Pasadena, CA 91106	James' cousin, parents of Darianna Resides next door to Dorothy
Meyer	Darianna "Dada"		Second cousin
Mitchell	Starsha		Daughter of Annette Wilson

People vs. Wilson
Mitigation Witness List
Angela Mason, LCSW

125

**North	Richard	Lancaster, CA 93535	Sister's husband Unemployed truck driver, formerly incarcerated for selling drugs
North	Rianna	Lancaster, CA 93535	Daughter of Patrice and Richard North DOB: 8/12/94
Pickens	Ricky		Distant relative of Tyrone's family. Gang counselor from the police department who facilitated meetings.
**Piggee	Connie	Pasadena, CA 91103	Mother-live in home assistant DOB: 8/4/48
**Piggee	Dorothy	Pasadena, CA 91103	Maternal Aunt Resides with Aaron Haggerty
Pool	Mr.	Pasadena	Manager at King's Manor and an activist in the neighborhood
Pulphis or Pulphus	Ms.		Former typing teacher (son Willie was killed)
	Rianna		Cousin
Reddix	Johnnie		Cousin, daughter of Annette Wilson and Eugene Reddix
Reddix	Eugene	Incarcerated for spousal abuse	Father of Johnnie Reddix (mother is Annette Wilson)
Reddix	Eumeka		Daughter of Annette Wilson and Eugene Reddix
Thomas	Joe	Retired Sanitation worker for the city of Pasadena	Boyfriend of Connie Piggee, had a son; Jonathan
**Wallace	Lt. Rodney	Pasadena	African American police officer since 1978 in Pasadena area.
Ward	Jason		Pasadena police officer, worked the same precinct as Wallace.
Washington	Kenny		Roosevelt's former gambling buddy. Roosevelt was incarcerated after shooting Kenny in 1973 or 1974

People vs. Wilson
Mitigation Witness List
Angela Mason, LCSW

126

Wilson	Alicia	Community Arms Pasadena Mrs. Harper: Arkansas	Granddaughter of Mrs. Harper, Roosevelt Wilson's wife. Mrs. Harper and Roosevelt had 4 kids
**Wilson	Annette		Aunt; daughter of Jose Wilson and Johnnie Mae DOB: 8/16/63 Addicted to cocaine
Wilson	Hope		Aunt Addicted to cocaine
Wilson	Jerome	Work: Community Arms Pasadena	Brother Refused Interview
Wilson	Roosevelt		Father of Jerome and James Abusive gambler 18 years older than Connie Piggee DOB: Feb. 4, 1930 DOD: Nov. 12, 1999
Date of birth	Dec. 20, 1974		

People vs. Wilson
Mitigation Witness List
Angela Mason, LCSW

127

People vs. James Wilson
Confidential Attorney Client Work Product
Housing Locations

Address   **Approximate Dates**

2 locations on Summit across from Orange Grove, Pasadena
Connie grew up here

721 Garfield, Pasadena
Connie's first apartment with her sister, she moved here to get away from her drug addict, controlling mother (Johnnie Mae Edwards). She started getting her own county check at 16 (1964). James' older half brother, Tyrone Ferdinand, was born this same year.

840 Buckeye, Pasadena

831 Los Robles, Pasadena

1081 Morton, Pasadena   **1973-1974**
Adjacent to the King's Manor, torn down, now being made into a football filed. James was born while they lived here (in Monterey Park

45 Hammond, Pasadena
King's Manor   **1976-1987**
They were kicked out of the project and lost their Section 8 due to Damon Barnes' drug sales.

68 Pepper Street, Pasadena   **1987**
From school records, not sure of exact dates

279 1/2 Park Street #3, Pasadena   **1988-1989**
Upstairs, the yard was all dirt. They place was falling apart with no metal gate

369 Astrabula, Pasadena   1970's-1980's
Roosevelt lived here with his girlfriend Mary Brooks while alternating time with Connie at 45 Hammond

Chronology Address Index

Address	Address
68 Pepper St. in Pasadena	1948 Birth Certificate of Connie Piggee
831 North Los Robles #4, Los Angeles, CA 91104	1973 Birth Certificate of Jonathon Thomas
45 W. Hammond St. Pasadena, CA 91103	1984 School Letter to Connie Piggee
279 1/2 Park St., Pasadena	1990, CYA Records
2383 North Olive Ave, Altadena	1994, CYA Records
279 Park St. Pasadena (mother)	1995, CYA Records
1518 Fair Oaks in Pasadena (mother)	2002, Rent Receipt

12/01/05 12:05:04   Message received from CLETS for unit 5384
CA0195300.09141311.LEMOS 0   DATE:20051201 TIME:12:04:57
RESTRICTED-DO NOT USE FOR EMPLOYMENT,LICENSING OR CERTIFICATION PURPOSES
ATTN:LEMOS 05042204 INV5384
****
DO NOT COLLECT DNA. DNA SAMPLE HAS BEEN RECEIVED,
TYPED, AND UPLOADED INTO THE CAL-DNA DATA BANK.
FOR INFO (510) 620-3300 OR PC296.PC296@DOJ.CA.GOV.
****
** PALM PRINT ON FILE AT DOJ FOR ADDITIONAL INFORMATION PLEASE
E-MAIL PALM.PRINT@DOJ.CA.GOV
** LASO RECORD
III CALIFORNIA ONLY SOURCE RECORD
CII/A09141311
DOB/19741220   SEX/M RAC/BLACK
HGT/600 WGT/255 EYE/BRO HAI/BLK POB/CA
NAM/01 WILSON,JAMES FLOYD
02 WILSON,JAMES
03 MONIKER,SLEPROCK
MON/SLEPTROCK; SLEPROCK
FBI/259992CB1
DOB/19741227 19741221
CDL/A9653165 D8087757 D8097757

SOC/███████████
INN/CYA-Y059870 CDC-K029628
SMT/TAT L HND; SC L CHK; TAT L WRS; TAT L FGR; TAT UR ARM; TAT LF ARM;
TAT RF ARM; TAT R ARM; TAT ARM; TAT L ARM
MDS/CTZ XX
 /STUDENT; CONSTRUCTION; CONSTRUTION; NONE
* * * *
ARR/DET/CITE: NAM:01 DOB:19741220
19881228 CAPD PASADENA
CNT:01   #138171
11352 HS-TRANSPORT/SELL NARCOTIC/CNTL SUB
DISPO:RELEASED TO PARENT/GUARD
CNT:02
11351.5 HS-POSS/PURCHASE COCAINE BASE F/SALE
DISPO:RELEASED TO PARENT/GUARD
* * * *
ARR/DET/CITE: NAM:01 DOB:19741220
19890722 CASO LOS ANGELES
CNT:01   #1519855-01470577
11352 HS-TRANSPORT/SELL NARCOTIC/CNTL SUB
* * * *
CUSTODY:CYA   NAM:01
19901011 CAYA NORWALK

CNT:01   #Y59870
-777 W&I
11352 HS-TRANSPORT/SELL NARCOTIC/CNTL SUB
SEN FROM:LOS ANGELES CO
* * * * * * * * * *
**   POTENTIAL FELONY STRIKE ENTRY   **
 * * * * * * * * *
 * * *
ARR/DET/CITE: NAM:01 DOB:19741227
19921120 CAPD PASADENA
CNT:01   #138171 1470577
-JUVENILE

00082

130

12/01/05 12:05:04   Message received from CLETS for unit 5384
CA0195300.09141311.LEMOS 0   DATE:20051201 TIME:12:04:57
RESTRICTED-DO NOT USE FOR EMPLOYMENT,LICENSING OR CERTIFICATION PURPOSES
ATTN:LEMOS 05042204 INV5384
* **
DO NOT COLLECT DNA. DNA SAMPLE HAS BEEN RECEIVED,
TYPED, AND UPLOADED INTO THE CAL-DNA DATA BANK.
FOR INFO (510) 620-3300 OR PC296.PC296@DOJ.CA.GOV.
** *****

** PALM PRINT ON FILE AT DOJ FOR ADDITIONAL INFORMATION PLEASE
E-MAIL PALM.PRINT@DOJ.CA.GOV
** LASO RECORD
III CALIFORNIA ONLY SOURCE RECORD
CII/A09141311
DOB/19741220   SEX/M RAC/BLACK
HGT/600 WGT/255 EYE/BRO HAI/BLK   POB/CA
NAM/01 WILSON,JAMES FLOYD
02 WILSON,JAMES
03 MONIKER,SLEPROCK
MON/SLEPTROCK; SLEPROCK
FBI/259992CB1
DOB/19741227 19741221
CDL/A9653165 D8087757 D8097757

SOC/563453747
INN/CYA-Y059870 CDC-K029628
SMT/TAT L HND; SC L CHK; TAT L WRS; TAT L FGR; TAT UR ARM; TAT LF ARM;
TAT RF ARM; TAT R ARM; TAT ARM; TAT L ARM
MDS/CTZ XX
    /STUDENT; CONSTRUCTION; CONSTRUTION; NONE
* * * *
ARR/DET/CITE: NAM:01 DOB:19741220
19881228 CAPD PASADENA
CNT:01   #138171
11352 HS-TRANSPORT/SELL NARCOTIC/CNTL SUB
DISPO:RELEASED TO PARENT/GUARD
CNT:02
11351.5 HS-POSS/PURCHASE COCAINE BASE F/SALE
DISPO:RELEASED TO PARENT/GUARD
* * * *
ARR/DET/CITE: NAM:01 DOB:19741220
19890722 CASO LOS ANGELES
CNT:01   #1519855-01470577
11352 HS-TRANSPORT/SELL NARCOTIC/CNTL SUB
* * * *
CUSTODY:CYA   NAM:01
19901011 CAYA NORWALK

CNT:01   #Y59870
-777 W&I
11352 HS-TRANSPORT/SELL NARCOTIC/CNTL SUB
SEN FROM:LOS ANGELES CO
* * * * * * * * * *
**   POTENTIAL FELONY STRIKE ENTRY   **
* * * * * * * * *
* * *
ARR/DET/CITE: NAM:01 DOB:19741227
19921120 CAPD PASADENA
CNT:01   #138171 1470577
-JUVENILE

00002

130

12021.1(A) PC-POSS F/ARM W/PR VIOL:MURDER/ETC
DISPO:RELEASED TO PARENT/GUARD
* * * *
CUSTODY:CYA   NAM:01
1[ ]0201   CAYA NORWALK
CNT:01   #Y59870
12025(B) PC-CARRY CONCEALED WEAPON ON PERSON
SEN FROM:LOS ANGELES CO
* * * * * * * * * *
**   POTENTIAL FELONY STRIKE ENTRY   **
* * * * * * * * * *

* * * *
ARR/DET/CITE: NAM:01 DOB:19741220
19941109 CAPD PASADENA
CNT:01   #4186366 01470577
12021(A) PC-FELON/ADDICT/ETC POSSESS FIREARM
- - - -
COURT: NAM:01
19941213 CAMC PASADENA
CNT:01   #94M06263
12031(A) PC-CARRY LOADED FIREARM:PUBLIC PLACE
*DISPO:CONVICTED
CONV STATUS:MISDEMEANOR
COM: 180 DAY(S) JAIL
COM: DCN-N0014681519600004901
* * * *
ARR/DET/CITE: NAM:01 DOB:19741220
19960131 CAPD PASADENA
C[ ]:01   #4706021 1470577
2[ ](A)(1) PC-FORCE/ADW NOT FIREARM:GBI LIKELY
CNT:02
187(A) PC-MURDER
- - - -
COURT: NAM:01

19960927 CASC SAN BERNARDINO
CNT:01   #FVA05381
245(A)(2) PC-ASSAULT WITH FIREARM ON PERSON
-USED FIREARM
*DISPO:CONVICTED
CONV STATUS:FELONY
SEN: 7 YEARS PRISON
* * * * * * * * * * *
**   POTENTIAL FELONY STRIKE ENTRY   **
* * * * * * * * * * *
* * * *
ARR/DET/CITE: NAM:01 DOB:19741220
19960201 CASO SAN BERNARDINO
CNT:01   #9602340025
187(A) PC-MURDER
ARR BY:CAPD FONTANA
* * * *
CUSTODY:CDC   NAM:02
1[ ]961121 CASD CORRECTIONS
[ ]:01   #K29628
245(A)(2) PC-ASSAULT WITH FIREARM ON PERSON
-USED FIREARM
SEN FROM:SAN BERNARDINO CO

00093

131

SEN: 7 YEARS PRISON
COM: COM-CTN FVA05381
COM: CCN-6126D253516
* * * * * * * * * *
*   POTENTIAL FELONY STRIKE ENTRY   **
* * * * * * * * * * *
* * * *
ARR/DET/CITE: NAM:01 DOB:19741220
20030516 CAPD PASADENA
CNT:01   #7696375-03027112
11351.5 HS-POSS/PURCHASE COCAINE BASE F/SALE
COM: ADR-051603 (6245, SACRAMENTO,, E, ALTADENA, CA,
91001,)
COM: SCN-43331360020
- - - -
COURT: NAM:01
20030707 CASC PASADENA
CNT:01   #3PA0176301
148.9(A) PC-FALSE ID TO SPECIFIC PEACE OFICERS
DISPO:DISMISSED/FURTHERANCE OF JUSTICE
CNT:02
11357(B) HS-POSS MARIJUANA 28.5- GRAMS
DISPO:DISMISSED/FURTHERANCE OF JUSTICE

* * * *
CUSTODY:CDC   NAM:01
20030905 CASD CORR DELANO
CNT:01   #K29628
VIOLATION OF PAROLE
) FINISH TERM
COM: SCN-91632520031
* * * * * * * * * * *
**   POTENTIAL FELONY STRIKE ENTRY   **
* * * * * * * * * * *
* * * *
ARR/DET/CITE: NAM:01 DOB:19741220
20040329 CAPD PASADENA
CNT:01   #8068280-01470577
3056 PC-VIOLATION OF PAROLE:FELONY
COM: ADR-032904 (1518, FAIROAKS AVE, 1, N, PASADENA,
CA, 91103,)
COM: SCN-43340890010
* * * *
CUSTODY:CDC   NAM:01
20040921 CASP CHINO
CNT:01   #K29628
VIOLATION OF PAROLE

-TO FINISH TERM
COM: SCN-92542660025
* * * * * * * * * * *
**   POTENTIAL FELONY STRIKE ENTRY   **
* * * * * * * * * * *
* * * *
ARR/DET/CITE: NAM:01 DOB:19741220
)50727 CAPD PASADENA
CNT:01   #8672911-01470577
3056 PC-VIOLATION OF PAROLE:FELONY
COM: ADR-20050727 (624, SACRAMENTO ST,, E, PASADENA,
CA,,)

00094

```
COM: PHOTO AVAILABLE
COM: SCN-L3252080008
* * * *
ARR/DET/CITE:          NAM:02  DOB:19741220
20  0901  CASO LA INMATE RECEP CTR
CNT:01      #8719253-01470577
-WARRANT
3056 PC-VIOLATION OF PAROLE:FELONY
ARR BY:CARA OTHER LOS ANGELES CO
WARRANT  #K29628
COM: ADR-20050901 (624, SACRAMENTO,,, ALTADENA, CA,

91001 ) TIME AT ADDRESS-(02 YEARS, )
COM: SCN-45552440056
**********************************************************
**********************************************************
NOTE:  6 POTENTIAL ENTRIES WITH FELONY CONVICTION DATA WERE
FOUND FOR THIS SUBJECT. SEE ENTRIES IN THE RECORD ANNOTATED
WITH "POTENTIAL FELONY STRIKE ENTRY" FOR DETAILS. THIS RECORD
MAY ALSO CONTAIN ADDITIONAL DATA RELATED TO "STRIKE" CONDITIONS.
**********************************************************
**********************************************************
*    *    *    END OF MESSAGE    *    *    *
```

00095

MASTER NAME FILE
PASADENA POLICE DEPARTMENT

N 3	DOB	S R HGT WGT HAI EYE	MNI	FP
WILSON,JAMES FLOYD	12-20-1974	M B 509 280 BLK BRO	123971	
624 E SACRAMENTO ST	PASADENA			

- -

OLN/OLS	PKG	SOC	SID	FBI	JID	AKID MNI
A9653165/CA	138171			259992CB1		
D8087757/CA						

FPC:R/5-6553 L/4-5444

- - - - - - - - - - - - - - - - - H A Z A R D - - - - - - - - - - - - - - - - -

PDL - BLOOD GANG AFFILIATION

- -

ALIAS	DOB	SR
SLEPTROCK	12-27-1974	MB
SLEPROCK	12-20-1974	MB
WALLACE,JAMES FLOYD	12-20-1974	MB

CONT   ***CONTINUATION***   00.60

00006

MASTER NAME FILE
PASADENA POLICE DEPARTMENT

REF	REF-NO	DATE	INV	REASON	SEC-REF
					8672911
BKRP	050042285	07-27-2005	ARR	PC3056	
CITE	BL00181243	07-11-2005	CIT	CDL NOT IN POSSESSIONGET NEW C	
BKRP	040017817	03-29-2004	ARR	PC3056	8068280
PDEF	030002290	05-19-2003	DEF	DEF	
BKRP	030027112	05-16-2003	ARR	HS11351.5	7696375
BKRP	960006652	01-31-1996	ARR	PC1320(B)	4706021
PERS	950083333	12-30-1995	SUS	ASSAULT WITH A DEADLY WEAPON	ASSU
BKRP	940074690	11-09-1994	ARR	PC12021	4186366
BKRP	940072993	11-01-1994	CIT	VC12500A	B212382
VEHC	940068488	10-13-1994	OWN	VEHC/REC	
BKRP	940063687	09-23-1994	CIT	VC12500A	B197664
BKRP	920084687	11-20-1992	ARR	PC12021	J302357
X PERS	890075490	10-11-1989	SUS	ATTEMPTED HOMICIDE	
BKRP	890003070	01-13-1989	ARR	HS11352	
BKRP	880092401	12-28-1988	ARR	HS11352	
PERS	880034814	05-20-1988	SUS	WEAPONS ON SCHOOL CAMPUS REPOR	
INTL	850037803	06-08-1985	VIC	ALL BICYCLE REPORTS	
CONT	***CONTINUATION***				04.58

00097

<u>CASE USED TO VIOLATE MY PAROLE</u>
<u>Note</u>: J.R. was killed by
Pasadena Police in 2016.

STATE OF CALIFORNIA
CHARGE SHEET/REVOCATION TRACKING/SCHEDULING REQUEST
CDC 1676 (4/91)

TRIBUTION: DEPARTMENT OF CORRECTIONS
JIGINAL - BOARD REPORT
1ST COPY - R.H.C.
2ND COPY - H.A.
3RD COPY - PAROLEE
4TH COPY - U.S.

REPORT TO: [X] BOARD OF PRISON TERMS

[ ] NARCOTIC ADDICT EVALUATION AUTHORITY

UMBER	NAME (LAST, FIRST, MI)	NAME BOOKED AS	REGION/UNIT	CSTCU - ST
K29628	Wilson, James	Same	III/PASD 3	[ ] YES [X] NO

ARREST DATE	ARRESTING AGENCY	BPT REFERRALS:	BOOKING NUMBER AND/OR LOCATION
03/29/04	Pasadena PD	[X] MANDATORY [ ] NON-MANDATORY	80682807LACJ

ARREST CODE *	* ARREST CODES:		
B	A P&CSD STAFF ALONE AB P&CSD ASSISTED BY LAW ENFORCEMENT AGENCY	B LAW ENFORCEMENT AGENCY ALONE D LAW ENFORCEMENT AGENCY WITH INFORMATION FROM P&CSD	

HOLD DATE	DISCOVERY DATE	HOLD REMOVED DATE	AGENT OF RECORD	CONTROLLING DISCHARGE DATE	DISCHARGE REVIEW DATE	IMMINENT DISCHARGE
03/29/04	03/29/04	N/A	K. Johnson	08/12/06	03/02/05	[ ]

CHARGES AND CODES
1. Gang Association (013)
   Association w/ Persons prohibited
2. Failure to follow instructions from P&CSD (024)
3.

CHARGES AND CODES
4.
5.
6.

REASON FOR RETAINING PAROLE HOLD: PAROLEE DANGER TO:
[ ] ABSCOND [ ] SELF [ ] PROPERTY-OTHERS [X] SAFETY-OTHERS

DATE COPY SENT TO PAROLEE	INITIALS OF PERSON SENDING

SUPPORTING EVIDENCE:

CHARGE 1: On 03/19/04, a victim was "kidnapped" and robbed in Pasadena at the eastbound 134 Fwy. at Figueroa Street. The following day, Pasadena Police Department Detective Devis #1855 received information that Pasadena gang members CKB, JR, and Sleprock were involved in the incident.

CK Boo's true name is Maurice Taylor and he is a project gangster gang member from Pasadena. A computer check revealed Sleprock to be (James Wilson), the Subject who was recently released from custody. Pasadena Police Department Detective Clawson discovered that the Subject is Maurice Thompson's uncle. On 03/22/04, Detective Devis spoke to LASO Comnet Team Member Detective Lord about the robbery. He stated that on 03/17/04, a confidential informant informed him that Sleprock and Boo were involved in robberies against drug dealers. The informant stated that Sleprock (the Subject) and Boo (Maurice Thompson) were putting victims into their Mercedes and then ripping them off.

On 03/17/04, at approximately 3:00pm Detectives Lord and Ferguson saw the Subject in the passenger's side of a Mercedes Benz with Maurice Thompson driving down Mentone Avenue in Pasadena. The informant also stated that on 03/22/04, Sleprock and Boo were responsible for the robbery and shooting of the man found on the 134 Fwy. On 03/22/04, Detective Lord drove by 1190 Mentone Ave., saw the same Mercedes parked at the location and took photographs of the vehicle. On 03/22/04, Detective Davis went to Huntington Memorial Hospital with the photograph of the Mercedes provided by Detective Lord. He showed the photograph to the Victim who positively identified the car as the vehicle he was forced into.

On 03/23/04, at approximately 1:15pm, Detective Lord stated that a surveillance was being conducted at 1190 Mentone Ave., and he saw Maurice Thompson and the Subject enter the door directly facing Mentone Ave. The informant informed Detective Lord that the Subject was at the location with family members. Detective Lord stated that the Subject was seen driving a white MonteCarlo that was parked at 1190 Mentone Avenue. The detective's surveillance team saw the car parked at the location with a man resembling the Subject's description sitting in it. A DMV check revealed that the car was registered to a man in Hawthorne. On 03/23/04, at approximately 4:40pm, Detectives Clawson and Devis drove past 1190 Mentone and observed the Subject standing in front of the location speaking to Franklin Thompson (AKA hardrock) who is a known Sguigley gang member. Per the Pasadena Police Department Franklin Thompson is the leader of the Sguigley Lane Bloods gang.

137

001848

PAROLEE'S NAME	CDC NUMBER
Wilson, James	K29628

Page 1 of 4

CLASSIFICATION: PC 3056 Parole Violation	LOCATION: 1190 Mentone Ave. #a	DATE: 3/30/2004	CASE NUMBER: 04017817

Introduction:

On 3-19-04 at about 1434 hrs. a man named Adonis Towles was robbed, kidnapped from Pasadena and shot in the head on the E/B 134 Freeway at the Figueroa St. on ramp. The following day, I received information from a confidential informant that a Pasadena gang member named CK Boo, JR and Sleprock were involved in the incident. The informant went as far as telling me that Sleprock had recently been released from prison.

Investigation:

I immediately knew who CK Boo was. His true name is Maurice Thompson. He is an admitted Project Gangster from Pasadena and is actively involved in gang activity (see attached Field Interviews documenting admitted PJG membership). I conducted a Pasadena PD computer check on the name Sleprock and discovered that James Wilson used that moniker. Detective Clawson checked Wilson's parole status and discovered that he had recently been paroled. In addition, Detective

Clawson told me that James Wilson was Maurice Thompson's uncle. On 3-22-04 I spoke to Detective Lord of the LASO Comnet Team. Detective Lord told me that on Wednesday 3-17-04 a confidential informant told him that Sleprock and Boo were involved in robberies and extortion against drug dealers. The informant told Detective Lord that Sleprock and Boo were luring victims into their Mercedes then ripping them off.

That same day (3-17-04), at about 1500 hrs., Detective Lord and his partner Detective Ferguson saw James Wilson and Maurice Thompson in the listed Mercedes Benz on Mentone Ave. just north of Hammond St. Thompson was driving and Wilson was the front passenger.

Detective Lord also told me that on 3-22-04 his CI called him and told him that Sleprock and Boo were responsible for the robbery and shooting of the man that was found on the 134 Freeway.

On 3-22-04 during the early morning hours, Detective Lord drove by 1190 Mentone Ave. and saw the same Mercedes parked across the street from 1190 Mentone Ave. Detective Lord photographed the vehicle, due to the information he was receiving from his CI.

On 3-22-03 at about 1450 hrs. I went to the Huntington memorial Hospital with a photograph of the Mercedes provided by Detective Lord. I showed Towles the photograph and asked him if it was the vehicle that he was forced into. Towles positively identified it as the suspect vehicle.

On 3-23-04 at about 1315 hrs. Detective Lord told me that while he was conducting a surveillance at 1190 Mentone Ave. and the Mercedes in question, he saw Maurice Thompson and James Wilson go into the only unit that has a front door directly facing Mentone Ave. In addition, Detective Lord's CI told him that James Wilson lives at the location with a family member.

Detective Lord told me that he has seen James Wilson driving a white Monte Carlo (Ca# 2CHB158) and that he has seen it parked in front of 1190 Mentone Ave. During a recent surveillance, Lord's surveillance team saw the car parked in front of the location with a man resembling Wilson sitting in it. A DMV check of the Monte Carlo's license plate number revealed that it is registered to a man named Dakar Tims in the city of Hawthorne.

138

COPIES: N/C	COPIED BY:	APPROVED BY:	OFFICER / ID: E. Devis 1855

CONTINUATION REPORT PPD 5206

CHARGE 2:

The Subject has a special condition of parole for, "no gang association". On 03/26/04, the Subject called the AOR and stated that his sister's home was searched by the Pasadena PD on 03/25/04, due to the Subject's connection with a robbery and shooting. The Subject was angry because he does not live there and the officer's had a search warrant. The Subject was instructed to report to P&CSD immediately due to the AOR knowing nothing about the charges. The Subject stated that he was going to clear his name before reporting to P&CSD. A case conference was conducted with the US and a miscellaneous decision was submitted immediately (the Detectives were not available for interview). On 03/29/04, the BPT acted to suspend his parole effective 03/26/04.

On 03/29/04, the Subject reported to P&CSD as instructed after speaking to the AOR earlier that day, and was taken to Pasadena Police Department for questioning.

The Subject declined to speak about the robbery without a lawyer present and was taken into custody for the gang association. The robbery and assault with a deadly weapon case is still pending.

PAROLEE STATEMENT: On 04/02/04, the AOR interviewed the Subject via-telephone. The Subject denied ever being in the car with a Maurice Thompson or being involved in any shootings. On 03/21/04, he reported to P&CSD for an office visit and informed the AOR that his sister was getting married that weekend and some individuals with gang ties were coming to her house for a tuxedo fitting. During the office visit, he stated that numerous individuals were coming by the house to get fitted for tuxedos but he avoided association with them and would often leave the residence despite helping his sister with the wedding. A Charles Mohammed called the AOR and stated that the local mosque (the victim of the shooting was a Muslim) conducted an investigation and the Subject was not involved.

POLICE STATEMENT: On 03/26/04, the AOR spoke to Detective Davis about the case. He stated that the Subject was a suspect in a shooting and robbery that took place on 03/19/04. He also stated that another gang member was possibly involved in the investigation. He also verified that he positively, identified the Subject speaking to Franklin Thompson, a Squigly Blood gang member.

COURT INFORMATION: None.

ATTACHMENTS: Pasadena Police Department arrest report #04017817.

WITNESSES:
Pasadena Police Department Detective Davis #1855.
LASO Comnet Team member Detective Lord (800) 451-1228.

001849

139

The Next Chapter

> *"It is not about doing time; it is about doing something with the time."*

My name is James Wilson, CDCR # AU5200. I am 45 years old. I am convicted for manslaughter, carjacking. And possession of a fire arm. I have been incarcerated 15 years. Since being in prison, I have completed the below-listed academic, rehabilitation, and pro-social activities, seeking to amend for my crimes, improve my life and community.

They are as follows:

1. Truly Redefine Yourself (T.R.Y.), a group I co-founded.

2. Criminal Gangs Anonymous (C.G.A.)
3. Alcohol Anonymous
4. Narcotics anonymous
5. Leadership Workshops, Inmate Organizer
6. Reaching out from within, A group I Co-Founded
7. Pledge of Peace, Inmate Organizer
8. The Day of Peace and Reconciliation, Inmate Organizer
9. Stop the Violence Talent Show, Inmate Organizer
10. Staff Appreciation Day, Inmate Organizer
11. Cash Donation to Veterans Group, Inmate Organizer
12. Veteran's Walk, Inmate Organizer
13. Financial Literacy Class, Inmate Organizer
14. Path to Restoration, Inmate Organizer
15. Ironman Challenge, Inmate Organizer
16. Racial and Cultural Tolerance Class, Inmate Organizer
17. Various Book Reports
18. Received G.E.D.!
19. Lifer Support Group
20. Peer Health Course
21. GOGI – Tools for Positive Decision Making
22. T.R.Y.s' Advance class
23. NEW H.E.A.R.T.s' Self-Help Group, Co-Founder
24. Suicide Awareness and Prevention Week, Inmate Organizer
25. Alternative to Violence Project (A.V.P.)
26. Inter-Faith Religious Seminar, Inmate Organizer
27. Islamic Study Courses and Practices (from different Islamic schools of thought)
28. Purpose Driven Life Seminar (Christian-based study)
29. Study of the Human Brain Course
30. Initiate Justice Legal Conference and Workshop, Inmate Assistant
31. Initiate Justice Self-Help Class
32. Civil Rights Peace Project, Inmate Organizer
33. Black History Month Celebration
34. Cancer Prevention Walk
35. Self-Improvement and Human Development Class, Co-Founder
36. In-Cell Writing Activities Programs (promoted by the CRM's Office after Covid-19 outbreak)
37. I have received various Laudatory Chrono's, from Chaplain's and Free-Staff Self-Help sponsors.
38. Besides Co-Founding Five (5) Self-Help Groups (T.R.Y., new H.E.A.R.T.S., Reaching Out from Within, Self-improvement and a Sports Activity Group (G.A.M.E.), I have Co-Organized several community events, Such as:
    ➢ Talent Shows
    ➢ Pledge of Peace

- ➢ Sports Tournaments
- ➢ Facilitates Symposiums
- ➢ Inter-Faith Religious activities
- ➢ Staff Appreciation Day
- ➢ Racial Tolerance Conferences
- ➢ Iron-Man Positive Competition Challenge

39. Participated in writing a Victims Impact Anthology with several inmates (most of them Are included in this profile) with future hopes of publishing the project and donating financial proceeds to Victims Impact Inmates. (title: "Writing our Wrongs")
40. I paid off my restitution fees
41. I am a regular mentor of men of all ages in the prison.
42. I have a strong and long standing support base on the outside. All of my friends are career people and active in their communities.

I have been offered a place to live and a job by Nate Williams with his organization "Choices for Freedom."

Following this list is a short selection of my personal achievement chronos and certificates. A complete list is documented in my CDCR file for further review. Additional insight about me is inside my Bio-Sketch on: prisonfoundations.com, under: Brains Behind Bars. Author: Adrian Woodard and Christopher Compton.

I WOULD BE REMISSED IN MY DUTY IF I DID NOT MENTION THE JUNIOR
MASTER,MARTY LEMASTER, WHOM I MET AT 41 YEARS OLD IN HIGH DESERT
STATE PRISON(2016).

THIS YOUNG BROTHER WAS INSTRUMENTAL IN HELPING ME TRANSITION INTO
A COMMUNITY LEADER AND SELF-HELP GROUP CO-FOUNDER. MARTY, LIKE
REUEL AND BARRY, HAVE BEEN INDISPENSABLE IN MY GROWTH AND
DEVELOPMENT AS A HUMAN BEING.

(YOU CAN READ MORE ABOUT MARTY IN "PROFILES IN REHABILITAYION"
ANOTHER BOOK I CO-AUTHORED).

Marty LeMaster, T.I.

QUOTES ON SUCCESS

" I did not create the car.
I only put together all
  the pieces other men
before me discarded. "
   - Henry Ford

" I am smart because I stay
 with my problems longer
     than others "
   - Albert Einstein

" I had a dream, and in the dream
   there were two doors: one had
music written on it and the other,
   Islam. I chose the door which
had Islam on it and never imagined
the level of success it would bring
me. What I gave up for God I never
            loss. "
   - Minister Louis Farrakhan

" I study from A - Level material,
and I'm a C - Level person but, I've
managed to bring myself to a Level - B . "
   - Unknown Author

DONEL POSTON

Cultural Outliers

In mathematics, an outlier is a value that is inconsistent with the rest of the data. It is defined as a value that is more than 1.5 times the interquartile range - the absolute numerical difference between the first and third quartiles - smaller than Q_1, or larger than Q_3. In relevance to this discussion however, an outlier is someone who sits outside the range of normal activities, situations, or circumstances. Not so much an outcast, but one who is looked at as unfavorable to succeed in any certain outcome.

Ironically, outlier and outcast share the same root word: _out_; which can be defined as situated outside, or at a distance. In relation to the title of this book (unlikely success), outlier and outcast are synonymous. That is, someone positioned outside the average group of people who are likely to succeed. For example, one may ask the question, "what is the probability of (someone like myself) a 45-year old Black man with a criminal history becoming a CEO of a Fortune 500 company?", or simply, "what is the likelihood of [that person] succeeding?"

Surely, it takes a certain level of self-esteem. Even moreso however, it's going to be centered around self-efficacy - the learned expectations of success that what we do, or try to do, is controlled by our perceptions or beliefs about our chances of success at a particular task, or problem. Along with these, it's going to take a high level of self-motivation. People who are self-motivated are inclined to set their own goals, and monitor their own progress towards those goals.

Seemingly outside the factors that contribute to this internal locus of control, what about data that is quantifiable? According to a November 2020 article in Forbes magazine, "Black men and women together held only 486 (8.6%) of 5,670 board seats of Fortune 500 and equivalent companies, 332 by Black men (5.9%) and 154 (2.7%) by Black women." "Other recent surveys do not improve these statistics. Black CEOs of Fortune 500 or equivalent companies, as of September 2020, still total less then 1%, none of them women."

Imagine if I add another all important criteria such as having served time in prison. I surmise that this value would decrease to a fraction of a fraction of 1%. The deck becomes even more stacked as we add other internal, and external, factors such as substance abuse, domestic abuse, your environment, your living conditions, etc. These aren't excuses, these are facts of life that demonstrably lower one's chance of success. These, and other conditions, are what a vast majority of young Black men face in this country. This is our reality.

Consequently, Covid-19 may have been both a gift and a curse bundled into one. Covid has illuminated the disparities that minorities had been experiencing all along. According to a July 11, 2020 article in The Economist, "One in three African-American men born in 2001 can expect to be imprisoned at some point in his life, compared with one in seventeen White boys. The sons of Black families in the top 1% of America's income distribution are as likely to go to prison as White sons from the bottom third."

Not withstanding zoning, voting restrictions, and redlining, childhood poverty plays a major role in who succeeds. When you're young - the time when your core values are shaped - if all you know is an environment full of drug abuse, subsidized housing, and poor economic attainment, your likelihood of success is lowered fairly significantly. Just over one-in-six children are poor. Poor children have a high tendency to grow up to be poor adults with lifestyles conducive to increased drug abuse, higher risk of criminality, and shorter lives.

I am a prime example of all the aforementioned statistics. My life circumstances have made me an outlier, or an outcast. However, because of these stats, my more recent history of self-educating, remaining curious, receiving a college education, learning the responsibility of running a legitimate business, and my great level of self-motivation has put me on track to become an unlikely success.

By: Donel Poston

"We live in a world that assumes that the quality of a decision is directly related to the time and effort that went into making it.

- Malcolm Gladwell

Chapter 9

Some days, I look back and try to figure out where I went wrong. Other days, I'm happy at the outcome, as opposed to the journey that led me to where I'm at right now. Living inside of a California state prison at the age of 45.

As I settle in on my eighth year of a 72-to-life sentence, I'm rather happy with where I am at in life. Not in my physical location, of course, but in my mental state. Had I been able to predict the future, would I have chosen this journey? Probably not. In hindsight though, being where I currently am only reaffirms my spiritual faith. My path has been decreed.

In the 1980's I was this innocent child being exposed to everything under the sun. I took in so much information from my surroundings that, at times, it was a convoluted process that required me to absorb it all, and make a decision, all in a moment. That quick thinking out of environmental necessity bred a whole generation of individuals like myself. Individuals who are able to take knowledge and manipulate it for all the wrong reasons.

An oft repeated statement directed at me when I was coming up was, "you are so smart that you're stupid." Had I been able to process this in the moment, I would have figured out that instead of talking down to me, people were actually praising me for having an ability that wasn't as common for them as it was for me. I don't think that I was gifted, or anything like that. Not like Olitio "Red", Sean, or Romeo (schoolmates of mine). All three of these young men are probably why I longed for an education, or at least for an intellect. The contrast between the four of us couldn't have been greater.

Poor doesn't begin to describe Red's living conditions. When he came to school, he always reeked of urine. His clothes were tattered, his shoes were useless (although somehow he managed to wear them anyway), and he was so dirt-covered that his skin was caked like the foundation on a beauty queen. In class, however, he was brilliant.

In elementary school he was already a backflipping, mathematical word smith. He could do mental math given the most complex of problems. In my mind, that was gifted. I once watched him do a complete aerial assault of flips, twists, and tumbles across the entire schoolyard. At that time, he possessed talents that could have taken an olympic gymnast all the way to a gold medal. Sadly, he died in the 7th or 8th grade.

Sean was a Jehovah's Witness, living in a sheltered environment. He never came outside to play as he was always with his parents. When he came to school however, he loved to play basketball. He was modest in his dealings, and always expressed answers matter-of-factly.

Romeo was a really short and very dark Hispanic kid. So dark that you could be forgiven for mistaking him as being Black, if it wasn't for his curly afro. He was a very talented sketch artist, and could read and write elaborate stories even better.

These gentlemen were my inspirations. In my mind, I didn't possess the wit that they did. Somehow though, I always ended up on the math team and in the Science Club right beside them. We travelled in Mr. Collins car alongside Melissa, Giovanni, and a few other girls. I loved it.

The walls of that elementary school were adorned with pictures of Nikki Giovanni, Tony Morisson, James Baldwin, Ralph Ellison, Maya Angelou, Malcolm X, and the like. That environment nurtured me. Nevertheless, the streets of Oakland formed my nature. It would seem that this contrast would shape my life.

I was moved by so many situations in my life; some devastating, others downright disgusting. I've lost plenty of friends to the streets, and nearly lost my own life on several occasions. Before this period would end, I would manage to survive a brazen break-in by an intruder, only to acquire a life-sentence for protecting myself from an idiot.

Oftentimes, I do believe that I'm that rose that grew from concrete, however unimagineable that may seem. I have managed to blossom in situations that don't usually permit growth. It may be providence, or maybe it's just that ineffable will to succeed when all else says otherwise.

While I may have not been as poor as Red or as sheltered as Sean, I have lived a life of volatility. Like most households in the 80's prior to the crack epidemic, all was well; until it wasn't. Then you were forced to regroup, gather yourself, and put the past behind you as best as you could. After crack burned through a neighborhood, it left a stench. There was no shaking it, no matter how much scrubbing, rubbing, or soaking you did to get rid of it. Crack left a stain in so many households, communities, and urban cities, and it definately damaged my outfit.

In most cities outside of low-income neighborhoods adolescents played recreational sports, got ready for their first dinner dance, or found a penchant for the opposite sex. However, in junior high school my brothers started smoking crack. As bad as crack is, there was an era when smoking it was actually acceptable. Unsurprisingly, this turned into a disaster. Then, my parents seamless progression into the lethal substance as well was just short of a conspiracy to contaminate my childhood.

My dad was such a good man. Being the youngest of five, my dad was vibrant, wise, and loving. His country roots instilled in him hospitality, manners, and chivalry. Characteristics long lost to another time. He served in the military, which landed him in Oakland, California, after a tour in Korea.

Mommy's journey was a tad rough. Not to say growing up in a rural town in Alabama during the Jim Crow era isn't tough, but having a mother herself that performed abortions, migrating from Texas, and having four daughters and a son couldn't have been easy itself. After my mom went through a rough patch with my brother's father (more on this in the book "Freedom by Degrees"), it's amazing that she continued searching for love.

That being said, the stars must have aligned for me to come along. Cue "Family Affair', by Sly and the Family Stone. That's how I remember the early years. Dominoes and Spades, Marvin Gaye and Frankie Beverly, and cookouts in the backyard or at a park. I value these memories because it reminds me of a time when life could not go wrong.

Then it happened. Between '84 and '88, things seemed to go down the drain. It started as small as the centrifugal forces in the flush of a toilet, and ended in a Cat-5 hurricane. Our living conditions went from a house, a Porsche, and a happy family to an apartment, a bucket, and no furniture.

What I've learned since then has definately contributed to my recent outlook. Never be overwhelmed or surprised about the unknown. Just be ready. One of my favorite mantras: Create your own space, and then own it.

Berry Park

Rock and Roll has been an American staple for almost 75 years. Most credit it's up-start to a young black man named Chuck Berry. Berry knew that he had something special. So much so, that he demanded his money be put in a bag because he knew that promoters were stiffing him. Chuck Berry is the reason why The Beatles, The Rolling Stones, and Elvis Presley exist. They all recognized his greatness, even emulating his style before their big breaks.

Most people do not remember (or never knew), however, that Berry did two stints in the penitentiary. One for allegedly bringing a 14-year old back to St. Louis from one of his tours, and another for tax evasion. Yet, he still managed to have an illustrious career after falling to rock bottom twice.

Eventually, he would build Berry Park in Berryville, Missouri. Here, he'd throw these wild desegregated concerts, at a time when integration was unheard of. Black and White kids partied and sang songs together throughout the night, until the venue was eventually shut down.

Like most Black artists of the 50's, 60's, and 70's, Berry was an unlikely success. He slept in his car, he demanded that he be paid, and he didn't take shit from any one. Berry's zeal and drive for success enabled him to create many decades worth of top 10 hits, and a legacy that was unmatched in his time.

Ironically, Berry's journey mimics the life of many entertainers and athletes. Less than 1% of athletes who play sports make it to the pros, and for thespians, the number that make it as actors and actresses is even less. By the time an individual makes it to the top of their respected field they have endured countless rehearsals and practice sessions. They began on the smallest of platforms. From talent shows and Pop-Warner leagues to hustling through high school and college, until they finally get to try their very practiced hands in a field so saturated with people that are trying to achieve the same thing that "making it" is very unlikely.

The truth is, we are all stars and professionals in our own right. Depending on what you deem success, life has prepared for you (and you for) a platform that you can stand on. Longevity is the key to prosperity, and consistence the key to existence. It takes a series of small accomplishments, and an unlimited amount of failures in order to see success all the way through. The likelihood of your success depends upon your unwillingness to give up.

"And all people live, not by reason of any care they have for themselves, but by the love for them that is in other people."

- Leo Tolstoy

Chapter 10

After a tumultuous upbringing, turbulance was destined to follow:

By the time I reached the sixth grade I had already watched the crack epidemic destroy my family. My brothers, to this day, have been crippled by the drug. To add to this, my mother and father were never to occupy the same living space again. For myself, I was left lost, wondering what my future might hold.

In 1988, my dad and I were to leave California on a sour note. Prior to leaving, we occupied a two bedroom apartment on the third story in the 'Murder Dubbs' (East 19th and 25th in Oakland), a dead-end cul-de-sac full of low-income apartment buildings. My parents managed to secure the spot after chaos had erupted at our previous residence.

The fighting had continued to escalate since we left our house on 73rd. Everytime the dope was absent, the arguments were present; my mom usually being the aggressor. She would slam doors, yell, and generally cause a real big stink. Not only was it embarrassing, it was scary, hurtful, and uncomfortable in so many ways to me. It never got old either, because I never got used to it.

These apartments were a complete downgrade for us. We had lived in a house at first, then we moved to the Skyline Hills apartment complex, which was lavish compared to where we had lived on 73rd. Here on East 19th though, was the definition of the term 'G-H-E-T-T-O'! Mind you, due to our temporary stay we didn't have much furniture (it was in storage), so our apartment was empty. We were without a car, and my parents were fully strung out.

If I recall correctly, my dad had even drawn his pension from working at Alameda County Transit, where he had worked as a bus driver for 14 years. They blew through that money so fast that you'd assume they had stolen it. In the end, they didn't have anything to show for it.

I remember one day in particular very vividly. They had been on a three or four day run, locked in their room, getting high. I'm assuming that my dad had run out of money, as my mother wanted to leave. Normally, that wouldn't have been a problem; if only the person that had come to pick her up had been a woman. My dad wasn't going for it.

My mom had gotten all dolled up while my dad sat there shirtless and exhausted. There was nothing he could have done to stop what was going on with my mom. She had secretly been involved in a relationship for a few years already by this point. Whether my dad ever confronted her however, I don't know. Before this, she would always dip around the corner, go up the street, or sometimes just wait until my dad left. That day, my mom was bold enough to have her friend come directly to where we lived.

When the car pulled up, this very fit young man was sitting in the car. When my mom went to leave the apartment, my dad took it upon himself to follow. In his hand was an aluminum baseball bat. This is when all hell broke loose.

Trailing my mom by a couple of a yards, bat in tow, he was adamant about not letting his wife leave. In doing so, he jumped behind the car as it backed up. When the driver slammed on the brakes, my dad slammed the bat into the trunk. The driver was livid, but my dad didn't care. Once the driver hopped out though, it was apparent that my dad was in trouble. The guy was huge.

They played cat and mouse around the car before the driver finally grabbed hold of my very frail dad and shook him like a rag doll. I stood on the side in disbelief and crying. I thought that the big man was about to hurt my dad. My mom sat in the car as if nothing was happening. She may have been crying herself.

Eventually, my dad got loose and made it to the car he'd borrowed from his nephew. During all the commotion my mom had exited the car, and made it upstairs. My dad was trying to maneuver his way out of the parking lot as my mom was upstairs cooking up another plan.

As my dad eased out of the parking lot my mom came bursting out of the apartment with an M1-30 semi-automatic rifle. Smooth and swift, my mom slipped down the steps. The car my dad was driving was a disaster. He had to pop the clutch to even get it started. As the car coasted down the hill my mom appeared from the side of the building, firing shots from her military style weapon.

My emotions at this point were in disarray. I was devastated, mortified, and extremely scared. The hubbub had the whole hood hollering. "Donnie mama a fool"; "Damn, she go crazy"; "That shit was sick"; all eyes were on us. If you looked at every apartment from the ground at this point people were either lining the balconies, in their windows, or down on the ground themselves. Each one tracking events play-by-play.

My mom found me at the back of the apartments sobbing, knees in my chest, and my head in my lap. She grabbed me by my hand and led me upstairs. She may have said sorry, she may have said nothing; it was all a blur to me. Once the door shut I found myself in the apartment, all alone. I cried myself to sleep.

A week later, my dad returned. We sat on the floor of the apartment watching a music award show on our floor model Quasar television. Music was my dad's and my favorite pastime. When Lynard Skynard took the stage, they belted out "Sweet Home Alabama". My dad sung along, tears blanketing his eyes. He turned to me and asked If I would move to Alabama with him. I gladly accepted.

With two Greyhound tickets, what little belongings we had, and a couple hundred bucks in my dad's pocket, the two of us left for Alabama. I'll never forget the look on my grandmother's and auntie's faces when they came to the bus station to pick us up. Upon seeing my daddy they looked like they had just stepped in some shit.

My father had contracted some type of lung disease while he was in the army. Even walking, his breathing was labored. He always wore this tattered ball cap cocked 'ace-deuce', his shirt open - kinky haired chest showing. His stroll made him look like he was gliding.

As we approached their faces began to droop, and their collective disgust became increasingly evident. Even at the tender age of 12, their body language was speaking volumes to me. I understood every word, audible or not. The ride back to the Poston cul-de-sac (my family was so prevalant there for so long that the street was named after us) was vicious. The criticism, the condemnation, the complaints. What made matters worse was my dad farting and snoring next to me in the back seat. What jumped out to me was the mention of Jim Crow.

The Jim Crow era was a few generations removed from my own, and outside of my understanding at the time. Although I had grown up in predominately Black neighborhoods in California, the racism wasn't as explicit as it was in Alabama. Though diversity did exist (for the most part), in 1988 Alabama segregation was as flagrant as it had been in the 60's. I wasn't quite prepared for what I was about to experience.

Standing at my locker one day, I encountered an incident that was rather novel to me. Usually a happy kid, Chad (my neighbor) was apparently having a bad day. If memory serves, I was also in a rush at the time. I was searching for my English book, and had my belongings in front of his locker. While I scrambled to gather my things, he kicked the neighboring locker in disgust.

When I asked him what was wrong, he replied, "shut up nigger!" (yes, with a hard 'R').

I was flabbergasted. Once he said it the world seemed to begin to move in slow motion. As the words echoed down the small corridor I knew that I had a choice to make. It didn't consist of alerting someone, or walking away, either. Although I don't think much (or if any) blood was spilled, I do remember that I beat the brakes off of that young man. To (literally) add insult to injury, I found myself the only one being suspended.

When my dad picked me up from school, the second confusing thing happened that day. He wasn't mad. I didn't understand. Once I got back to the trailer where my grandmother had invited my dad and I to stay, she couldn't help but snicker and throw an, "I told you so," my way.

That was the first of many incidents that left me by the side of my bed, in the back of the trailer, hating myself. I developed anger issues that left me "foaming at the mouth" over things as simple as not being included, not being able to spend the night at a friend's house, or just not understanding something. The anger I had long harbored over my situation had finally begun to reveal itself as hatred.

I had suppressed the many goings-on of, and between, my parents. I acted like the infidelity and drug affairs didn't bother me. Now, day after day, I would come home from school and just cry.

My grandmother thought that it was because I missed my mom. Really, I just wanted to die. I recall telling myself that I wished I wasn't Black, which really made me cry. I did miss my brothers. I missed my friends. I missed Oakland most of all.

For the two years that I stayed in Alabama, I had one good friend outside of my cousins. His name was Louis. He was White, and he was very understanding. He lived in a nice house with his family only a couple of miles from where I stayed. He didn't judge me, nor did he care that I was poor, Black, and from California. I created some good memories with Louis. He helped me get through my time in Alabama.

When I was with Louis' family, I felt welcome. They showed me love, asked me questions, and taught me things. Most importantly, they helped me deal with my anger issues. For this, I have been forever grateful.

I moved back to California in the summer of 1990. I already knew that the situation hand't changed much with my mom from the visits with her every summer. So, instead of being excited to see my mom, I was just excited that I had made it back to California.

Due to my anger issues, and subsequent hang-ups, I hadn't been able to flourish or see my real potential while in Alabama. School simply did not excite me. I was unable to find that drive like when I sat next to my childhood classmates. I still received decent grades, but I wasn't willing to overachieve. I just wanted to "get by".

These Crises Were Not Created Equal

> "The clear majority of all Americans have violated
> drug laws in their lifetime. In fact, in any
> given year, more than one in ten Americans violate
> drug laws." (Alexander, 2012, p. 104)

Unfortunately, the amount of people in urban neighborhoods that recover from the resulting addictions is far less than one in ten. Those who grow up in households saturated in substance abuse are far less likely to succeed than those who grow up in households free of such maladies. In the course of any human life, far more people will experiment with drugs than is ever reported. Of this number however, only a fraction will become truly addicted.

At the height of the crack epidemic, no one sought to bring charges against the government for single-handedly injecting the lethal substance into urban communities. Crack cocaine shattered the entire identity of America's urban city dwellers. Seemingly overnight, "Crack Babies", "Crack Whores", and "Crack Addicts" became a favorite topic of our media. All too often, the face of this media blitz was Black people, from all walks of life. This painted a negative image of Black Americans, and helped to ruin much of the cultural respect we had gained in the 60's and 70's.

Fast-forward twenty years to the opioid crisis. The 'invisible hand' had come to correct what seemed to be attacking the suburban youth of America. While the images were horrific, the tales helped foster an environment where communities of suburban parents, looking to avenge the loss of their loved ones, would sue big drug manufacturers.

This was unheard of in the 80's and 90's. Even in the early 2000's, when both drugs seemed to be running a neck-and-neck race of destruction, no one was advocating for those families already swallowed up, and spit out, by the crack epidemic. Both eras had lived through irreparable tragedies, yet assistance would only be provided for the latter; in the form of monetary settlements and drug treatment programs. A bid to help slow the affects it would have on future generations. An about face had occurred from the policies during the crack epidemic that aided in the perpetuation of America's mass incarceration problem, which had already long held Black and Brown people as it's most revered occupants.

Run both generational crises in parallel and it becomes easy to see the disparities, and disadvantages, for one community as opposed to the other.

Both are equally devastating, but they were never equally treated in the media, by the government, or by society. The likelihood of making it out of either situation is discouraging, but the children of the crack epidemic are still struggling to succeed nearly 40 years after the war on drugs were declared.

I am an offspring of the crack epidemic. While I never smoked crack myself, I was, nonetheless, one of the many victims of the generation that crack destroyed. I didn't need crack to fall into the same pattern of addiction so prevalent in my formative years in any case. Out of my current 45 years, I spent close to 25 of them addicted to a controlled substance. Had I not spent the majority of my early (and now adult) years in prison, the years I spent addicted would probably have been even longer.

"All things are not explained by one thing, but by all things."

- Albert Camus

Chapter 11

I arrived back in California in the summer of 1990. Ironically, my mom had returned to that lush apartment complex at the edge of the Oakland hills. Furthermore, she was now sharing a living space with that muscular mystery man.

I didn't harbor any ill will for this gentleman. Over the previous few summers I had a chance to get to know him. I had actually come to both respect, and like him. I admired him for still being there for my mother as she continued to struggle with addiction. As for myself, I made it a point to get back into school and excel. It was my Freshman year in high school, and I remained on the honor roll the whole year. I attended weekend college programs, and went to Cal Berkeley in the summer.

Being back in Oakland had placed me back in my element. I was making it work, and working hard. Although I noticed that my mother was still stuck in a bad place, I felt that if I brought home good grades she would acknowledge what I was doing, and support me in the things that I was trying to accomplish. Just maybe my successes would rub off on her.

Not surprisingly, no matter how much I excelled, it wasn't enough. At least, it wasn't enough to receive any affirmations. My overachieving seemed like a challenge. I don't think she even realized all that I was doing to make her happy. It became exhausting.

For that reason, my transition from the 9th to the 10th grade proved to be life changing. I began to rebel. It started with drinking and moved into smoking, as well. Then, I started selling drugs and stealing. All this negativity garnished me some of the previously craved attention, so I kept doing it.

Before long, my life had spiraled out of control. I managed to find myself in the wrong places with the wrong people, doing all the wrong things. I began to care less and less about school, and more and more about that false attention.

It was this attention seeking behavior that lead to my illicit drug use. Once the attention from my mother began to fail, I sought it from my friends instead, and my friend's brothers. While one of my friends was in the living room playing 'Tecmo Bowl' (a football game for the original Nintendo),

I was in the other room smoking weed with his brother. This began a toxic relationship where I would visit when my friend wasn't even home. I had placed myself in a position where I was learning things that I shouldn't have been learning. Before the summer was over I had acquired plenty of new knowledge, like the finer points of smoking, and selling, weed. As I was still hanging out with my friends, I began to influence them as well.

While I was still going to school, I was creating a new identity as a weed dealer. Those whom I had gone through elementary and junior high school with were confused at my new development. Some believed it was a phase, others shook their heads in disappointment.

During this time my mom's drug use was continuing to increase. It consumed her, causing her to pay increasingly less attention to what I was doing. This painful development also gave me the room to begin to manipulate, rob, and steal. Whenever I could I would make up an excuse to get money from my mom's boyfriend, only to go spend it on weed and alcohol. When that got old, I would take his service revolver and go rob people on the other end of the complex.

In a single school year I had done a complete 180. I was shooting dice, stealing from supermarkets, and getting high. Whenever an opportunity presented itself to get some fast cash, I went for it.

My mom was so oblivious to what I was doing that I could lock the door to my room and stay out practically all night, sneaking back in through the window or balcony when the excitement was over. I began locking my doors because my mom would come into my room at night and steal money from the drawers in my bathroom, and harrass me for the money that I kept in my pocket (for further insight read 'Freedom by Degrees'). It spiraled from there. At the time, my knowledge about addiction was shallow, so I didn't understand what she was going through. This lack on my part meant that my default emotion became hatred.

Not long after this started we moved to a house in the flatlands. The first night at the house, before we moved our belongings from the apartment complex, some friends and I smoked out my bedroom and got really drunk. When my mother came to the house in the morning, she was fuming. That incident set a precedence for how I'd continue to act.

I was smoking so much weed that I'd fall into debt with the people who were fronting it to me, so I began robbing people to get the money back. I participated in a few brazen heists; breaking into department stores and ransacking the place. Most notably were the daily runs to the supermarkets where we'd

163

steal top-shelf alcohol to sell back to the neighborhood liquor stores.

Consequently, I started living homeless. My good friend Carlos, who I met in high school, allowed me to stay at his place on and off. Most of the time we'd get so high that I'd simply find myself waking up on the couch in his room. We'd wake up, go to school to round up more friends, and be off on our mission for the day.

In high school my drug habit only increased. I was high all day long. So much so that I couldn't even apply myself to my school work, or learning. I was content with not graduating. My attempt at taking the high school proficiency exam ended with me failing by a single point. Carlos passed. From there, I dedicated myself to the street life.

One night, I was out robbing and stealing with my friends. We had rented a car from a dope-fiend, using it to do any and everything. We sold crack from it, robbed and stole out of it, we bought drugs in it, and we drove it erratically throughout the Oakland streets. The two guys I was with snorted heroin and coke. They were both maybe a year younger than me.

At the time, those drugs were out of the question for me. I stuck to the traditional mind-altering substances like alcohol and weed. However, because they used those heavy drugs, they could consume large amounts of alcohol. By the end of the night our young minds and bodies were at their limits. While driving up one street at excessive speeds, my friend lost control and drove us into a house.

When I awoke, I was handcuffed to a gurney at the county hospital. From what the police report said, there was a gun laying by my side. The entire front of the car was in someone's living room. The courts gave me an ultimatum; either go to jail, or go back to Alabama. This was a no-brainer to me. I wasn't going to do either one of them.

This escapade definately got me some attention. My mom was pissed. The following day, she put me on a plane to Alabama. I got off in Arizona though, and told the ticket agent that I'd left some turntables in California. They ended up refunding my ticket and flying me back to Oakland International Airport. This gave me a pocket full of cash on top of what I already wanted. With no supervision, and being off "the hook" (no jail), I decided to go directly to my friend's house that I knew would let me stay. All was well on the home front too; until I never showed up in Alabama.

In the following days, my mom was in a panic. She called around to all the police agencies, and filed an FBI, as well as a missing child's, report. Had I not went to another friend's house to get a haircut, I would've stayed off the grid for even longer. However, my mom conned this friend into telling her where I was sleeping.

On a positive note, the friends I had attached myself to at the time had just received a major record deal with Jive Records. They were only two years removed from high school. This was a dream come true for me (more about this in 'Freedom By Degrees').

By the time I finally moved on from my friend's house I had already become an alcoholic and marijuana addict. While this may not seem extreme, my addictions had me stealing and hustling just to get high. This creates a problem, no matter the substance. It eventually left me homeless.

Im sure I could've returned to my mother's house, but I still harbored resentment towards her from my experiences as a youth. For that reason, I chose to sleep in cars, couch surf, and rent motels whenever I could afford it. The irony about being homeless is that it still costs money. Survival is never free. I already had experience with stealing alcohol. Now I would walk out of supermarkets with bread and meat as well. This soon evolved into pushing out full shopping carts.

While homelessness definately increased my bad habits, it also increased my vulnerability. I was exposing myself to dangers that should not have had a place in my life. I began hanging around my turf, selling drugs for my older homeboys, packing guns, and committing robberies. These robberies were different from those of my past. Now that I was robbing drug dealers and drug houses, they were much more dangerous. In my state though, I saw nothing wrong with it. Luckily, I was never caught or injured because of these actions.

However, I did go to jail for robbing a bike store. Luckily, this time I didn't have a gun. This relatively minor crime (for me) would begin a long relationship with the penal system. By this time, I was 18 years-old (a couple months prior, I had been put on probation for selling weed).

At the time I didn't know that probation for a young Black man in the United States is like signing a lease for housing at the county and state prison systems. For the past 25 years now, I have spent at least part of every one, with the exception of 2012, inside of a jail cell. I have discharged two prison numbers, and have visited institutions at every level. I have been on ranches, CCFs (County Correctional Facilities), and level two's, three's, and four's.

Each time, I believed that I had a new lease on life, yet I would always return to society faced with the same challenges. Nowhere to go, no job, and not wanting to live with my mother. This inevitably pushed me back into criminal activity. Although I managed to land a few legitimate gigs between prison stays, they were never enough to amount to much.

My friends in the music business were always present in my life. I'd paroled from Solano State Penitentiary in 1999, and when I got home I went on tour with them as a roady and intermittent ad-lib vocalist across the states. This gave me time to regroup and get in touch with myself. We performed shows in the states and in Canada. It was a surreal experience.

When I got home, I met this young lady (Angie) at the store. We began dating, and built a strong relationship. For a little over a year we were inseparable. However, in 2000 I came into a boat-load of cash through a settlement from a car accident. True to the statement, I was "acting like a person who ain't never had nothing." I blew through thousands in weeks. Before long, a high speed chase and possession of a firearm had me back in jail for a 12-month violation. Because of the half-time rule[*] I would only do 6 months of it.

My girlfriend was pregnant with my first child at the time, and I was looking forward to being a father. She had complications in the pregnancy, so she gave birth on September 30, 2000 to a premature baby while I was still 3 weeks away from my parole date. Unfortunately, the baby didn't survive. I lost my first born, Anada-dei, on October 19, 2000.

This was a hard time for me and my girlfriend. I had no idea how she felt, and found it difficult to understand her pain. I was so immature that all I wanted was to kick it with my friends, not taking into account that a life was lost. Between doing shows with my friends and selling drugs in my neighborhood, I was never there to care for my distraught girlfriend. It only took me three months to find myself back in jail.

During our relationship, my girlfriend and I got hooked on Ecstacy. We popped pills every night, drank excessive amounts of alcohol, and smoked excessive amounts of weed. This trip to jail would be the end of our time together. The old adage, "you never really miss something until it's gone," sums it up nicely in this case. I was lost when I got home. My drinking picked up and I found myself angry all the time. This was the first time that I was

---

[*]Half-time (50% of max time) is offered to incarcerated individuals whose crime doesn't consist of any violence.

166

ever love sick. It made me realize how big a void she filled in my life. So much so that I began calling her phone at all times of the night, and showing up at her place unannounced; I was terrible.

All this anguish opened a wound that I attempted to bandage by getting high, and staying high. I hung out at a club called The Vintage Inn that sat on a street next to a barbershop that I used to go to with my dad. I spent many nights in this club hustling, getting high, and running amuck with my friends. I would stay in the club until it closed. Within the next few years I would have children with two women that I met there.

Elena, who I found parked across the street from the club looking for a place to hang out in the middle of the day, was from Seaside. Her and her friends were sitting in a car smoking weed when I stumbled upon her. I introduced myself and we had a few laughs, but that was the last time I saw her until we magically reconvened in Las Vegas. This was in 2002. Oftentimes, I would drive to Seaside to spend the weekend and party with her and her friends. She stuck by my side when I got arrested in Utah and in California on fraud charges. We had a long distance relationship, which kept me less than honest with her.

Leah was a student at Cal Berkeley who just happened to be having a girls night out with her friends when she crossed my path in the club. This was later on in 2002. We began chatting, which lead to us hanging out a few times, but because of her school schedule we ended our short friendship.

I became incarcerated in March of 2003. Unbeknownst to me, Leah was pregnant and had been searching for me. At the time, my neighborhood was feuding with a rival neighborhood, which caused me to expand my own territory to a place where I could sell drugs without worrying about getting killed. When Leah came searching for me near The Vintage Inn, I had already temporarily relocated to another neighborhood on the other side of town. Unfortunately, when she finally found me I had already gotten nabbed.

In May of 2003, I received a letter while incarcerated in the county jail. It was from Leah. She asked me if I wanted to be a part of the child's life that she was about to give birth to.

Prior to going to jail, I had picked up another habit. I started using cocaine. I had experimented with the drug once or twice with a friend, a couple of more times with a cousin of mine, and a few times on my own. By the time I relocated to the other side of town, snorting cocaine was already a thing I did with my peers there. This kick-started my heavier usage. Eventually,

I would begin experimenting with heroin, cocaine, and ecstacy to go along with the marijuana and alcohol habit I already had.

As much as I despised my parent's and brother's drug use, I fell right in-step with their same addictions. The correlation between my and my parents drug use was that none of us knew a healthy way to cope with life and it's many obstacles. Drugs have been a staple in my life for as far back as I can remember. It's poison ruined my parent's relationship, as well as my own with them, and any other that could have been meaningful. It also caused me to veer from every positive path that was presented or available to me, leading me to a dead-end road instead: prison.

Desperate Conditions Will Always Breed Violence

Gun violence is plaguing America at an alarming rate. In May of 2021, when we first thought the Covid pandemic was over, gun violence had surged in suburban and urban communities alike. The administration is blaming the makers of ghost guns and backdoor gun shops for this uptick in violence. However, in cities like Chicago, Oakland, and Los Angeles, gun violence has been a mainstay since the war on drugs in the 80's.

NBC Nightly News has reported that Black men are 14 times more likely to be killed by gun violence than a non-Hispanic White man. Most of the time, gun violence is attributed to gangs, which are birthed from environments that (non-coincidentally) are always underserved and lacking in proper resources. Squalid living conditions and minimal opportunity for economic advancement creates these cutthroat environments where those already strapped for cash must fend off attacks from individuals that exist in the very same environments.

The violence in these communities stem from this lack of resources (proper education, lucrative employment, effective social services, food deserts, the digital divide, etc.), not the makers of the ghost guns or the illegal gun shops. Those are just tools that exacerbate the root problem. The likelihood of people succeeding in these conditions run concurrently with the conditions themselves. This cause-and-effect relationships recognizes the disparities of people in these low-income communities. No money, no education, no food - high rates of crime and violence.

A recent study of 22 states shows gun violence up 16% from 2020 to 2021 (as of August). In 2020, gun violence was low partially because America was locked down, businesses were closed, and Covid was ravishing the country. The after-effects have shown that this "down-time" created a vacuum of activity from which minority youth became over-eager to get out and provide for there families, no matter what it took to do so, making up for what they could not do while locked down.

Most of the households these youth come from have broken families. Most are missing at least one parent either to incarceration, death, or substance abuse. Those missing both live either within the system, or are with relatives. Most often this means grandparents, who are already up in age, and mainly survive off of government assisted living such as welfare or social security. Those who do work are often burdened by doing menial labor jobs with low pay and long work hours, leaving the children at home alone to get into any- and everything.

I am a product of a broken family, and an underserved community myself. The lack of proper education and guidance contributes to the need for acceptance, leading towards gang creation and membership, and these gangs participate in violence. The youth growing up in these communities are fighting a steep uphill battle, and are very unlikely to succeed.

"The powerless have to do their own dirty work, the powerful have it done for them."

                                          - James Baldwin

Chapter 12

As my drug addictions increased, my visits to the penitentiary would follow in lock-step. At one time, I was snorting at least a quarter of an ounce of coke every two or three days. Add all of the ecstacy pills, alcohol, and marijuana I was doing to this, and that bright school kid I used to be was now deeply buried under all of it's weight. I was constantly going back and forth to jail for selling dope, or committing fraud.

In addition to this, I was about to be a new father. After the loss of my first daughter you would think that this news would give me hopes of settling down and getting off of the streets. Neither was the case. I continued my narcissistic and selfish ways. Any money that I hustled up would be spent on myself, or my drug habit. When I did want to look out for Leah and the baby I spent on material items, not necessities like the rent or bills.

Consequently, upon release I started off in a bad situation. I was sent directly to a halfway house. Not before long, I was bringing alcohol, weed, and cocaine back to the transition house. When the administration locked us in for the night we'd all cram into the bathroom to get high and tell war stories. In this, it would be me that would always be holding court, leading the discussion about whatever adventure I had gotten my self into. It wasn't long before I found myself on the run. 90 days later I was back in jail for a three month stint to finish off my sentence.

This vicious cycle would continue over the years; in and out of prison, one false promise after the next. I managed to get myself enrolled at Ex'pressions Digital Art College, where I thought a renewed penchant for learning was about to turn my life around. However, with both Leah and Elena pregnant again (both mine), and me hocked on drugs like a research monkey, my future was already a foregone conclusion.

Even though I was maintaining a 3.83 grade point average ,I still somehow managed to get myself kicked out of school. Two months later I was locked up again for 16 months, for possession of fraudulent check paper. When I paroled from that term, I began attending school for C++ training. Two months later, I was imprisoned again for possession of marijuana. This term would last eight months, starting in the summer of 2009.

Time had run away from me in those previous five years. My kids were getting older, the relationships with my children's mothers were becoming increasingly strained, and my addictions were a constant that hung over it all. While my inner-self yearned for education, my addictions and the street life always took precedence. While on the one hand I wanted to be in school learning, the other only reached for fast money and a party, and the gangsters and hustlers that I gravitated towards always kept both of them full. I could never find a balance. Even in my attempts to find it, I always failed to take into account that my kids were on those same scales.

In July of 2010, I (once again) was headed back to prison for passing counterfeit checks and possession of fraudulent check paper, for a 12 month stint. By this time I had found a new lady, and she was pregnant with my fifth daughter. I knew her all of two months before going back to jail.

I met Shelly at a night club in Oakland and we hit it off fast. She was crazy, fun, and beautiful. I paroled in July of 2011, and moved to Las Vegas with her and her three kids. No sooner had we landed in Las Vegas however, that she began to constantly (and falsely) accuse me of cheating. These accusations caused me to increasingly stay away from her, which caused us to fight. A heated argument, and a visit by the police later, and I was headed back to the airport. When I arrived at the Oakland International Airport, my parole officer was there to take me into custody. I spent three weeks in jail, and was released a few days before Christmas.

My mom and I were on better terms at this time, and she wanted to help me stay out of trouble. Because of this, she gifted me the house that we lived in when we moved from the Oakland hills. The one that I smoked out as a teenager when it was still empty.

In January of 2012 I got a job at Cal-Trans through a prison release program and moved my childhood friend in with me. I began to stack my money, and take responsibility for myself and my kids. Unfortunately, just when it seemed like I had turned over a new leaf, someone broke into my house and shot me several times. I would spend the next month in the hospital recovering.

As crazy as it may sound, I was inclined to return back to the street that I hustled on for so many years. The Vintage Inn had been closed down, but the street still maintained a heavy flow of traffic. For some reason, I felt like my old neighborhood would give me power. I wanted to show whoever had shot me that I wasn't scared. Ironically, I decided to buy a firearm, learn how to shoot it at the shooting range, and kept it in my room for safety.

Ten months after being almost fatally attacked in my bedroom I found myself under siege once again, this time at the gas station. Consequently, someone would lose their life. A stray bullet, intended for me, found it's way into a passersby driver-side front window, nearly instantly killing the driver.

A year later, after a speedy trial, I was sent to prison for a 72-years-to-life sentence. Because of my ego, my carelessness, and my unwillingness to back down to the streets, I was now committed to prison for life. I had left my kids with no father, their mothers with less help, and my mother with one less son.

After eight years in prison now, I have accomplished more than I had in the previous 37 years of my life. I continue to push myself "110%", my priority being to realize my true potential. I have earned four Associates Degrees, authored three fictional novels, and co-authored four rehabilitative projects and several self-help groups.

Throughout my prison journey I have managed to shed my selfish past, and become a more giving person. For the past two years I have been a certified Peer-Literacy Mentor, teaching adult basic education to men trying to earn their General Education degree or High School Diploma. I also lend my assistance to college students trying to earn their own degrees. This fall I will be graduating with a Bachelors Degree of Science in Small Business Management / Entrepreneurship.

I will continue to push myself to new heights. My past would suggest that I would never be able to get back to where I was as a child. I have beat these odds. I have dedicated myself to giving back, and moving out of the space that I occupied for so many years: addiction.

My next step is to attain my Masters Degree, and get back home to my children and my mother, who need me the most. At this point, I am an unlikely success, but in order for me to fulfill my full promise I need to get home and be there for those who have always been there for me.

Profile Presentation

Of

Donel Poston

"Tough times don't last, tough people do!"

(Me in the center)

My name is Donel Poston (AT-2512). I am 44 years old. I am convicted of second degree murder, under the Provocative act Doctrine. I have been incarcerated for seven years. Since being in prison, I have completed the below-listed academic, rehabilitation, and pro-social activities, seeking to make amends for my crimes and improve my life and community.

They are as follows:

- ❖ 12/17/15 AVP Participation Chrono/Certificate
- ❖ 01/16/16 AVP Advance Workshop Chrono/Certificate
- ❖ 03/17/16 Training for Facilitators AVP Workshop
- ❖ 04/20/16 Criminal and Gangmembers Anonymous (CGA) Chrono
- ❖ 06/08/16 Strong Man Competition Chrono
- ❖ 06/15/16 CGA Parenting Workshop Certificate
- ❖ 08/01/16 CGA Facilitator Chrono
- ❖ 09/07/16 Field Day Event Chrono
- ❖ 12/16   Certificate of Completion/Entrepreneurship
- ❖ 04/17/17 Juvenile Diversion Program (JDP) Membership Training
- ❖ 05/27/17 Houses of Healing, A prisoner's guide to inner power and Freedom
- ❖ 06/15/17 Donated a Book I authored to The Library
- ❖ 08/18/17 The positive things I learned in Prison Chrono
- ❖ 08/20/17 AVP Facilitator Chrono

- ❖ 11/18/17 Fatherhood Focus Parenting Program Certificate/Chrono
- ❖ 11/25/17 30 hr. Positive Parenting Program Certificate/Chrono
  Victims Impact Workshop Certificate
- ❖ 01/21/18 AVP Facilitator Basic Chrono (Facilitated a Group)
- ❖ 01/24/18 RAC Credit
- ❖ 04/15/18 AVP Facilitator Chrono (Facilitated a Group)
- ❖ 05/08/18 RAC Credit
- ❖ 05/17/18 Facilitator Completion Chrono/Certificate
- ❖ 05/25/18 Presidents Honors GPA 3.75 or higher
- ❖ 10/31/18 Individual Works Initiative from Chaplin
- ❖ 05/13/19 Pledge for Peace
- ❖ 06/03/19 Life Skillz Facilitator Chrono
- ❖ 06/03/19 JDP Mentorship Chrono
- ❖ 06/18/19 Organized Structured and Prticipated in Community Event
- ❖ 07/18/19 AVP Facilitator Chrono (Facilitated a Group)
- ❖ 07/25/19 TRY Advanced Chrono
- ❖ 08/06/19 New H.E.A.R.T Co-Founding and Facilitating Chrono
- ❖ 08/07/19 RAC Credit
- ❖ 08/20/19 Organized Stop the Violence Talent Show
- ❖ 08/27/19 Talim Chrono
- ❖ 08/31/19 Ramadan Chrono
  Path 2 Restoration Chrono
- ❖ 09/07/19 Night of Power Chrono
- ❖ 09/26/19 Suicide Awareness and Prevention Week
- ❖ 10/06/19 Path 2 Restoration
- ❖ 11/18/19 Path 2 Restoration
- ❖ 11/18/19 Cash Donation
- ❖ 11/18/19 Veterans Walk Certificate
- ❖ 11/27/19 Reaching Out From Within Co-Founder/Facilitator Chrono
- ❖ 12/21/19 Giving Back Hygiene Drive/Donation
- ❖ 12/06/19 Leadership Workshop
- ❖ 01/06/20 Reaching Out From Within
- ❖ 01/28/20 Day of Peace and Reconciliation
- ❖ 02/16/20 AVP Facilitator Chrono (Facilitated a Group)
- ❖ 02/25/20 Path 2 Restoration Chrono
- ❖ 03/12/20 Staff Appreciation Day Speaker/Organizer Chrono
- ❖ 02/12-3/11/20 Mind Over Matter Seminar Certificate
- ❖ 03/17/20 Initiate Justice
- ❖ 04/27/20 In Cell Covid 19 Packet Chrono

I haved also earned three degrees, including AST: Business Administration, AS: Social Science, AS: University Studies. I am currently in my second semester at Adam's State University, looking to achieve a BA: Small Business Management in two more semesters. I have published three books, all available at Barnes and Noble or on

Amazon. I have Co-written several Self-Help groups and have completed an unpublished book, Co-written with 11 other inmates.

Following this list is a short selection of my personal achievement Chronos/Certificates. A complete list is documented in my CDCR file for further review, additional insight about me is inside my bio-sketch on: prisonfoundations.com – under: Brains Behind Bars. Authors: Adrian Woodard and Christopher Compton.

QUOTE ON SUCCESS

" To laugh often and much; To
win the respect of intelligent
people and the affection of
children; To earn the
appreciation of honest critics
and endure the betrayal of
false friends; To appreciate
beauty, to find the best in
others; To leave the world a bit
better, whether by a healthy
child, a garden patch, or a
redeemed social condition; To
know even one life has
breathed easier because you
have lived. This is to have
succeeded. "
- Ralph Waldo Emerson

FREE SESSIONS

Brains Behind Bars

"To fall in love with yourself is a life-long romance."

Session 1
An Alternative Point of View

Early Years

I was born in the city of Santa Clara, California. Somewhat unusual to my direct peers, I grew up in a two parent household. This addition, however, turned out to be a subtraction.

Both of my parents were drug addicts, and eventually suffered unemployment. The combination of drugs and a lack of income led to our family's first experience with homelessness. This happened when I was no older than three years old, and we would move frequently throughout the Bay Area until I was about six. Our transient housing was a Motel 6 in Menlo Park. It was here that I got introduced to criminality and child abuse as my father began to service out my older sister (who was also a drug addict) for money. After about a year, the family packed up and moved to Hayward, California, and life for us appeared to improve.

My father, still applying his hand to being a pimp, had expanded his harem. To some extent we were living, what I recall as, a "middle-class" existence. We had a home with a two-car garage. There was no sign of material destitution for us, and the community we lived in was crime-free and decked out with spectacular accessories: a fine park, gym, a pool, a computer room, and security guards. Things began to seem normal.

The turning point for me came on a New Year's Eve when my mother introduced me to hard liquor. I was just nine-years old. From that day forward, I would have a secret craving for alcohol, and me and my friends started stealing from grocery stores to supply my budding habit. I lost touch with the reality of my being a child and started cutting up at school, even while my teachers tried to remind me of my potential.

It was no match for my father's approval of my bad behavior, however. Subconsciously, I wanted to be like him; I idolized my father. Even prior to acting up in school, I had no parental restraint. There was no curfew enforced in the home, and I was allowed to run the streets at all times of the day and night.

Eventually, my brazen behavior led to my first encounter with the law. It was for stealing from Toys-R-Us. There were 10 of us kids who were caught. The cops counselled is, then released us to our parents. However, this did

not have the desired effect of curtailing our mischievousness. We resumed
stealing, and engaging in other forms of criminal behavior. We even committed
a serious act of arson that caught the apartment building I lived at on fire.

I was snow-balling out of control. My teacher sensed my decline, and
sought to intervene by getting me involved in school sports. While I enjoyed
playing on the football team, I was unwilling to accept structure and discipline.
The team ended up being red-flagged (penalized) for my being on the roster,
and for my unruly conduct. It became apparent that I wasn't one to adhere
to anyone's rules.

One day, my bike got stolen while I was at football practice. Upon finding
out, my father grew angry at me and drove me all over the neighborhood looking
for the thief. We were not successful, and my father took it upon himself
to berate me constantly for "allowing someone to take something" from me.

To my surprise, and relief, a friend of mine eventually found out who
the thief was and pointed the way to him. Unfortunately, I also learned that
the thief was also in possession of a firearm. The combination of pressure
from my father, my own anger, and the presence of a weapon allowed for my
next set of foolish choices. I decided I would hunt the other kid down, and
shoot him. Luckily, I missed at my attempt, but the act brought me a reputation
in my community that made others fear me. With the other kids, I was a celebrity.

It was during this period that I also started to have sex. First with
a girl I used to cut school with, then other girls from my school joined the
"party". By the time I turned 15-years old, I had impregnated three of the
girls from my high school. None of the pregnancies would be taken to term.

My first "real" arrest came as a teenager, deriving from one of these
adolescent relationships. Proving that "the fruit doesn't fall far from the
tree," I assaulted one of the girls at school, and the police were called.
Being less verbally savvy than my father, I relied instead on my next option:
fighting to compensate for my inadequate communication skills. In hindsight,
it was also a signpost to my tumultous inner world.

To some extent, I had "died" on the inside due to the unsuccessful pregnancies
(one through drug-use, another a miscarriage, and the last due to a physical
altercation). The other huge blow to my will to live came at age 17 with my
father's unexpected death. I was devastated. To add to this, my mother abandoned
me during these "tipping point" crises, and I became homeless. She banned
me from even coming to her home at all. I was now on my own, taking this cue

from my mother to take to the streets with reckless abandon.

Before long, I was committing armed robberies to survive. Not the most mature choice, but I had to eat and clothe myself. Eventually, my older brother caught wind of my situation and took me in. This was not the ideal situation, as my brother had seven kids of his own, imposed rent on me, and when I couldn't fulfill my share would physically accost me. This caused me to lose all respect for him, and I began to steal from him.

Not long after this our relationship tanked, so I decided to find my way out by joining the military. I enrolled, but no less than six months later I was forceably discharged for drug possession and sales. I went from bad, to worse.

Adult Years

I was 18-years old when I was sent to the county jail in San Joaquin County. I stayed for about three weeks, and was released. My brother met me in front of the jail and delivered some choice words to me. He also had all of my possessions with him. He verbally grilled me, and left all of my things there in the jail parking lot.

Now I was to be officially homeless (I had nowhere to turn this time), and by extension, despondent. I was fresh out of hope, and jumped head-long into the funk. I decided to go back to my familiar territory of Hayward.

Along with my property, I was carrying the baggage of pain, guilt, resentment, and depression. I hooked up with an older friend from the neighborhood, and he put me on to breaking and entering into peoples' homes. While the money could be good, it was risky, and he was not an honest crime partner. He would finagle most of the profit. So, I resorted to my own strengths by assaulting and robbing him. I decided to strike out on my own, but was arrested fairly quickly for burglary, and was back in county custody.

This time I would experience something new for me. I was actually looking at prison time. The charges would be settled, however, and I was released on probation. I decided to head to Sacramento, where I knew no one.

I survived by stealing money from tip jars at restaurants. Fortunately, I met a military vet who taught me how to live "the homeless life". It kept me above water physically, but I was still in above my head and would consistently find myself in and out of jail.

Eventually, I met an older woman that I had a good relationship with

for a time, but my old habits and trauma inevitably surfaced, and we began
to fight like cats and dogs. I finally left her once I accepted that it wouldn't
work. Not following this internal voice for long though, I let her convince
me to resume our battered, and broken, relationship. It would land me in prison
for 14 years.

The Transition

Entering prison at 24 was a challenge. I was both distraught, and angry.
I responded to these emotions by fighting with cell-mates and engaging in
other misdeeds. This characterized the first year of my sentence. I really
didn't care what happened to me, or what I did to others.

As a routine, I used books to escape from the negativity of my circumstances.
This proved a choice that would pay dividends as I happened upon a book that
shook me out of my lethargy. It was "Think and Grow Rich", by Napoleon Hill.
I came into contact with this book by way of an older cell-mate. Both it,
and he, would start me on my new trajectory.

This amazing book taught me that my poverty was not financial in nature,
but my economic destitution was instead really a result of my conditioned
thinking, my learned fears, and my lack of a quality outlook. This new point
of view for me opened my eyes to the fact that my brokenness originated from
within and shaped every aspect of my life. Despite my domestic upbringing
and the socio-economic factors (driven by capitalism) that informed the circumstances
of my formative years, there were still things that I could do to gain control
of my destiny.

This book encouraged the direction of further reading, like "The Perpetual
Paycheck", by Lori B. Ross. This book taught me the power of networking and
investing in people, as very little is accomplished without the aid of others.
Something Napoleon Hill calls "the mastermind counsel". By tapping into the
needs of others, and leveraging that against my own success, I would be creating
a self-perpetuating cycle of service.

Most of these new books that I was reading came from Adrian Woodard,
my older celly, who had (at that time) been incarcerated for 24 years. He
came into prison the same age (24-years old) that I had, and had developed
much the same insight I came to rely on for my own growth and development.
On top of helping me to become an avid reader, Adrian also created the perfect
environment for me to exercise my new knowledge by having daily discussions

179

on the material.

Amongst my readings, I came across "The Willy Lynch Letter" and "The Future of the Race", by Henry Louis Gates and Cornell West. This gained me a more historical perspective in relation to being a Black man in America. Something I lacked growing up in a mostly White community. As a child, I lacked a self-image rooted in my ancestry, as did my parents. My world-view as it relates to my place within it, especially concerning how I could help others within my environment to get ahead, began to expand.

I became a minor philanthropist, and started using my meager income to help people in need. I also became an unofficial tutor and physical training assistant. I knew that there was something I could, and needed to, do to improve my life, and the life of those around me.

The law of attraction being what it is, I met other men that showed an interest in my educational development (Bobby Ladelle and James Wilson, to name a couple). They offered me access to additinoal books, positive friendship, and self-help group platforms I could utilize to articulate my new-found beliefs. I was becoming the change I wanted to see in the world.

Through this gradual change of beliefs, my values became much more worthwhile and reflective of a progressive mindset. I had learned to invest in myself and my social capital, and it was reaping obvious benefits. I became resourceful, and learned that there were people and agencies willing to help me, even with housing. Excuse-making and playing the victim were now concepts of powerlessness. Through knowledge gained, and concepts practiced, I now walk through my life with the full understanding that there is always something we can do about our situation. A point of view worth it's weight in gold.

Andre Jenkins
(#BF8601)

"Doors are locked from the inside."

Session 2
The Inside Scoop

There is a natural tendency in our psychology to look at a circumstance, an event, or a person, and make some form of hasty judgement. In limited circumstances we can make true judgements, but we often allow our egos to become so wrapped up in the judgements we make that we don't leave room for the possibility that we may have made a mistake, or are in err.

Would you like a doctor to make the wrong judgement on an issue of your mind by just looking at your brain? The mind cannot be adequately explained just by studying the physical brain. Your thoughts, memories, and knowledge have no individual location in the brain. They are a collection of connecting parts just as complex as the experiences that comprise them. Similarly, you can not simply look at a person and say with objectivity that your judgement(s) are correct.

Preconceived notions may, at times, serve us well in life, but not always. Human relationships are a growth process, built upon getting to know the other person. It's only through further interactions with an individual that we truly get to know them, and get beyond our hastily made judgements to learn more of the complexities that make up a fully realized human being.

All things that we wish to learn about, and understand fully, take looking into with an open mind. A closed mind can not get beyond our preconceived notions in order to learn and grow. You must be willing to delve into the subject to discover it's true nature, it's intricacies, and it's flaws; just as a mechanic must first run their diagnostic to see the specific issue with your vehicle, or a doctor that must probe deeper by running specific tests to reveal the patient's true ailment. Diamonds are dug for, pearls dived for, and oil drilled for. To truly know someone beyond what appearances may suggest one must take the time to dig, dive, and drill.

Our eyes can play tricks on us, though we have a tendency to always believe what we see. The lens of our minds only refracts from the surface of our own knowledge and experiences. It is not until we look through the lens of our hearts and empathy that we truly allow for a clearer vision of people. With people we love, or are very close to, we tend to see them through a magnifying glass; through a thicker lens of emotion. We exaggerate their eccentricities because we feel that we know these people, and if they act differently than what we feel is the norm, we exaggerate these actions as well.

If we look at ourselves, we find out that we are impermanent, and subject to constant change; sometimes for the better, and sometimes for the worse. Man is complete, yet imcomplete. It's hard to recognize our own incompleteness, but we must accept this, understanding that our belief in completeness (our own perceptions of it) damages our perceptions of reality.

In life, we tend to believe that the people we come in contact with, or feel that we know, are somehow already complete. However, this would mean that they are not changing, do not have the ability to change, or are not in a period of transition, just as we are. Why do we not allow others the same grace we allow ourselves?

This period of change is the most difficult in human development. Trying to transition from a negative mindset and bad choices, dealing with the consequences, understanding that they are (at times) irreversible, to feeling that there is the possibility of redemption. Yet we increasingly seem to accept as a culture that once a person is labeled a thing, that they will always be so. The old adage, "once a criminal, always a criminal," seems to be a widely held belief in our society. It is this group, it turns out, that is one of the few in America that we have been given permission to hate, oppress, hold down, and ostracize; in perpetuity.

Criminals have been entitled to no respect, and little moral concern. They are deemed a characterless, and purposeless, people deserving of scorn and contempt. These people, however, are more than the label(s) placed upon them. They are fathers, brothers, sons, uncles, husbands, nephews, friends, teachers, leaders, and much more. They contain within them aspirations, empathy, insight, and emotions like love, longing, and care. More importantly, the majority of them have the desire to change, thus they have the capacity to do so.

The negative side of <u>every</u> human situation is always the easiest, and thus the first, to be recognized. Allowing ourselves to take a beat and look beneath the surface of (often) complex situations though, gives us the ability to see that everyone has purpose for good, and the ability of achieving meaningful purpose. The more that understand this, and play their positive role in society, the better place it will be for all. To think that once a person makes a mistake, no matter how big, that they no longer deserve (or can learn) to fulfill this role, is wrong. Some of the greatest unmined potential is locked away in jails and prisons. Aiding, and allowing, men and women who have erred to discover, and realize, this potential would leave society all the greater (and more moral) for it.

The modern criminal justice system has been put in place to not just punish criminals, but also to rehabilitate them. Rightly, society has come to believe that a more true criminal justice system not only seeks to punish criminals to serve justice for those effected by crime, but must also take an active role in the process of rehabilitation. To aid the person entering the system through a process that can change one's thinking and behavior from criminality, to understanding their ability to relate, and gain harmonious = willing cooperation with both nature's and society's laws.

What does rehabilitation look like?:

1) Helping people who have engaged in criminal behavior understand that change is possible.
2) Impart the belief that society will accept them after growth and progress have taken place.
3) Those incarcerated accepting accountability for their negative behaviors.
4) Identifying factors that brought them to criminal behavior, and incarceration, in the first place.
5) Imparting / making accessible the proper tools that will aid in the correction of these criminal factors, as well as an education that will aid the individual attain economic stability upon release.

At least three factors are commonly associated with incarcerated people:

1) Poor Education - Poor meaning less than adequate; education meaning formal knowledge or training, with a skill being obtained.
2) Poverty - The lack of information and resources.
3) Poor Social Conditioning - Less than adequate ability to relate to human society, often due to the above two. A major cause of a person's inability to put themselves into the proper condition for action, or use.

To combat these three factors, the individual meeting at least one of their criteria must be provided with the proper corrective tools. Adequate education must address the discrepancies between the learned habits that can lead them to harm themselves and/or others, and that which properly equips them to take corrective action. Most importantly, it must provide the person with an education that has the capacity for social and vocational use so they feel confident in their ability to adequately provide for themselves, and their family. With proper knowledge, education, and resources, any willing person is able to change their actual conditions to a new, more desired one.

While understanding these three common factors of incarcerated people is important, providing the tools to cure these issues is just one part of the solution. Convincing people to believe in the process of self-help and development is the first necessary step, and sometimes the most difficult one. The process of becoming a person who relies on crime to survive is just that; a process. As with all processes, it takes time to evolve. For most of those incarcerated, crime has/had become their life and livehood. Most of these people come to believe that it's their only way to a means. Convincing people to try something new long enough for it to show results is the true task of rehabilitation. The old saying from most incarcerated people that, "this is all [they] know", is not just a saying or excuse, but an in-depth look into the mind, and lack of education, of this subset of society.

The task of undoing the mind-state that believes poverty, crime, and (ultimately) prison is somehow it's fate is daunting, but not unachievable. To rehabilitate is, by definition, to restore to a former capacity, or to restore to good condition. By itself, this definition lacks the fundamental aspects to truly restore these people to a good condition. You must first address the current condition before you can restore it to any other. Providing the means to self-development and knowledge is not, in itself, rehabilitation. To simply have someone memorize a few facts and sayings should not be the approach to "rehabilite". Instead, rehabilitation must be rooted in an approach that guides individuals towards the realization that the results we have in our lives are the sum-total of the decisions we've made in the past.

By acquiring self-knowledge the individual can get to know their own minds, and the processes therein, so as to better understand not just _that_ the thinking of criminality can be changed to a more productive mindset, but _how_ they can achieve this end. The saying, "this is all I know", can then be lengthened to, "this is all I know, but not all I have the capacity to learn". Rehabilitation starts with changing this mind-state. The thinking must be broadened beyond a one-track way towards achieving a goal. Their "tool box" must be filled with a different variety of tools that will help them to construct a better, and more stable, end result.

Most important for those just starting on their rehabilitative path is the ability for the individual to see that the process can, and does, work. Most criminals are in a life of crime out of necessity, and with a belief that the way to achieve their goals is to commit crimes. One's basic needs like food, clothing, and shelter must be attainable, and met, before they can have piece of mind. Most people aren't cognizant of how these necessities weigh on a person. To know where you're going to sleep, get adequate clothes to protect you from the elements, or find nourishment to keep you going.

To rehabilitate, or return to a good condition, we must first address the bad conditions that leave the mind desperate, suffering, and/or fearful from which criminal thoughts are birthed; growing into actions. We must understand that people are afraid to learn something new because they might lose that which they already know. To condition a mind to return to good you must show, and convince, it's owner that it's okay to forget their old means of survival. That this process towards new (positive) thinking and behavior will lead them to an objectively better one.

The way to build a new mind is with the right education. Knowledge being the foundation of all things in existence; it's information, data, and actual facts, and how to apply these things properly to a growing knowledge-of-self. The likelihood of success for a person increases as their (proper) education increases. The more "right" information one has, the better the outcomes that will naturally progress from them. After the acquisition of knowledge comes an increasing wisdom. Being the interpretation, or application of knowledge, wisdom is knowledge in motion, or activation. If the new learning does not have a capacity for use, it is of no value.

Understanding is the ability to see things for what they are. It is also a picture one draws from knowledge and wisdom. It's growth and development, once achieved, stimulates the elevation of the person mentally, intellectually, and morally.

Freedom is the ability to express yourself unrestricted. Given proper knowledge, freedom gives the individual the ability to apply it in a way that causes elevation in the individual. Freeing them from a destructive mindset and lifestyle.

Justice is a reward, or penalty, given to one according to their deeds or actions, or deeds or actions that are done to them. Justice is served not only by convicting someone of a crime, but by correcting criminal behavior. By giving someone the means to help themselves end criminal acts, and develop positive actions. By stopping crime from the inside-out society would not only find itself to be more moral, but also be rewarded in the long run.

Equality is to deal equally with all things in existence with the same measure of devotion to criminality, positive thinking, and equal effort to growth and development. Rehabilitation can only take form with an equal amount of support from the justice system that the justice system gives to convicting criminals in the first place. If the system were to give this level of support to the process of, and belief in, rehabilitation, we could (as a culture) truly begin to serve justice.

Peace is the absence of confusion; a state of calm, and public security under law. When you have piece (and peace) of mind there is no confusion, because you have things in order. People in a life of crime never get to enjoy peace. By ending their thoughts of criminality, no longer having to look over their shoulders, peace of mind naturally comes. The new mindset takes the person from the low plane of criminal, to the necessary plane of citizen. This allows public security under law to truly take place not just for society at large, but for the reformed criminal as well.

Happiness is the state one achieves out of love, peace, and total satis-faction with one's own actions. At the end of the day, happiness is what we all strive for. For the system, this occurs when justice is served. The law was broken, and time was given out with the hope that it will deter that person from committing criminal acts again. If that doesn't work by itself (and we know that it often does not), the knowledge that there is also a rehabilitative process set in place to help change, and end the criminal cycle, aids towards the system's (and society's) end goals. Happiness, for everyone involved, has a much better chance of being the end result with successfully proven processes in place that help change criminals into law abiding, and positively productive, citizens.

In the end, we need people from all walks of life to help make our society better. When the hands are many, the work is light! The people who have the power to pass stringent laws must know, and believe, that people have the capacity for change. Look at the common factors already mentioned that most criminals have. Adequate knowledge, information, resources, education, and belief from society are the foundations from which rehabilitation must stand.

The old approach of, "lock the door and throw away the key," is not just antiquated, but immoral given the human capacity for learning, and the implication for the resulting loss for society and (especially) the reformable person's loved ones (whose own lives are perpetually made worse in very tangible ways). The future is always forward looking, and forward thinking for rehabilitation will get us there in better shape.

Contrary to what some people believe, a lot of the people behind bars want to change their lives around. The inadequate know-how, and the lack of adequate resources to get us there, is the problem. Though it's true that "you can't lead a horse to water and make him drink", you can bring the water to the horse so he can lower his head into it when he's ready.

Belief in humanity, understanding that everybody has the capacity for good, and the change that is sometimes necessary to achieve it, would be a great step towards the future, and the betterment of society. To give up is to die. Let us lend a hand to the forgotten, and aid those people who have victimized themselves in their victmization of others to become contributors to the advancement of life, and make the world a better place to live and grow for it.

Criminals are more than you think they are. In fact, what you just read was from the mind of a criminal.

B.J. LaDelle
(#AW1161)

"Every saint has a past, and every sinner has a future."

"You will be judged by the same measure you judge with."
- Bible

Session 3
A Prisoner's Plea for Mercy when Everything Else Fails

During my educational journey, I discovered that our English word for "think" has it's origin in a Greek word that means, "to add up the numbers and [then] recheck them." In other words, when we "re-search" (Re, meaning to "do over again"), our search for answers and final judgements on people, things, and ideas should bring us to revisit our old assumptions, opinions, and biases in order to weigh them against our newly discovered information. In prison lingo, we call it a second chance.

In this, "second" is not a simple numerical formula (as in the number two), but is instead tied to the concept of rehabilitation, or redemption. Both long-term processes that merit the same understanding we lend to our religious and academic training. In mathematical terms: FS = L (Failure multiplied by Success equals Learning).

This formula (FS = L) has underlying factors that determine it's effectiveness:

1) The mental and physical health of the individual.
2) Their situation (what kind of environment fostered, or hindered, the individual's growth).
3) The conditioned person you have before you in whatever learning environment you encounter them in (home, society, school, or prison).

There is a "normal" degree of failure that attends any attempt to learn something new. No child "succeeds" at walking for the first time. It takes successive failed attempts to accomplish such a task. The same is true, for instance, for learning, writing, and mathematics. No one just "gets it" the first time. You try, you fail, you work at it (with assistance), and then you say: "Oh, I see."

Someone brings out your hidden potential for learning from the darkness of ignorance into the light of a new realized capability. With this trajectory towards continued learning and cultivation of skills as a goal, you can plot your gradual advancement towards greater success. Even so, something abnormal (i.e., mental or physical trauma) can offset these learning capabilities.

The Bible has God saying that he is "long-suffering" in order that no one will be left out of His plan of salvation. This plan, according to Christians, has been in effect since the "beginning of time". It took thousands of years to manifest this redemption model for human salvation.

In Islam, we learn that Allah (God) created the world twice. The first world was built on justice (you sin, you die). In realizing that no one could survive in this "justice" model though, Allah implemented a "second world" (so to speak). He added mercy as the new model. Instead of every sin leading to judgement (death) there would be a "way out". In the Bible and the Hadiths (saying of Prophet Muhammad) it is written: "The mercy of God triumphs over His judgement."

Imagine it this way:

Sin ───────── Mercy ───────── Judgement

When it used to be like this:

Sin ───────── Judgement

The Jewish scriptures (Torah; Old Testament) talks about something called "the mercy seat" residing inside of the Ark of the Covenant. This seat (where the priest met with God) sat in between two angels. In other words, the seat (God) stands between "our sin" and "His judgement". This is called mercy. This "grace period" (patience while others grow and change) is similar to our formula for learning: FS = L.

Within our American penal code (the book that defines crime and punishments) is a measured structure that we apply to various criminal behavior. There are:

1) Infractions.
2) Misdemeanors.
3) Wobblers (between misdemeanors and felonies).
4) Felonies.

These categories have subsets (not every felony is considered equal). A judge can rely on aggravating, or mitigating, factors during the time of sentencing. A severely disturbed person, even in a serious case, could get a relatively light sentence, for example. These infractions, or crimes, can incur a varied sentence: fines, time in county jail, probation, prison, or a combination of them. In extreme cases, the state can deem your crime (sin) worthy of the ultimate judgement (death). The only semblance of "mercy" in this category is your right to appeal.

In criminology, a convicted felon's incarceration is supposed to operate by three phases:

1) <u>The sentence</u> (punishment for the crime).
2) <u>Rehabilitation</u> (atonement for the crime and a change in thinking and behavior).
3) <u>Restoration</u> (returning the changed person to the community from which they came).

These condepts and practices are to teach us that:

1) Formative growth takes time.
2) The person (their experience and circumstances) matters.
3) We must temper our judgement with wisdom.
4) Repair (change) takes time after trauma.
5) People can (and will) change if given the opportunity, and assistance.

According to scientists and theologians, we live in a "falling world". Whether it's seen through the lens of the Biblical "falling man" belief, or through the scientific theory of entropy (all systems deteriorate), the fact is the same. Things fall apart, for normal or abnormal reasons. Much of our scientific, religious, political, and psychological research efforts are an attempt (sometimes failed) at trying to mitigate, or reverse, an apparent endemically declining Creation. Like the titan, Atlas, who is condemned to support the world on his shoulders, we need "mercy" (leverage against judgement) in a "fallen world".

Medical professors have found that there are thousands of mental diseases, and therefore thousands of ways for our brain (and thus, the behavior birthed from it) to fail us. There is evidence that, aside from developmental diseases, many of these mental conditions are genetically transmitted. Many that are genetically predisposed become exacerbated by environment, or displayed from unintended injury, trauma, or stress. The human, despite it's resilience, is beset by potential problems both internal, and external. In these cases, we use medicine (like mercy) to give us a kind of "intervention" - a fail-safe method - that attempts to counteract the effects of our continuing chances of failure.

The original word for 'education' had nothing to do with pounding facts and data into people's head, requiring that they memorize all of it so they could recall it when called upon. Instead, it meant: "The process of leading out from." This makes an educator a leader, or an interventionist, who brings their pupil gradually from darkness into light, weakness into strength, and ignorance into knowledge. Our word 'educe' - to bring out - is synonymous with education.

In ancient Egypt, education was based on the understanding that all one needs to know is inside the self (soul, mind, etc.). This view of education recognized the structuring of an environment to educe the higher potential of that person. Based upon this research, we further learned that the 'logos' (meaning) of the 'psyche' (mind, soul) is the concept that the Greeks learned from their teachers in Egypt. This is how the Greeks received their word "psychology". They were instructed to view the objective of psychology as the object of life: to gain awareness of the full dimensionality of the soul.

Psychology in Egypt was called 'sakhu' (self, mind, soul). Within the "self", like a multidimensional seed, is everything one needs to achieve success. Like any seed (potential, capability), it must be put into a cultivated environment and given the proper care in order to grow properly.*

In the case of Egypt, teachers (parents, relatives, etc.) were responsible for creating, or finding, the best environment suited for a pupil's growth. These environments included: the person, the home, the community, school, society, religious institutions, etc. Education and health (growth) was structured on a holistic model. The whole person was "greater than the sum of its parts", so to speak.

We know relatively little about this amazing tool we call the brain. This places us in a position where we have to use a "tool" with infinite potential with our limited know-how for usage. There is a built-in hinderance, even against our best intentions, to ameliorate and augment our anticipated failing condition. This demands our humility. It requires that even the greatest teacher (or best parent) be a constant student, opened to learning, as "there is so much we don't know about what we think we know". One problem with our limited humanity is that we don't know what we don't know. This makes it even more imperative that we remain humble, and open, as we pursue research into matters that escape our current understanding, or are yet to be explained. The absence of evidence isn't evidence of absence.

As a child, the Buddha (a prince and prospective king) was sheltered in the palace by his father. This kept him ignorant to much of life but that which his father deemed necessary for his station, and blind to the true reality of life: that nothing is permanent, and everything is unaligned (out of balance).

---

*See: Naim Akbar's book, "Light From Ancient Africa".

A concept he later called "dukkha".

One day, the Buddha tricked his charioteer (and chaperone) to take him out of the palace so he could "see things for himself". During his escape, the Buddha came across four things:

1) A poor beggar.
2) A sick man.
3) A dead body.
4) A seeker of truth (or ascetic).

The Buddha decided to leave his pampered existence in the palace behind him in order to search for the true meaning of life. He would later conclude that, "everything a man is, is the result of his mind." Thus, he proposed a philosophy that could bring one to 'enlightenment' (peace with how things actually are).

The cornerstones of his philosophy came to be called "the four noble truths". I'll list the ones (hopefully all four, if not, forgive me):

1) There is suffering in the world.
2) The origin of suffering is attachment.
3) There is a way out of our suffering.
4) Here, I will need mercy myself as I forget the fourth phase.

The Buddha saw this concept of suffering not just in the human condition, but in the entirety of Creation. Everything was out of alignment (out of order - dukkha). Only enlightenment could put things back into proper alignment (cosmos). Until then, we'd suffer chaos (disorder) and suffering.

Every well-meaning teacher has taken part in the noble cause of trying to solve problems created by the human condition. This was the ambition of Confucius, Loatzu, Moses, Socrates, Jesus, Muhammad, Elijah Muhammad, Nelson Mandela, Malcolm X, and Dr. Martin Luther King Jr., to name a few.

The Christian doctrine of salvation through sacrifice in order to compensate for the original sin and the sinful nature of human beings is comparable to dukkha in Buddhism, and Ammārah in Islam (the soul that wants to command evil). This state of the human is the base nature (hunger, sex, violence, desire, lust, etc.) that leans toward excess, pleasure, greed, and chaos. Everything harmful, and that brings about suffering within the human condition.

This is to be checked by the growth state (called lawwāmah), known to us as 'conscience' - our ability to distinguish right from wrong. The highest state of consciousness / conscienceness in Islam is called 'mutma-innah' (a soul at rest, not struggling with God's will, or tempted by evil). It is for those who attain this "perfect" state that are spoken of as, "those on whom my Lord has [mercy]."

From the time of our mythical utopian state of Eden (a plush garden) to the "wilderness" of North America, mankind has groped in darkness, seeking solutions to our failed human experience (experiment). Sadly, every human disovery, along with their uses, also leads us to further peril (hydrogen bomb, fire, atom bomb, metal, weapons, etc.). The more we learn, the more dangerous we become! Moreover, our laws become constructed (qualified immunity) for the people with the most power to legislate death:

1) Military
2) Congress
3) Presidents
4) Police Officers
5) Corporations
6) Nation States

As the saying goes: "If you kill one person you're a villian; kill a thousand people and you're called a hero."

Yes, we need mercy and humility in everything we do. Like Voltaire stated: "If God didn't exist it would be necessary to invent him." We need "God" (intervention) in a machine that is designed to (and pushed to) constantly fail. That is to say (notwithstanding "God"), there are problems created by man that only man can solve. God is not going to fix gang violence, drug trafficking, homelessness, climate change, racism, or mass incarceration, to name a few. Superman is not coming!

We need to take off our willful "blinders" and see reality for what it is: the poverty, the mental and physical sickness, massive death, the researcher (truth-seeker), and the miserably wealthy are all in trouble. When the boat (Earth) sinks we are all going down with it.

The band continues "singing on", attempting to put lipstick on a pig (of tragedy). This type of window dressing only creates more problems, and exacerbates our collective misery, delaying solutions. My plea is: until we come to our collective senses, and find real solutions to our real problems, can we just show each other (even grudgingly) a little bit of mercy?

By: James "Ansar" Wilson

"I can't change the direction of the wind, but I can adjust my sails to always reach my destination."

                                                    - Jimmy Dean

Session 4
More Than You Think

I am the very definition of "More Than You Think". The reason I say this will be revealed as you continue to read this brief essay. Before you start thinking, "WOW this guy really has an enormous ego," or that I'm simply a narcissist, let me assure you that nothing is further from the truth.

What I am is a prisoner within America's justice system. An inmate, or incarcerated individual within California's Department of Corrections and Rehabilitation ('Rehabilitation' being a new addition); and I am only one of over a hundred-thousand others in this same overcrowded prison state (yes, this is numbers just for California). There are so many of us now that we have begun leaking out of it's seams, and are no longer silenced by the concrete and steel that bind us within it's walls. Most important of all, I am a human being, a voice, and activist for: Self-Improvement, Insight, Change, Reform, and finally - Rehabilitation. So, while I can confidently say that I am "More Thank You Think", I am also here to tell you that we all are!

In introducing myself I don't want to sound cliché, so I'll focus on the essence of what makes me the definition of "More Than You Think". My name is Dylan Dunn, I'm a 46 year-old White male, and I've been incarcerated now for more than 25 years due to the worst law within California's Constitution: the Three Strikes Law. In the time since becoming incarcerated on that life sentence, and giving myself up to the hopelessness and despair that comes with it, I've caught a few extra determinant sentences that keep me buried in this pit of misery.

Now that you might be thinking, "Hmm, this guy seems like a real dumbass," I can tell you that you wouldn't be wrong, or even the first person to think or tell me that. No, it's called self-destructive behavior (or self-sabotage), and it's part of a cycle of addiction to a certain lifestyle, as well as a symptom of the hopelessness that comes with the term 'life-sentence'.

From the earliest days of my youth, I immersed my developing psyche in a negative outlook about the world around me. I would like to say that I learned all of my bad habits and character defects from my parents, television, or my social environment, yet I can't attribute but some of it to these influences. Most of it was my inherent need to get attention. I thought that if I was different from those around me that I'd be recognized and stand out.

As I said, I can probably attribute some of it to my parent's influence. After all, they were bikers, and basically raised me and my twin brother while living that outlaw lifestyle. From my earliest of memories, they were revered amongst the members of their club. I grew up on stories of how much of a badass my pops was, so it was only natural for me to want to be like, and impress, him. Having a twin brother to contend with only intensified this, creating a competition between us for who would get the most attention. This not always being me caused me to unconsciously program myself to resent those that didn't recognize my intentions, or the effort that I put forth to be noticed in the first place. Ultimately, this led me to seek attention elsewhere.

At this point, I was already lost to the dark side, and lacked any regard for rules, responsibility, or any other such thought that my own perverse longing for attention and a popular reputation. Being that the only other social structure I had at the time was school and the streets, I became a class clown, and bully. Although this got me some of the attention I craved, it wasn't until I started playing sports that I would achieve the attention that would sate my need and, at the same time, gain me my sought for social status.

Not surprisingly, this only led me to new people, places, and things to influence my developing adolescent character:

The people - teammates from my football team, who also happened to be a part of a street gang in the area where I lived.

The places - The city and county streets, back-alley hangouts, dope spots, and public territory claimed by this gang.

The things - Guns, drugs, crime, fast women, and so much more...

Already being a misguided, rebellious, naive, and impressionable teenager, I started to glorify this gangster, hustler, and criminal lifestyle. Unconsciously, I was programming myself to believe that this type of lifestyle was right. Why wouldn't it be? My parents were already living a similar lifestyle, and it worked for them, so I started to condition and define myself through this lens, and justify the aggressive mentality that came with it as cool.

It was with this mindset that I took all my grandiose thoughts and ideas of this lifestyle and wove them into a whole other personality. I made a mask of the gangster I wanted to be for myself, and made it a reality. Add my previously discussed attention-seeking complex and I began to pretend that I didn't fee.

195

any pain, instead hiding it behind a persona of no fear, and resentment. This culminated in my joining a street gang in my second year of junior high (8th grade).

The cold part about this is that, at just fourteen years-of-age, I thought that I was the ultimate gangster. After all, I had grown up drinking alcohol by sneaking beers out of the refrigerator, smoking weed with babysitters by pinching it from my parents stash, and fighting with my twin brother constantly over one thing or another. In this I was delusional, but it was training for my brain, preparing my psyche for those things I allowed myself with the gang.

When it came to those more legitimate criminal activities (i.e.; "putting in work" - shooting at rival gang members, or "being down" to "hit a lick", or other such gang-related activities), I found them easy. I had grown up shooting guns by hunting, and skeet shooting with a shotgun. More importantly, I was taught early to be comfortable with a firearm; to respect the rules that came with shooting or possessing them. This knowledge put me in a higher regard with my peers, as well as the "big homeys". They were impressed that I essentially knew how to handle myself, and was confident doing so in any situation. It's easy to disregard this, but imagine for a second a person on the streets in action, in a life-or-death situation, having never truly handled a gun before. You're liable to shoot yourself, your homeboys, or even an innocent bystander.

I did these things because I had already given up on the good values that I was taught by my parents, school, and society in general. Instead, I chose to rebel against everything that was good and decent in life and society. I chose the criminal and gang lifestyle over being responsible and respecting the rights and the freedoms of others in society. I consciously became the total opposite of what someone from my background would normally be expected to become.

Unlike my outlaw biker parents, and their poor White privileged social background, I chose to become a "Crip" and immerse myself in "the ghetto" social lifestyle. Rebelling against my parents while still ultimately achieving my illegal desires. By wearing this mask, I became the epitome of a gangster: taking whatever I wanted, not caring, and hating authority. This resulted in me abandoning my family and their values, and resenting everything they worked hard to provide me growing up.

I sought to embody this fake cover so much that I ran away so I could

live in the "hood", dress the way my homeboys dressed, and act the way that
I believed would win me the respect I deserved as a gangster. By wearing this
mask 24/7 I would become more confident and secure in my persona. I couldn't
stand anyone who said I was just going through a phase, or that I was a wanna-be.
These "insults" just made me try harder to prove that I was the "real deal",
when in reality I was just deceiving myself to fall further into everything
that the cycle of addiction perpetuates.

Consequently, this addiction to the criminal and gangster lifestyle
didn't do anything but get me caught-up in the position for which I sit now:
writing this essay from my cell in High Desert State Prison. Like I mentioned
in the second paragraph of this essay, I started off this term having fallen
victim to the "Three Strikes Law". For twenty-one years, I lived the existence
of a lifer in California's penal system, traveling up and down this state
to many of the thirty-plus prisons in this state; some three or four times
over.

The reason this brief story is entitled "More Than You Think" is because
I did all of this as a "White Crip", and while maintaining one thought, and
one thought only: "I'm going to die in here". To me, this was to come either
by the other prisoners I lived with in here, or by the long, and slow, death
sentence that 'life' in prison promises. Yet somehow, I broke this mentality.

Personally, I did my time for 24 years as an active Crip, and prison
gang member; a man with something to prove. I'm not going to get into all
of the bad things I did to other people here in prison as this, to me, would
just be an exercise in either glorifying or attempting to justify my behavior.
Suffice it to say, I was a self-motivated violent, aggressive, hateful, angry
person hopelessly lost to this lifestyle that acted out of self-preservation
and egotistical and selfish beliefs with a complete lack of humanity and empathy
for far too long. It led me to hurt a whole lot of people, not least of which
was myself.

To be completely honest, I'm ashamed of the things I've done, the people
I've hurt, lied to, and hustled or manipulated for the furtherance of my addiction
to my chosen lifestyle. So, let's just leave the details for another time.
If you're still interested at all in seeing a snapshot of who I used to be,
then you can look up an interview I did in 2006 for MSNBC entitled "Locked-Up
Raw: Ganging Up". It was about the last prison they opened up in the state
(Kern Valley). A super-max, level-4/180 design institution. Or, you can wait

197

until I get out on this last in-house determinant sentence, and buy the book
I plan to self-publish: "The Last of a Dying Breed: The Story of a White Crip
and the B.O.S.S.'s of the California Department of Corrections".

In reality, I completely institutionalized myself by completely immersing
myself in the prison culture that was just a continuation of my criminal,
and gang, lifestyle. All because of some warped belief that I was honoring
the code of loyalty, pride, and an obligation to my homeboys, the gang, and
to the B.O.S.S.'s (Brothers Of the Same Struggle).

I was laced up by this prison system. The worst part of all was that
I knew that I was harming myself by doing these things, and living this way.
I even went so far as to tattoo a necklace around my collarbone: "Feel My
Pain And Loyalty". Now I sit here and wonder: "Do I fit the definition of
insane?" But, the truth of the matter is that I really had to be crazy to
continue to live this way for so long, all while knowing that it was wrong.
Ultimately though, all the warped beliefs that I trained myself to believe
were a weight I could not carry forever. Once my exhausted psyche could no
longer find the energy to justify it's own bullshit, all the things my loved
ones were trying to tell me throughout the years began to break through.

So it was, that after twenty-some years of living a criminal, gang,
and prison lifestyle (or, as we like to call it - "pushing the line"), it
all finally dawned on me. For me, the last straw came in the form of another
case. I know... you're probably wondering again how I could be so stupid,
and once again, you wouldn't be wrong. This is the reality of the path I chose,
though.

Now, thanks also to my beautiful wife Desiree, this is it. God bless
her good, kind, and awesome heart for having the faith in me that she maintained,
supporting me to the breaking point. Once again, I am not going to get into
the semantics of the case, as I don't wish to glorify my old lifestyle in
any way. I'll only say that it was for possession of a weapon with intent,
and it has cost me six more years in this hell-hole.

A large part of what close this chapter for good in my life was an ultimatum
by my wife. This came a month after our prison wedding, while I was doing
my last S.H.U. term (time for an in-prison offense in the Security Housing
Unit) in 2016. Since it ultimately came down to losing someone I love or continue
on the same road I have been on since I was a teenager, I finally chose to
quit because I just couldn't stand to lose another thing to my criminal addiction.

This is when I chose to become S.N.Y. (an inmate on a Special Needs Yard instead of General Population), and give up the gang lifestyle. Although it hasn't been easy to quit being the person I was, accepting that I can no longer be a man who hides behind a mask, I can say that, if it wasn't for a few of the good people I have met on this side of the fence, I don't think that I could have accomplished many of the things I have.

It has been people like Philip Lozano, James Wilson, and a few others, along with the love and support of my family, and (of course) my wife that have gotten me through it - reminding me of who I am becoming when I struggle with my old thought patterns. I also must credit the C.G.A. program in here, as well as numerous other groups, that have influenced me to become a group facilitator, a mentor to the newly incarcerated, a seeker of continuous self-improvement, and a college graduate with a degree in sociology.

I look forward to all of the things to come for me now (that I will let you all know about in the years to come) as I continue to strive to be an advocate for future incarcerated individuals who I want to help to not make the same mistakes I made on this long journey. Thank you for taking the time to read this along your own.

By: Dylan Dunn

199

"Allow yourself to have a weak moment, and not a weak mindset."

- Devon

Session 5
The Sum of All Parts

All of these stories are more than the sum of the their parts. They tell the many unwritten stories of the millions of men and women who are faced with the same near insurmountable obstacles from the day they're born. You can take a piece of that story, add it with a little bit of this story, and sprinkle a taste from another to get the complete story of a generation of individuals. At some time along the way our stories have crossed paths, our circumstances and situations were each others, and each face in every story was forced to deal with it in their own individual, yet very collective, human way. Sometimes cautiously, sometimes recklessly, or sometimes a mix of the two, yet no matter what, we all maintained our will to survive.

Ultimately, we're all seeking change. By this, and in this entire session, the "all", "us", and "we" I am speaking about (and, at times, too) are those who exist within lower economic conditions and/or are marginalized by the culture at large. Change from our conditions, our environment, or from a lifestyle. We all want out; some by whatever is holding them back, holding them down, or holding them up from overcoming what is holding them back. We find ourselves held down by our environment, trying to hold it down for our community (through peaceful protest, "go to the poll" initiatives, and community events), but get stepped on, or stepped over, searching for opportunities.

After perniciously pummelling the pavement, parading the streets carelessly, we have all been hauled through the halls of hell because we didn't value a life, someone's property, or otherwise recklessly endangered a community because of a false bravado, or ego, born and cultivated in desperation. This brings me to the question that undergirds this entire book's thesis. One that demands an answer for the sake of the future of our communities, and society as a whole. Do we, as society's failures, even deserve success?

Seemingly, success is a measurement of your own personal greatness, but success to me may be different than success for you. To understand how one defines success, you must first ask what unit of measurement one is using to measure success with. Is it financially, academically, socially, emotionally? What does sucess mean to you?

At some point, we all had to ask oursaelves if we would even make it to see 25 years of age.* According to scientists, the human brain isn't fully

---

*In most urban ghettos, kids feel that by the time they are 25 they will either be dead, locked up, or an O.G.

developed until the age 26. Unfortunately, by this age many men and women
in urban neighborhoods nationwide have already been through a lifetime of
trauma. Most grow up fast experiencing domestic abuse, substance abuse, and
gun violence. Others are faced with taking care of siblings while still being
children themselves. Success in this context may just be surviving to see
another day.

On the other hand, success may be financial freedom (generally meaning
bills paid up, car paid for, and minimal debt) or even a financial fantasy
(think "Lifestyles of the Rich and Famous"). While for the mid-to-upper middle-
class financial freedom is a reality that is taken for granted, for those
of us at the lower end of the economic food-chain (still a large chunk of
society) both remain largely unobtainable.

Academically, many are proud to receive a GED or high school diploma.
Others receive a two-year degree (Associates), and have done what most people
in their families have never done. Those who allow themselves the luxury of
a bachelors degree or higher are outliers, at least in underserved communities.

Emotionally, success falls under such a large umbrella that it becomes
almost impossible to fully measure. First, let's talk about the mothers who
go to sleep scared every night hoping that their child makes it home. Many
have already experienced tragedy. All they hope for is not to bury a loved
one by years end. Additionally, we have children and adolescents who are constantly
hoping that their parents stop fighting and/or using, and start loving,
and paying proper attention instead. There are mothers who hope that they
just don't get that phone call that begins, "I have a collect call from...",
once again (to the unaffiliated, this is how all calls from jail and prison
begin).

On the other hand, you have the proud mother who gets to see their child
walk across the stage at a high school graduation, or experiences the shared
joy of a child that gets accepted to college, or even (rarely) when all a
parent's worries are over because their child has been drafted to some professional
sports organization. This (obviously) is only to name a few of emotional successes
and distresses, but hopefully is enough to define it's multitudes.

Social success implies what we do for our community, as well as what
we do to improve our community. Some just hope that the murder rate goes down,
or seeks to bridge the divide between rival gangs so that the violence can
cease. Sucess may come when you have community events that brings everyone

together without any violent incidents. Others hope to lift up those who have
fallen so hard that they've met homelessness first hand. A good recent example
is the hopes of helping those displaced by Covid-19.

Here again I ask, do society's failures deserve sucess? I suppose first
I should ask: what is, or who are, society's failures? I dare not say our
prisoners. Some of our most prominent citizens are felons: Martha Stewart,
Michael Vick, Nelson Mandela, and so many others. Are we failures because
jail is where they send failures? Are we failures because we got caught for
not following the laws of the land? In this case though (with the exception
of infants and small children), society as a whole has failed. While we, in
the United States, have the highest incarceration rate in the world by far,
given our laws we still could say that the majority of society is deserving
of incarceration, if only they would have been caught. Our question then remains
the same, yet given our context here it seems like we have collectively only
succeeded in filling the nation's jail cells. Validating eager politician's
abuse of our instincts given the impulse of fear in a bid for votes, then
justifying to themselves, and us, the issuance of disproportionate sentences;
as evidenced by our existing tough on crime bills.

However, prison reform has taken center stage in the past few years.
More and more advocacy groups are emerging, gradually turning the key to free
individuals who have turned to faith and/or fate to combat hopelessness. Success
to a prisoner, especially one who has spent a quarter of a century incarcerated,
is freedom. As of recently, the California Department of Corrections and Rehabilitation (CDCR) has incentivised incarcerated individuals by providing a way
to earn their way out of prison. Though they could do much better to fulfill
the promise of this name, the current model allows prisoners the opportunity
to earn Rehabilitative Achievement Credits (RAC), Milestones, Education merits,
and extraordinary conduct to incrementally take time off their sentences. Incarcerated women/men can also reduce their sentences by participating in rehabilitative
groups, achieving an education credit, and an education merit upon completion
of a GED, Associate's degree, or any other progressive educational accomplishment
thereafter. Moreso, they have amended the sentencing structure recently for
incarcerated individuals with indeterminate life sentences, and below.

First, they changed 85% to 80% (percentage of full sentence a violent
offender will serve without departmental disciplinary infractions) with the
passage of Proposition 57 in 2016-17. More recently, they have changed 80%

to 66.6% (they have made changes for non-violent offenders as well). Those hopeless individuals can now see the proverbial "light at the end of the tunnel". So, in a sense, if freedom is success for an incarcerated individual, then success is on the horizon.

Furthermore, how can those of us on the inside find a legal avenue for financial success when the state currently has the power to take this away by operating under the protection of the 13th Amendment (legalized slavery). Since CDCR already offers mental health services, higher learning, and ways to donate to non-profit organizations, shouldn't their remit to create future productive citizens be widened to include financial stability through legitimate means? I read a recent article in the San Quentin Newspaper entitled, "Gate Money: Is It Time for a Cost-Of-Living Increase?", and I thought that was an adequate assessment of what we're experiencing as transitioning citizens.

Frankly, this process must begin long before an individual leaves the cell block. It's probably safe to say that the majority of the incarcerated population would like to see an increase in our pay wages (it ranges from $0.08 - $0.37 per hour for the overwhelming majority, and no one earns more than $1 per hour). This would allow those strapped for cash an opportunity to earn their keep. If you were to ask any incarcerated individual nationwide, they could describe to you the ways that occupants of our jails and prisons are instrumental in keeping each prison running from the bottom-up.

This is only a fraction of the market standards for doing the same jobs (i.e.; plumbers, janitors, maintenance workers, cooks, etc.). If being a moral society is important to us, we must seek to increase those wages to something that will allow an individual to both pay off their restitution (their financial debt to both society and their victim) and still have enough to survive, and help their struggling families to survive, for the month. How do we evolve from a society that wants to bury slavery in our schools (the current political debate about teaching critical race theory), yet still treats it's lowest citizens like slaves.

We should also wonder why there hasn't yet been a mandate on financial literacy. Had the prison population had an inkling of financial literacy when they received their economic impact payments (from the federal government during Covid), by in large they would have thought of ways to save for the future, or even increase their future wealth, as opposed to squandering it within a year. You can't expect an already poorly educated individual to understand the intricacies of investing money when they have never had any to invest. For an economic system that touts the importance of both spending and investing properly (in fact, economist's predictions rely on the spending of a "rational" individual), it is obviously poor planning to not educate it's citizens to it's inner workings. In this way, the benefits would cut both ways, allowing the individual's legitimate investments to move them closer to financial freedom (success). The more a person understands, and feels a part of, the inner-workings of society, the more they respect other's property and values their own. If we were to thusly concentrate on fixing our problems at their root (below the surface), the more we prevent the weeds from running wild.

The more I've spent my days mentoring, teaching, and maintaining my own self-education, the more I've noticed that, while people want all different types of success, most are either intimidated, or don't want to put in the work to achieve it. The average incarcerated individual is so used to seeking (and, at times, attaining) instant gratification that, if the success they visualize does not promise to be instant, then they are not even willing to entertain it. It's almost like, if they don't see instant success, then they don't believe that ultimate success is possible.

Could that mean that they don't have any faith in themselves? Or, has our culture of convenience created a stigma that has a person telling themselves: "If I don't get it now, it'll never happen"? What happened to hard work paying off? The path to ultimate success is always a culmination of many steps.

In closing, I want to say that it's important to restructure our core values as a culture, and as individuals. The only way to influence people is to connect their needs to their actions. One must first ask the question, what do you (or I) want? In this case, success. Whether it's freedom, financial, academic, emotional, or social. What do you want for yourself, and others, if you achieve this success? How do you want to put your success to use?

So, the question remains: do society's failures deserve success? This depends if you feel like you failed society. The only way a person truly fails society is if they go to their grave without evolving as a human being. Otherwise, while life remains, you still have an opportunity to make a difference. If you change what you tell yourself about something, you will change your response to it.

The American economist Milton Friedman said, "there is no such thing as a free lunch," because "everything that has benefits also has costs." Your opportunity cost is that which you are willing to give up for any given opportunity. For those incarcerated, are you willing to give up the gangs, the lifestyle, the way of thinking? Or, perhaps your packages, your store, or your tennis shoes, to achieve a higher goal? How do you expect to swim in the ocean on the outside when you can't yet tread in shallow water?

It's time to broaden our understanding about life. That is, stop claiming street signs, blocks, or colors that don't really belong to you. Get away from seeking acceptance from another person, especially without even finding a way to accept yourself first. This constant inner-battle that we are faced with is because we struggle with deinal. Once you accept change, then success becomes more clear.

Yes, you do deserve success. You are not a failure. You may have failed, but failing is not perpetual, unless you resist learning from your mistakes. Even then you will find new ways of failing that will inform how you must continue to evolve for a better future. We are the sum total of all our parts, which always allows for the opportunity to become an unlikely success.

By: Donel Poston

A Little Bit About The Editor (and Typist)

I have known Donel Poston now for nearly six years, having met him soon after arriving at High Desert State Prison in 2015. A little over a year ago now he introduced me to James Wilson, who was looking for someone to type his (and his various co-author's) many proposals and curriculums for self-help and rehabilitation groups for both the organization 'Initiate Justice', and his own personal book projects. Though, at first, I looked upon the opportunity as a way to make some extra money, I quickly realized that (though most of these men's backgrounds greatly differ from my own) James', Donel's, their co-author's, and Initiate Justice's ideals and goals greatly aligned with my own.

Though I grew up in a middle class family, largely sheltered from the neighborhoods and circumstances that these men describe in their own histories, prison has only acted to confirm, and further, my own knowledge and ideals concerning humanity. I've always believed that any act of, or endemic, oppression and impoverishment that lessens an individual's sense of well-being (I'm not just speaking economically here, but impoverishment of hope, of respect - self or otherwise, of voice, of equity, of opportunity, and/or any other physical and psychological necessity) will often lead to a sense of desperation and lack of belonging that bastardizes the "normal" social character, even if only momentarily.

Not only do these mens' histories attest to these conditions, but equally does our justice system (mass incarceration, over-sentencing structures, and relative lack of a path towards rehabilitative release) perpetuate it. We must do better, in this land of plenty, to combat this (largely) self-created reality. It is largely for this reason that I have taken great pleasure in attempting to aid these men's voices and true stories in edit, and type. The projects I have (thus far) provided this service for are as follows:

- "Evidence of Long, Lost Letters"
- "Why We Must Initiate Justice"
- "Write Our Wrongs"
- "Unlikely Successes"
- "Nagy Notes"
- "Profiles in Rehabilitation"
- "Freedom By Degrees"

Lastly, in answer to James' question in his introduction of "Unlikely Successes", asking (in short): "What is, and do society's 'failures' deserve, success?", I wish to share a thought that I wrote down a few years ago from one late night spent contemplating my own, and other individuals', failures that will now follow us for the rest of our lives:

The Next Chapter

OTHER THAN GANGSTER

From Gang-Bangers
to G.A.M.E. Changers

"Everyone can be great
because everyone
can serve."

- Martin Luther King Jr.

By: James Wilson

Contributing Authors
Anthony Thomas
Michael E. Scott
Gary Figueroa
Darnell Dorsey
Christian Smith

Being a Gangsta is Stupid

I don't know anyone who can honestly say that
being a gangsta was the smartest choice that
he or she has ever made in their life.

Except perhaps an actor or rapper being paid
to portray an image of one.

I don't know how you call yo'self a gangsta if
you have killed someone you grew up wit', or
someone you didn't even know. That's not gangsta.
That's shady and evil, and if that's your version
of being a gangsta, then being a gangsta is stupid.

I don't know how you call it gangsta if you ridin'
around shooting up parks with little kids and
innocent by-standers in 'em enjoyin' they life.
If that's gangsta, then being a gangsta is stupid.

I don't know what's so gangsta about calling
home to yo' people, who out there workin' hard
for they money, askin' them to send you some
to reward you for being stupid; thinkin' that
is something to be proud of and call it gangsta.
If that's gangsta, then being a gangsta is stupid.

I don't know how it's okay to double-cross someone
you supposed to love and then call it gangsta.
If that's gangsta, then being a gangsta is stupid.

I ask someone to please explain to me how continuing
to mess up your life more and more to prove to
your so-called friends that you are a gangsta
is somethin' to be proud of? If that's gangsta,
then being a gangsta is stupid.

I ask every one of us that has been infected
wit' the delusional street life, that has ruined
a lot of our own lives, how inflicting unbearable
pain on other people in our own communities is
something to be proud of? And then, have the

nerve to call it gangsta.

If that's gangsta, being a gangsta is definately stupid.

I would also like to ask how bein' locked up forever, faced with the possibility of never comin' home, and livin' wit' another human being in a closet-bathroom is a badge of honor you want to wear and call it bein' a gangsta? If that's being a gangsta....

I'm done, cause I'm not built like that, and I don't want to live in a dark world where I'm the cause of turmoil and strife in other people's lives. That's not how I was raised and brought up by my people. Being a gangsta is stupid!

I have been blessed to have avoided much darker circumstances that come wit' bein' in prison, so I'm bowing out gracefully while I still have a chance. If you have the courage to admit that you have been a dark cloud storming on other people's lives, use that same courage to bring some light and sunshine to the people's lives you touch instead.

The street life is delusional darkness. Turn on the light and be a guide to others living in the darkness while you still have a chance. Let love and light be your guides.

By: Michael E. Scott
#K31521

"Show me the heroes (or sheroes) the youth of your country
look up to, and I will tell you the future of your country."

Introduction

Every great story has a hero. As humans, we are fascinated by the central
character in a book or movie who overcomes various odds and challenges to
secure a victory for themself and/or others. It is that aspect of a story -
the triumph - that drives our interest, compels our attention, and demands
our appreciation and allegiance. We can talk about thousands of years of ancient
history, covering great nations of antiquity such as Egypt, Babylon, Greece,
Rome, China, or the early America's, and the discussion will inevitably have
it's focus on some person whose legacy survived the ancient ruins of their
nation, and the annuls of time, to capture the imagination of millions of
their fellow human beings.

It is fascinating to note that most of us don't even know very much
about the totality of most of the figures who have come down to us through
history. Instead, many are remembered for just a single quality. Take, for
example, some of the following individuals thusly associated:

- Osiris = Mysticism
- Nimrod = Warrior
- Hammurabi = Lawgiver
- Nefertiti = Beauty
- Hercules = Strength
- Caesar = Conquerer
- King Tut = Royalty
- Confucius = Wisdom
- Venus = Love

Whether these were actual people or myths, these mostly one-named figures
are summarized by one enduring quality, or act.

Now, fast-forward and think about the modern day mythical heroes like
Superman, Batman, Wonder Woman, or Black Panther and what comes to mind? For
me: strength, ingenuity, fascinating, and inspiring (respectively).

Here are some other more recent people we know by a single name, are
known instantly, and are associated with something great:

- Jordan = Unstoppable
- Kobe = Fearless

- Jesus = Sacrifice
- Muhammad = Islam
- Elvis = Timeless
- Hitler = Hatred
- Madonna = Seduction
- Prince = Genius
- Obama = Charisma
- Adele = Unique (one of a kind, right?!)

Maybe you can think of other words that typify these individuals, but this is what I've heard (and imagine) when I see or think of them. At least, when I'm being superficial and awestruck.

Let's expand this schematic to states, cities, and regions. What comes to mind when you hear **South Central? Los Angeles? Chicago? New York? Watts? Detroit? Compton? Silicon Valley? Hollywood?**

Given the following categories, where would you place each of them?

Crime / Poverty

1.
2.
3.

Manufacturing / Vehicles

1.
2.
3.

Creativity / Technology

1.
2.
3.

Culture / Entertainment

1.
2.
3.

So, where did you list Watts? Chicago? South Central? Detroit? Compton? There is no need to actually say here. I'm sure I can guess where most landed.

There are some excellent people who have come from Watts (Watts poets, Tyrese), South Central (Ice Cube, Tiffany Haddish), Compton (Anthony Anderson, Serena, Venus, Easy E, Dr. Dre), and Chicago (Obama), just to name a few. There are also some horrible people who have come out of Silicon Valley and Hollywood (it isn't all about brains and fame) along with the greats. No person, or place, can be summed up completely by just one word. No "living" entity is homogenous as the real world is not a place that exists in a vacuum. There is crime, poverty, manufacturing, vehicles, creativity, technology, entertainment, and culture in every location mentioned above. Go visit each for yourself if you don't believe me!

Just as those examples above, most fictional characters (at least, the well written and memorable ones) are not one dimensional either. Superman isn't _all_ about strength. He had other strengths, as well as weaknesses (Lois Lane and Kryptonite to name two). Even mythical superhumans have made their mistakes, as well. Some real life examples that attest to this include:

- Jordan = Gambling
- Kobe = Infidelity
- Elvis = Plagiarism
- Prince = Drug Addiction
- You = ? (power lies in secrecy, right?)

If we were to add more to our descriptions of great people we could easily find ourselves filling sentences and paragraphs. Basically, a story that has some mix of good and bad; some ups and downs. As I've heard it said: "The pancake, no matter how flat you make it, will always have two sides." This is the very reason why some have cautioned against meeting your heroes. Not all is sunny, and inevitably a person will let you down at some level. Often, the higher our expectations the greater the fall.

This is true of all of us: the criminal, friends, family, judges, prosecutors, cops, and our heroes. Don't believe me? Stick around!

This is what this short book is about. Dimensions, overcoming labels, shattering stereotypes, and (as the title suggests) picking up some G.A.M.E., even from the most unlikely of places (prison).

What Do You Think?

On July 4, 2020, Donald Trump gave a speech that sought to attack "the left" (or "Radical Democrats"). He accused them of four things:

1) Wiping out American history.
2) Defaming American heroes.
3) Destroying American values.
4) Indoctrinating American Children.

Chew on it as you read on.

By: James Wilson

"I touch the future; I teach."

Chapter 1
Walking On During Team Practice

Before I was 13 years-old I had no intention of becoming a gang member. It was not something I ever deliberately considered for my life. Like most youngsters in my community, our idea of an enemy was the other kids around the neighborhood our age whom we differed with over the small things of childhood. Things like whose bike, shoes, or family car looked better, or who was better at a particular sport or feat. While we were squabbling over marbles, baseball cards, and who should get the ball over a challenged foul call on the basketball court, a war was raging around us. As children in this environment, we were living in a parallel universe where we were constantly faced with intersecting doors.

I was born in Pasadena, California in 1974, just three years after the gang known as The Crips was founded, which was about one year before their rivals - The Bloods - hardened into a street gang. It didn't take long for these gangs to cross the 210 Freeway from Los Angeles to plant their flags in the city of my birth. Affectionately called "The City of Roses", Pasadena is the home of the Rose Bowl, the annual Rose Parade, the Jet Propellant Lab (JPL - a subsidiary of NASA), Cal Tech College (immortalized in the sitcom "The Big Bang Theory"), and where the Ninth Circuit Court of Appeals (the highest court in California) hold hearings and set legal precedent for a session out of each year.

From a tourist's or television viewer's perspective the city is as beautiful as a rose. This is also true for those of means who live comfortably within it's old (and new) money-sheltered spaces. For those of my demographic however (Black, Brown, poor, uneducated), we knew well it's thorns: the northwest sector of town that was fertile soil for gangs, drugs, violence, and generational poverty. The seeds of the Bloods and Crips would be nurtured there, and the resulting weeds were left to overwhelm and strangle an entire community. Close on the heel of this street gang infestation, the crack epidemic would then spark a fire that would consume the majority of households.

The low-income housing project my family lived in during the late '70s to mid-80's would become split territorially between Bloods and Crips. Most of the conflict was an obvious expansion of our childhood differences and squabbles. Now there were teenagers and adults fighting and jumping on each other for colors, territory, and gang sign differences. Occasionally, some type of weapon (a knife, a bat, even a small caliber pistol) would find its way into the scuffles.

When crack cocaine hit our streets, all of this changed. Simple gang beefs turned into drug wars where territory translated into profits. A battle ensued over who would run the projects, and in its wake the crime rate spiked, the body count increased, and incarceration numbers went up.

Culture is always one's prime behavioral instructor. By a mixture of proximity, osmosis, and indirect tutelage I learned how to speak slang, interpret gang signs, distinguish between rival parties, and ultimately how to purchase, market, and sell cocaine. Since the greatest existential context for me was poverty, I reached for a bag rather than a rag. I chose to become a drug dealer instead of a gang member.

The Northwest sector of Pasadena is relatively small. Despite some personal and family disputes, back then the bifurcated community along gang lines held no meaning for me. To my knowledge, prior to the uptick in gang violence people in our neighborhood had carte blance, and unlimited movement, throughout the community space we shared. We were united by both race and poverty. Crack would do what mere gangs could not. It exploited the cracks in our community bonds until the levies of love and support were breached and all hell broke loose.

Early Mistakes

By 1987, just shy of my 13th birthday, I was already a novice in the dope game. That year, I made a common rookie mistake and sold drugs to an undercover cop... twice. The first time, I was released from police custody into that of my mother. It would be while awaiting adjudication in juvenile court on that case that I caught the second.

The game had changed for drug cases by this point in the 1980's, and with the stakes higher I was sent for the first time, and on Christmas night, to East Lake Juvenile Hall in Los Angeles. It was just my luck that I happened to be dressed in red and burgundy that day (the official color of Bloods), and when the Crips saw me come through the reception unit they went into an uproar.

My brother Jonathen and I were dressed alike, and the unit staff had to separate us from the unit dayroom, occupied mostly by Crips. Getting a nudge from a unit worker (an older Blood from L.A.), he put it squarely:

> "Y'all are from Pasadena, a predominately Blood
> territory. All these Crips seen what y'all were
> wearing. When y'all go out to the units they
> are gonna label y'all Bloods, so y'all might
> as well claim P.D.L. There are some 'Lanes' out
> there, and our numbers overall are short. So,
> wherever y'all land, pave a way for the other
> homies coming behind y'all."

Pasadena Denver Lane (P.D.L.) was the largest gang in Pasadena, and encompassed most of the city. Including where I grew up all of my life. It wouldn't be hard to fall into this role as, via the social curriculum, we were "learned in all of the ways of gangsterism."

We knew the language, the signs, many of the members (including some of our family members), the rivals, and we were trained to fight. In a span of minutes, the scales of the conflict and violence for me had risen. Reckless and brash, I rose to the occasion, foolishly accepting this new challenge. Gangs had now melded with drug dealing in my mind. It would ultimately claim my heart. Some would even claim that it took my soul.

The Set Up

Joining a gang (also called "claiming a set") is not like adding a new feature to your life - a new patch on an old garment, to borrow a Biblical phrase. Instead, it brings with it a "new life" of it's own, complete with a new set of thinking and practices. It is a new game; complete with teammates, team colors, team rivals, team loyalty, and more. The playbook is simple: go out into the field; secure good positioning; make contact with the enemy by any and all means (fight, shoot, kill); score a victory for the team at all costs. At least, this is the generalized view of the game for the ambitious young novice. I dove in.

What is Game?

In the hood, almost all facets of street life is called "game". Game covers both language and practice. It is your learning (by whatever degree) and your skill (at whatever level).

Young boys, when they reach puberty and take to the streets to play on young girls, earn the title of "players". The goal is to play on (really, 'prey' on) the youthful naiveté of impressionable girls. In this context, "game" is individually crafted words, personal style, and the amusement and tact used to outmaneuver an intended target in order to "score" (have sex).

"Game" is also illegal schemes to defraud, steal, or "come up on" (take advantage of) unsuspecting people, businesses, or their possessions (homes, cars, credit, etc.). It is about one's ability to survive the often challenging criminal underworld lifestyle (by brains, brawn, or both). How you play will determine, in many cases, where you lay: in your bed at home, a bed in jail, a bed at the hospital, or as fertilizer for a bed of flowers.

One's game has life and death consequences, and because there are no official divisions in the street game (minor / major / amateur / professional), you enter as a kid "playing by the big boy rules". You are up against people with far more knowledge, experience, and skill than you possess. Everyone is playing, to a large degree, at their own risk. I have been in the game long enough to have seen young homies kill big homies, and big homies kill little homies. Age ain't nothing but a number in the streets. I was basically stepping through a door of no return.

To my advantage (and my mother's dismay), I gravitated towards older people as a kid. My father would discipline me for, what he called, "looking into the mouth of older people" as they spoke. He had a rule: kids should not be in the room when grown folks were talking. Playing towards my mother's affections and protection, I'd nestle next to her, shielded and incognito, to steal the covetted secrets of adults. I gained the dual reputation of being both a mature and quiet kid. In other words, sneaky and tactful.

From an older brother, I would learn how to masturbate in preparation for early sex. He would also teach me the intricacies of dealing drugs and being a more sophisticated criminal. My older sister taught me all of the gang signs and, via her company, kept me in the presence of all of the up and coming gang-bangers who came to hang out with her to buy weed and get their hair braided. It was through this venue that I learned more about gangs, drugs, and the use of marijuana, alcohol, and PCP by age 13. As they say, "culture is destiny."

Adults in the hood would call this upbringing being "fast". Basically, trying to do grown-up things while still just a kid. Drugs, gangs, and sex robbed me of a childhood. Eager to sharpen my teeth and claws, I started trying to run game (schemes) on everyone: my parents, my teachers, my probation officer, girls (and their parents), and my older homies.

Accused by my mother of "smelling my balls, and getting too big for my britches [pants]," she kicked me out of her house. Now having to lean moreso on what I'd learned up to this point, I hit the ground running and didn't miss a beat. By this time, I was spending more time in the streets anyways, and home was just a convenient place to shower and sleep. It felt like I was in my natural habitat. I fell in with the worst of my kind.

A New Set of Challenges

By this time, I had either stolen or bought enough guns from crack users to supply a small army. I was also taught how to shoot them, beginning with the biggest of all: a shotgun. Shooting these guns into the air raised the ire of the older homies, who accused me of making the hood "hot" (bringing the police around). One older homie told me that he was sent to California Youth Authority (CYA) for shooting a shotgun through some bushes, striking a lady in an adjacent home as she was washing dishes.

These encounters brought me into contact with older homies who, in an effort to scold me, would also become my street mentors. They were fascinated by how many guns I had amassed and kept stashed in the basement of my mom's apartment complex. This exposure also put me at risk of being targetted for theft, and tested to see if I'd actually use a weapon on someone.

I learned to keep shifting my stash and was encouraged to prove my mettle. My reputation with the older homies increased and my teammates respected me. The game had claimed me. Being out late at night with older homies gave me more access to learn from more seasoned players, make more money, and come across all the things that would give me an edge on most of the other youngsters my age flirting with the game. I bought guns, motorcycles, cars, jewelry, and sex from older women in the wee hours of the night. By breaking the rules, I was quickly closing the gap on the tier of players who'd been in the game much longer than I had. I was no child in their eyes. This was grown-up stuff.

By the time my gang career would end 21 years later (2009; 34 years-old) I had spent six-plus years in juvenile detention centers, approximately ten years in adult facilities (county jails, prisons), and had been accused of almost every crime you can imagine - including homicide. I had risen to the top of the food chain in the streets and while in custody. By age thirty I was being called both "the worst person of [my] generation," and "a living legend." I had, by then, fought two separate capital cases for murder. I also had beaten the odds. I had survived many life and death situations.

It was for all of these reasons that the other youngsters looked up to me as a hero. They were fascinated by my story, and the stories of others like mine. Not that they are short on a range of other heroes to choose from. In many poor and crime infested communities "gangsters" are the most visible representation of what power looks like.

Parents, teachers, preachers, and in some cases law enforcement, fear this type of figure. Proximity, influence, and consistency (like a relentless commercial) prevails over better judgement and decision-making. It's similar to a financial cost / benefit analysis. The greater the benefits people expect to receive from any given alternative, the more people are likely to choose the greatest amongst their options. The greater the perceived cost, the fewer people are likely to select it.

The perceived benefits of being a gangster (the illusion of success and power without legitimate responsibilities) has a certain allure. Like many marketing schemes (game), it appeals to your limbic system (emotions), not the rational part of your brain. Emotions are powerful drivers of actions. Who among us can't think of a specific incident driven by the following:

- Anger
- Fear
- Lust
- Greed
- Shame
- Disgust
- Appetite

In the context of the economic straits of many American communities where children consistently watch their parents work (or not) and are in a perpetual struggle to survive, why not get in the game and hustle? Further, why not put some muscle behind this hustle and join forces with the neighborhood gang? Like any group (or nation), the gang (citizens) wants authority (political, economic, and military power) to expand and protect their gains. After all, that is the American way, right?

Remember the quote at the beginning of the introduction:

"Show me the heroes the youth of your country
look up to, and I will tell you the future of
your country."

Prior to joining a gang and dropping out of school, the only "legitimate" heroes I had in mind were the ones promoted in music (gansta rap), on television (Different Strokes, A Different World, Fresh Prince of Bel Air), the movies (School Dayz, Do the Right Thing, Colors), and the litany of "White gangsters" provided to all kids in school text books: George Washington, Thomas Jefferson, John Adams, James Madison, Abraham Lincoln, Ulysses S. Grant, General Sherman, General MacArthur, and everybody else who "made and saved" America and Democracy. Then, there was Jesus. Every single black woman's mythical "man", as well as His Father, who made and saved us from our sins (while we starved on Earth trying to get to Heaven to eat and be free!).

There weren't many tangible examples for those of us from our side of the tracks to choose from. Unsurprisingly, our futures weren't promised to be all that bright. We perform (especially kids) as we see practiced (taught and modelled) in our immediate environments. To us youngsters, the person most likely to survive the trials and challenges of the hood (and even thrive, in some respects), despite the risk, was the gangster. The hood hero. They were our Zeus', Paul Revere's, and General MacArthur's. But, is this really the "quality" that I'd like to be remembered by?

Check List

James = Sleprock[*]
Sleprock = Gangster

Remember though, no one word can tell a person's whole story.

By: James Wilson

---

[*]Sleprock II was my nickname in the gang.

"If they can name you, they can tame you."

Chapter 2
Kicking Around Some G.A.M.E.

Here is a list of a few of the words that others have used to describe me. How many have people used to describe you:

- Nigger
- Criminal
- Entitled
- Angry
- Aggressive
- Rapist
- Racist
- Killer
- Gangster
- Jerk

Just to name a few.

Check out these two quotes:

"If they give you ruled [lined] paper, write the other way."

"Describe yourself in one word: I am a [rebel]."

(you wouldn't expect a rebel to follow the rules and use just one word to describe himself now, would you?)

The G.A.M.E. is Bigger Than Me

I did not intend for this to be an autobiography. I wrote enough about myself in the eight books I've written or co-authored so far (something you probably wouldn't expect from a "gangster", right?). The following is a list for those who wish to learn more about my story (some of which I've summarized in Chapter 1):

- Why We Must Initiate Justice
- Profiles in Rehabilitation
- Write Our Wrongs (I and II)
- Freedom By Degrees
- The Unlikely Success
- Evidence of Long, Lost Letters
- Nagy Notes

This book is really about 'G.A.M.E.':

Gaining A Meaningful Education

Basically, G.A.M.E. is knowledge. Everything we've learned of conceptual value and practical use. G.A.M.E. is the tools that assist us with leveraging circumstances to our advantage. G.A.M.E. is survival skills. G.A.M.E. is what took Jay-Z from the projects in Brooklyn to a penthouse in Manhattan. G.A.M.E. is insight. As Mark Cuban (owner of the Dallas Mavericks) said: "Life _is_ ball." Basically, life is G.A.M.E.

A Lesson on Education

Here is some insight into the root meaning of 'education'. Education isn't just one word. It's comprised of three:

_E_ = A Latin prefix that means "out from".

Duco = A root word that means "to lead".

tion = A suffix that represents the "process of".

Placed in it's root meanings, education is "the process of leading out from".

Kicking G.A.M.E.

To put it in slang terms: G.A.M.E. is know-how. It is guidance. When you reach a certain level of knowledge you develop the skills to lead (survive and progress) in any situation. For example, think of Lebron James. the man has G.A.M.E. on and off of the court.

It has been G.A.M.E. (and probably God's grace) that has allowed me to transform from gangster to guru. From troubled youth to youth advisor. From wild man to wise man. As one man said: "We are given the meaning of things that corresponds with our capacity to comprehend them."

Early in the game I began to see that there was more to life than running around the hood being a terror. To my advantage, I got my knowledge from older men and women. As a result, I got a glimpse of the end at the beginning.

I spoke with the killer who, after succumbing to the lure of crack, wouldn't kill a fly and became a punching bag in the hood. I witnessed the flyest girl that, out of desperation for love, turned into a hood-rat with multiple uncared for kids by various deadbeat dads. I saw the killer testify on his so-called homies. I had, what is called, ball skills (basketball). I had excellent comprehension of street-life, and it helped me to survive. It's why I still have my head while other people have headstones. Not to brag on myself (okay, maybe a little), but I took to the canvas with an understanding rare among my peers. It allowed me to excel beyond them. It wasn't because I had more guns or guts. It was because I had soaked up more G.A.M.E.

I had my mind in the G.A.M.E., and earned the reputation of being a "mastermind". A criminal mastermind, but a mastermind nonetheless. Now that I'm no longer a criminal, I still maintain the mental capacity of a "master". One with the ability to perform at levels, and accomplish things, that others find almost impossible. Like a game master.

Teachers are Leaders

When you are educated, you are equipped. Where others are failing, you have the capacity to succeed. When others are falling short, you have an abundance. When others are down and out, you find a way to overcome.

Education becomes the specialized training for your critical leadership skills. You can lead others out of their own difficulties and problems because you've overcome them yourself. It's the reason you receive G.A.M.E.: to assist yourself and others.

In this definition of G.A.M.E., you are a hero or shero. To others, you can accomplish anything. As we say in the hood: "turn shit into sugar." You make things happen. like all the other people who made the heroes/sheroes list in the introduction. People still talk about you (or your personage) because you've transformed and transcended the mortal into something more immortal; you've become an idea (gangster, soldier, warrior, legend, hero) that is no longer bound by time (read the book 'From Nigga's to Gods' if you haven't yet). This is when extraordinary people (Osiris, say) become legendary and come to be the central figure in myth (and mystery schools of Egypt) and history.

Longevity in the G.A.M.E.

This is all a gangster wants. He wants <u>name recognition</u>. He wants popularity. He wants to be, in a single word: immortal. So they take steps to achieve that:

- Accepting challenges and feats to stand out from others.
- Writing and spray painting one's name everywhere.
- Building a lineage of lil' homies or homegirls to carry on one's name.

(you got guys with lil', baby, junior, and infant homies!)
- Achieving unrivalled status, wealth, influence, and power (like the Mafia before us: Al Capone, etc.)
- After making the team, wanting to lead the team.

As it's said in the N.B.A.: "Make it to the playoffs, you make a name for yourself; win a championship and your name becomes famous." Even if we're not on a great team, we want to be great players. Sometimes the cost isn't worth the benefit, but in order to win it, you know you gotta be in the game. Especially when you find very few other pathways to greatness. Who doesn't want to be great?

Culture Wars

Culture is destiny. The culture, accelerated by the realities of every day life in our communities (that a Hollywood producer can only dream of) simply perpetuates our need to be famous. We try to "play up" (greater than our stature in the world) because society has never given us a good self-image, or relateable model to look up to. We had to repurpose our own lives, against everything else in society screaming that we are nobody!

We have to use our G.A.M.E. to defend ourselves at every turn. It's us against the world!

Word Up!

- KRS1 = King
- NWA = Gangsters
- Tupac = Thug
- Jay-Z = Emperor
- Wutang Clan = Gods
- Rick Ross = Boss
- Outkast = Players
- Too Short = Pimp
- E40 = Gamenologist
- Beyonce = Queen

Our Story, Not His-Story

Taking the game into our own hands, we took control (at various costs) of our own destiny. We created a culture that told the story from our perspective and now we could say, like Biggie Smalls: "I went from ashy, to nasty, to classy." Using our G.A.M.E., we narrated rags to riches stories where someone could actually start from the bottom (think of Drake) and get to the top. "Behind every great start," it's been said, "is a good story."

Just like ourselves, some of these men sat on the stoop and got their boots laced up (educated) by the old heads in our respective neighborhoods. What we learned was similar. To varying degrees though, what we did with it proves different.

The Difference A Name Makes

- California = Homeboys
- The South = Wody
- East Coast = Sun / Son / Shortie
- Bay Area = Folks / Bruh

Words Possess Power

It has been said that, "language is the thing of empires." With our language, we were simply trying to recreate a family (the nucleus of love) that American culture had destroyed. We were attempting to get back to our throne. To rule.

Check List

American History = Slavery

Americas Heroes = Racist

The old heads called us 'Brother' (or 'Blood' to symbolize relationship), regardless of where we were from. They taught us G.A.M.E. to simultaneously help us survive, and retain our pride, as we navigated an enemy culture.

Check List

American Values = White Supremacy

(By now you should know I'm responding to Trump's speech from the intro)

To memorioalize the efforts of those who came before me, I regularly kick around G.A.M.E. to the "loved ones" around me.

The Goal

- Black = Family (Human family, too!)
- Blood = Brother (World-wide Brotherhood)
- Community = Love (Love of all mankind)
- Struggle = Unity (Amongst all people, if you were wondering)

The game has got to change, but first we have to get in the G.A.M.E. Take the challenge!

By: James Wilson

"Do something you expect; but, do it in an unexpected way."

Chapter 3

G.A.M.E.: Incorporating an Educational Component

The following definition of 'education' comes closest to what I view as G.A.M.E.:

Education
1. A method of living
2. Strengthened by experience
3. Broadened by learning
4. Governed by intelligent and judicious thinking

The true meaning of a student-athlete! In the G.A.M.E., always discovering new levels of your potential, and curating your skills. Like Rick Ross writes in his book about being a boss: The boss remains a student and continues to work. Our knowledge and experience will distinguish us!

Game Tight

In this chapter, I want to outline the elements that I believe represent G.A.M.E. Before I do though, I want to quote something about G.A.M.E. I read in the great book "Contagious", written by Jonah Berger:

> "Game mechanics are the elements of a game,
> application, or program - including rules and
> feedback loops - that make them fun and compelling.
> You get points for doing well at Solitaire,
> there are levels of Sudoku puzzles, and golf
> tournaments have leaderboards. These elements
> tell players where they stand in the game and
> how well they are doing. Good game mechanics
> keep people engaged, motivated, and always wanting
> more."

"Contagious" is really about the best ways to spread ideas (like we kick G.A.M.E.). In it, Mr. Berger offers several insightful tips about the value of game mechanics, such as:

1. Increasing internal motivation to achieve rewards (being driven).

2. Interpersonal performance level (how well we're doing in comparison to others; i.e., our status in the group).

3. Elevating one's social currency. Basically, when you're doing well, you look good to others. We gain status because we talk about our achievements, and so do other people (you are hip; the life of the party).

4. We gain leverage (an advantage) that helps ourselves, and others, publicize achievements (like an insider; someone having the scoop on things).

5. Tranformative power - The ability to make things happen when nothing seems possible (the mover and the shaker).

Mr. Berger is certainly on his G.A.M.E., and is why we wisely position ourselves to learn from others. G.A.M.E. recognizes G.A.M.E.! The long G.A.M.E. (the one that plays out over time) requires mentors - teachers with visions - that give us a glimpse into our future.

Five Elements of the G.A.M.E.

My philosophy of G.A.M.E. rests on these five points:

1. <u>Knowledge</u> - You can't play any game, or accomplish anything effectively, without knowledge. Tyler Perry, Lebron James, and Big Meech are some well-informed people. If you want to be good at anything, mastering your craft begins with knowledge. This is why KRS-1 calls himself a king. It is because: <u>K</u>nowledge <u>R</u>eigns <u>S</u>upreme <u>O</u>ver <u>N</u>early <u>E</u>veryone! The king can't rule without power (knowledge). If you want to step your game up, then increase your information intake. Period.

2. <u>Skill</u> - This is the ability to use your knowledge readily and effectively, in execution or performance. It is the learned power of doing something competently (this is straight out of the collegiate-sized Webster's dictionary). Jordan had skills. Kobe had skills. Minister Louis Farrakhan and Jay-Z are skillful men. Have you ever marvelled at the language skills of Martin Luther King Jr. or Malcolm X? They were masters of their craft. So is Farrakhan. Floyd "Money" Mayweather has brilliant boxing skills just as Kanye West does with his business skills. Skill distinguishes us in the G.A.M.E., and puts us in a class of our own (leaders of the pack, right?).

3. <u>Rules</u> - Chaos reigns where there is no law and order, right? Rules provide both legitimate boundaries and meaning to the G.A.M.E. If there were no rules (principles) for truth, we could easily exchange truth for lies. There has to be standards. Without rules, buildings don't go up, there are more car accidents and people killed in them, and businesses cheat their investors without consequences.
Having rules doesn't mean we can't defy expectations, artificial boundaries, or other limited views of ideas or actions. Jordan changed the game and how rules were interpreted by how he played. It is how Henry Ford connected an engine to a buggy (which had always been lead by a horse) and made the first car. Einstein said he discovered his theory of reletivity by challenging an axiom (what others thought to be true at the time).
Don't confuse rules with expectations. We know by the historical record that observation and experimentation has prevailed over the contemporary authority (the "official" version of truth, rules, and boundaries of the day). "There are men and there are masters."

4. <u>Time</u> - The clock will eventually run out on all of us. Time puts us under pressure to get the job done without delay or procrastination. Time also dictates agenda, highlightning what it is we should be doing at any particular moment. Everything is governed by time - games, seasons, growth, and prison sentences! As Muhammad Ali said: "Don't just do time, make something out of it!"
Incidentally, time spelled backwards is emit (emit means to "bring out"). Time places a demand on us to be on our game. To execute; to finish before it's too late. A man plans his work and works his plan. The end game comes through the process of time. Time can help you win or lose the game.

5. <u>Purpose</u> - There is a saying in the NBA: "You can lose with a purpose or you can lose on purpose." Undoubtedly, if you play any game consistently, there will be times that you lose. I am not an expert on sports, but I am aware of a practice in professional sports where teams will lose on purpose in order to secure better players (picks) during draft selection. Unless you're already secure in your career (and just on a team that sucks) you want to <u>live</u> every moment with a purpose. What other purpose is there when we play a game other than to win?

The goal of (the game of) life is success. We want to achieve. It is why we enter any game, and is how we ought to view our lives. The knowledge we gain, our skill-level obtained, the rules we master (or excel at), and the time orientation we organize ourselves around should all be aimed toward a paricular purpose. Perhaps even the purpose for which we are born to accomplish. We are not born to fail. We are here to succeed!

What is Purpose?

One sportscaster, in attempting to define greatness as it relates to some of the greatest basketball players of all time, said: "Greatness can't be defined; but, you know it when you see it." In my humble opinion, unlike greatness, purpose can be defined.

The G.A.M.E. on purpose, as given to me:

1. It is something that you love to do (who excels at what they don't enjoy doing?).
2. It is something that (of course) takes time to master, but you are a "natural" at (i.e., a prodigy).
3. It is something that can bring you a livelihood - an income (even our word "talent" was once an ancient unit for money).

And, if God is your head coach:

4. Fulfilling your purpose will bring glory to your Creator (let your light shine so others can glorify God in Heaven; to quote Jesus).

I guess, to some extent, we all have a "game G.O.D." (Good Orderly Direction). It is the natural order and design of the universe that we have leaders and teachers.

We should pay homage to those who gave us the G.A.M.E. It is why the Negro League was finally elevated to the Major Leagues in baseball. Recognize greatness when you see it! You don't blaze trails without the fire kindled before you. G.A.M.E. is to be told. Pass it on!

By: James Wilson

"If you don't know your history, any history will do."

Chapter 4
The G.A.M.E. Ain't Over

In the Egyptian story of Ausir and Auset (the Greeks called them Osirus and Isis), Ausir is a civilization builder who comes down from Heaven to reveal gifts to mankind (agriculture, writing, art, science, etc.). He has a twin brother named "Set" (or, Seth) and a sister Auset / Isis (mentioned above, and whom he marries). Together Ausir and Auset have a child (yes, through incest - a commonality in ancient times), and they called him Heru (the Greeks renamed him Horus). Like his father, Heru is a protagonist in the story.

Set turns out to be the opposite of Ausir (who is good), and is cast in the story as the personification of evil. Long story made short, Set eventually kills his brother (like Cain did Abel, and the Bloods and the Crips), and Heru then avenges his father's death.

This ancient myth became a story of the fight between good and evil; light and darkness. Ausir in Egyptian mythology was a sun god, a bringer of light. Set, on the contrary, symbolizes darkness. When Set killed his brother (the light) the sun set. The light was overcome (as happens at night) by the darkness. The story not ending there; when Heru rose up and avenged his father's death by destroying his uncle, the light was returned (the sun rose again).

It is from that son - Heru - that we get our word hero: someone who steps up and saves the day. A version of this storyline is written into all of the cultural histories of the world.

Take Note

- For the Jews, it's Moses.
- For the Christians, it's Jesus.
- For the Muslims, it's Muhammad.

We can go down the list:

- Buddah = Hero
- Confucius = Hero
- Quetzalcoatl = Hero
- Spartacus = Hero
- Florence Nightingale = Shero
- Angela Davis = Shero

- Harriet Tubman = Shero
- Martin Luther King Jr. = Hero
- Malcolm X = Hero
- Pacchuco's (in their zoot suits too) = Heroes

I won't waste anymore paper here. You know the stories! When it comes to heroes, there are multidudes..... Okay, maybe a few more: S.D.S., Brown Panthers, Puerto Rican Independence Movement; yes, heroes!

The Egyptian myth - according to many great sistah's and brothah's who reached (researched) back to the motherland to bring us G.A.M.E. into the present - was left for us as an understanding that we would experience a great historical trial (e.g., slavery). It also promised a future that would eventually be bright - kind of like what God told Abraham about his descendants going into a strange land to suffer for 400 years before they would come out with great substance.

It brings to mind a saying like:

"If you want to learn about a culture, learn
its stories. If you want to change a culture,
change its stories."

That is how the enemies changed the game: they tampered with history! This is not some kind of big secret, either. It is why so many people get upset with the 1619 Project (Critical Race Theory) being taught in schools. If the historical record is critically examined and corrected, George Washington wouldn't be the hero he currently is looked upon as. Nor would many historical "heroes". Whoever it is that tells our story is the one that controls our history.

Check List

George Washington = Slaveholder
James Madison = Slaveholder
Thomas Jefferson = Slaveholder
(What about indoctrinating White children, Donald Trump?!)

G.A.M.E. From A Former Slave

"When lions write their own history, the hunters
won't be heroes!"

- Frederick Douglass

How did our ancestors' oppressors become our heroes/sheroes? A clue comes in a quote from Steven Biko:

"The greatest weapon of the oppressors is the minds of the oppressed."

Some Insight Into Stories

I could never list them all, but I do know that superheroes like Superman, Batman, Black Panther, and Wonder Woman were developed by Jews who escaped Hitler's Germany and fled to the United States. The producers and artists of this genre of books used imagery to develop a personage big enough, strong enough, and courageous enough to defeat evil (e.g., Hitler) in the world. Marvel at that!

Story-telling is a powerful vehicle. It is why, when the old heads "bend our ear" with G.A.M.E., they usually set it inside of a story. Here is one of my favorites. Two of them, actually:

The Bird Reluctant to Fly South

"I will tell you a story about a bird. There was once a bird that was always reluctant to fly south with the rest of it's flock. When winter came he delayed, and his wings froze, so he was grounded. While freezing to death in front of a barn, a horse backed out and took a shit on him. Quite naturally, the bird was upset. However, as he sat in the poop, he felt it's warmth begin to thaw out his wings, and he felt life returning to his being. He cheered up, and started singing, but his singing caught the ear of a wolf passing by. The wolf came over and removed the shit off of the bird, and ate him. Not everyone who shits on you is an enemy, and everyone who takes shit off of you is not a friend."

This story was told to a youngster when he first got to prison by an O.G. - an old head. The youngster was Jarvis Masters, who wrote about it in his book "Finding Freedom". He is now on death row (with hopes of getting off!) because of an "alleged" murder of a corrections officer in the 1980's. I think the brother had been a member of the Black Panther Party for Self-Defense. I'll leave it at that (can't expose too much G.A.M.E.!).

The second story was told to me around the year 2000 during my first prison term, at age 25. The O.G. was a Muslim, and wanted to share with me something thought to be conveyed in a speech by Minister Louis Farrakhan. The brother had a baritone voice like the singer Barry White. He almost sang it to me. And, the melody lives on:

The Big Fish and The Small Fish

"See that line right there? At the bottom is
a sharp object called a hook. On the other end
of the line is a man. He is riding on something
called a boat. If you take the food on that
line you'll be snagged on a hook, and that man
will reel you onto his boat. He will hit you
with a stick, cut you open, and throw you into
an ice chest. Later, he'll take you to something
called a house. Once there, he will put you
into another cold place called a freezer. When
he gets hungry he will pull you out, let you
thaw out, and season you to taste. He has something
called a stove, and it produces fire. Next,
he will place you in a skillet on top of the
fire, and cook you. Then, he will eat you. In
his home is something called a bathroom which
has a thing called a toilet. One day, he will
sit on it and shit you out, and you will return
back to the sea, but you'll never be the same.
So, the short cut is the long way home. Don't
take the bait!"

This allegory is a great explanation of how our ancestors got kidnapped and brought to America: taking the short cut. They started trading and dirty-dealing with thieves who had an agenda bigger than they imagined at the time.

Some of the tribes were funking back then. The rivals that they caught (P.O.W.s) they would trade to Europeans for whiskey and guns, which gave them an advantage over their tribal foes. Those prisoners of war would later find themselves on ships bound to America to be enslaved. Later, the Europeans came back and got the sellouts too. Sound familiar?

Check List

- Gangs = Tribes.
- Guns = Trade items.
- Drugs = We'll come to this later.
- Alcohol = Trade items (liquor store on every corner in da'hood).
- Snitches = Sell outs
- Prison = Slavery

Real Talk

In the 1980's, the United States was fighting several wars around the globe, including a war against their own Black and Brown citizens. They were fighting:

1. The Russians in Afghanistan - A good resource about this war is the book "Ghost Wars" and "The 40 Year War in Afghanistan" by Tariq Ali. The math: 1980 + 40 = 2020 (in 2021 the U.S. pulled out of Afghanistan. The war never truly ended. They never left and have secret military forces there to this day). This is how Osama Bin Laden came to fame. It started with the war in the '80s.
2. The Contras in Nicaragua (those "horrible" Commies!)
3. The Iranians through a proxy (Iraq) - The way Sadaam Hussein got into power and who the U.S. later overthrew after he helped fight their enemy (History doesn't repeat itself, but it sure rhymes!).
4. Black and Brown communities - Later called "the war on drugs".

So, how did they kill several birds with one stone (trickery)? Did I say trickery already?

The U.S. was actually funding both the Iraqis and Iranians. They couldn't directly sell weapons to Iran because Iran was under an embargo by the U.S., so the U.S. was using money from the cocaine trade that the C.I.A. and F.B.I. established in Black and Brown communities to buy weapons illegally and have them sent to Nicaragua, and secretly to Iran. A bunch of illegal business that destroyed millions of lives in America, and around the world. Like I said in chapter 1, this is how the gangs went from simple fist fights to all out warfare in the '80s (crack and those evil crackers in Washington D.C., and they're still cracking us over the head!).

Note: Oliver North took the fall for Ronald Reagan (illegal weapons trades) but got a pardon by Reagan's vice president (George Bush Sr.) when he became president.

Changing the Story

In a matter of a decade (from 1970 to the '80s) our communities went from Civil Rights to civil war. During the '60s and '70s we had some of the best sheroes and heroes organizing, protesting, teaching, and fighting the oppressor for our freedom:

- Marcus Garvey
- Elijah Muhammad
- Martin Luther King Jr.
- Minister Malcolm X
- Dianne Nash
- Josephine Baker
- Huey P. Newton
- George Jackson

Then, in the blink of an eye, there was a new set of role models given us to idolize:

- Felix Mitchell
- Freeway Rick
- Bunchy Carter
- Frank Lucas
- Ray Ray Browning
- Doc Holiday
- Supreme McGriff
- Big Meech

The rest, as they say, is history (or tragedy, depending on who's telling the story).

Before these models, our idea of being gangsters came from European immigrants (Mafia figures). This stuff ain't nothing new. Many immigrants came to America and used illegal drugs and organized crime (Lucky Lucciano) to make their "American Dream" (Italians, Irish; no, not Mexicans!). During prohibition, Jack Kennedy (the father of the first Catholic president, John F. Kennedy) was a bootlegger who sold whiskey illegally, using the money to fund his children's academic and political careers. Behind every empire exists a lot of crime. How do you think the forefathers of America built this country?

Check List

- Mass murder
- Stolen land
- Slavery
- War (expansion)
- Military industrial complex
- Prison industrial complex
- Wall street
- Imperialism

They have passed these levers of power onto one generation after the other (a 400-year on-going catastrophe for the victims of the "empire"), and it looks like everything is legit. Now that's gangster! There is an old saying that goes something like: "Kill one person and you're a murderer; kill a million and you're a hero." It's how Andrew Jackson got my elementary school named after him!

It was the government and their police (C.I.A., F.B.I., local cops, etc.) who destroyed and murdered Black leaders and their organizations during the Civil Rights era. Cops! Elected officials! Who does this (I'll let you fill in the blanks)? We need to step our game up, huh?

Body Count Check List

- Leonard Peltier - A.M.I. (American Indian Movement)
- Marcus Garvey - U.N.I.A. (Universal Negro Improvement Association)
- Elijah Muhammad - N.O.I. (Nation of Islam)
- Huey P. Newton - B.P.P.S.D. (Black Panther Party for Self-Defense)
- Martin Luther King Jr. - S.C.L.C. (Southern Christian Leadership Conference)
- Stokely Carmichael - S.N.C.C. (Student Nonviolent Coordination Committee)

• Malcolm X - O.A.A.U. (Organization of African American Unity)

Just take key words from these organization's names to see what they were trying to accomplish (their purpose) to put us back into the G.A.M.E.

- Improvement
- Nation
- Leadership
- Unity
- Self-defense
- Coordination committees

Where is the crime in that?

Stop playing! Get back in the G.A.M.E.! The G.A.M.E. ain't over. The light is well and alive. He who owns the ball (knowledge) owns the game!

Still we rise! (like Heru. And, can't forget: Tupac!)

By: James Wilson

Homework

Juxtapose (compare and contrast) these two quotes:

1) Every criminal is not in prison, and every prisoner is not a criminal.
2) Every saint has a past, and every sinner has a future.

"It is a crime not to increase the quality of life on this planet."

Chapter 5
Take The G.A.M.E. To 'Em

President Biden (America's second Catholic president) recently travelled overseas in October, 2021, to meet with the pope and attend the G20 summit (21 gansters!) with leaders from 20 of the world's most powerful nations in attendance. They all posed, for what is called, a family photo (the Mafia called itself a family too). They met in Rome.

These are O.G.'s (old game!) too. Can you imagine (just try for a moment) the full extent of the crimes represented on that stage? War crimes, war on the climate, war on poor nations, race wars, and more. Whew!

These are the nations responsible for:

- Colonialism
- Extermination of native peoples.
- Capitalism (the Communist countries didn't show up to the G20; i.e., Russia and China).
- Slavery
- Hundreds (if not thousands) of wars.
- Overthrowing countries.
- Robbing poor countries of their natural resources.
- Militarism
- Mass incarceration.
- Invading and occupying weaker countries.
- Using religion to control the minds of people (every major monotheism to one extent or another, depending upon the region).

and this is just the short list! It has been said that, "when business gets too big it becomes religion, and offices become temples."

Comparing Notes

- Roman emperors = Popes
- Roman senate = Bishops
- Senate buildings = churches

When the western Roman Empire fell (476 C.E.), what we know as the papacy (the Holy See) filled the political vacuum in Rome. The pope stepped into the role of the former emperor, and the bishops and delegates occupied the space that was formerly occupied by the senate representatives. The real estate of the emperor, including the emperor's palace (now the Vatican, and the pope's house) became the office of the Knights Templar (I'm slightly joking on this point).

Edicts were dictated from the temple (Vatican) to the European powers. The Vatican basically took possession of the vast resources of native peoples (called "heathens" by the church), sparking European expansionism and colonialism. Christopher Columbus, who worked for the Catholic powers of Spain - the king and queen - was part of this process. The king and queen being under the dictates of the pope in Rome. History may not exactly repeat itself, but it definately rhymes.

Targets

- Africa
- Asia
- Early America; Native America
- Pacific Islands

Clue: Darker inhabitants (those I refer to as Black in this book!).

I know how much Black people like a smiling, nice looking, White man with a comeback story (i.e., J.F.K., Bill Clinton, and now Joe Biden). I can't knock'em for knowing how to play the game, but here are some things about Biden in particular we should remember.

Check List

There is an interesting documentary out about Joe Biden that covers his almost five decades (yes, 50 years) in politics. Unsprisingly, it is called "Empire Politician". the man has been in that game since the 1970's (probably earlier). This goes all the way back to the Nixon era (where the first major "war on drugs" effort began). Here is a short list of some of the things Biden has stood for:

- Biden was for the Espionage Act (but not for foreign spies). The act was used to go after U.S. citizens. So-called leakers, whistle-blowers, etc. The same law President Obama revamped in the 2000's for many of the same purposes.

- He supported U.S. invasions, and coups, in Nicaragua, Grenada, and other poor countries where our country, with great help from the C.I.A., overthrew legitimate governments. We aided in, and looked the other way during, mass killings of citizens of those nations. We then established "puppet regimes". Remember the Contras!
- He supported the bombing of the home of former Lybian president Muammar Qaddafi.
- He voted for the first Iraq war in 1991 (the Gulf War) as well as the second in 2003 (shock and awe). Always remember that no weapons of mass destruction were ever found (a huge justification for the invasion). The intellegence on the war is now considered all a lie. How did Colin Powell, the man to perpetrate that lie to congress and the United Nations, ever fall for that game?
- He half-heartedly supported calling the slaughter of Muslims in Bosnia a "genocide". However, he soon backed off of this statement. After all, the only "real" genocide was the Holocaust, right? Biden is Jewish Catholic? Or, a person of Jewish ancestry who is a Catholic.
- He also supported the invasion of other weaker nations. Nations like Guatemala and El Salvador. Maybe he was a little soft on El Salvador because of the Catholic priest who got smoked (killed) for writing Ronald Reagan and asking him not to supply weapons to the military of El Salvador. Just weeks after the Reagan administration couldn't get the pope to shut that "radical" priest up, he was assassinated.
- He teamed up with segregationist Strom Thurmond on crime bills that incentivized locking up more people (hence, mass incarceration today). History is always in the present.
- He has close ties to banks and other financial institutions.
- He is still against debt relief for students who can't pay off their college loans (the kind of loans, unlike the loans of the rich, that are not forgiven after filing bankruptcy).

I know I went in on the guy a bit here (even as he's trying to clean up his record - second chances, right?!), but at least with open racists and White supremacists - like Donald Trump - we know exactly who we're dealing with. Malcolm X used to say, "it's better to deal with a wolf than a fox." They both want your throat. The only difference is that one comes straight for you (wolf) while the other creeps up behind you (fox).

I think it's time for us to face our enemies head-on and take the game to them. If we don't, they will decide:

- Who lives or dies.
- Who eats or starves.
- Who is employable.
- Who lives where, and in what condition.
- Who has access to the ballot box.
- Who gets to come into this country.
- How America is defined.
- What the truth is.
- Who is entitled to free speech.

As Tupac said, "we can either live like men, or die like cowards." That's a thousand deaths we don't have to give. Instead, remember another line from Pac (from his song "White Mans World": "Get my weight up with my hate and pay 'em back when I'm bigger."

Get your G.A.M.E. up!

By: James Wilson

"Power never changes hands without a fight."

- George Jackson

Chapter 6
A Lame G.A.M.E.

The "so-called" greatest accomplishment of many of the men that I speak with regularly is their record of harming and killing members of their own race and community. These men have (not solely of their own accord) erected a standard of violence as a metric for respect. The more people you've murked (slang for murder), the higher your repute. The American way!

In the book "All Gods Children" the author, Foxx Butterfield, asserts that during slavery Black men learned licentious violence from their only teacher: the slave master. One of the reasons White people believed they had power over Blacks was because Blacks were considered inferior and unworthy of any respect. The Dred Scott case (1857) almost cemented that belief when the Supreme Court, the highest court in the land, procaimed that:

1. Blacks could not be citizens of the United States.

2. Their presence in a free state did not mean that they were free.

3. Blacks, by this very ruling, were not equal to Whites.

4. Overall, Blacks had no rights that a White man was bound to respect.

I think it was Robert Greene in his book "48 Laws of Power" who said, "the smallest dog that loses respect for it's master will attack him." Blacks were more likely to be assaulted on this notion because respect was not their prerogative. Black people had no control over their labor, their wages, their bodies, their families, or their safety. Basically, they were considered property.

Not surprisingly, after slavery was finally abolished in the United States (1863-65), Black people craved nothing more than respect. With their freedom newly won, a "new negro" emerged. One who demanded respect and would fight, or kill, if disrespected. Especially when it came from other Blacks. As Carmello Anthony, the famed N.B.A. star, said, "in Brooklyn they kill you over disrespect; in Baltimore they kill you for sport."

As it was then, so it still is today. Too many Black and Brown men will still kill you simply for feeling disrespected. It is enshrined in hoods and prisons; especially in California. Wars and fights ensue when others believe another person or group has committed an act of disrespect.

The demand for respect (intra-personal respect) is literally killing us.

What we really should be asking ourselves is, what are we actually doing that is worthy of respect? "Who should respect someone with divine potential that behaves like an animal?" Minister Farrakhan once said, "after all, dog is god spelled backwards."

Check List - Are These Worthy Actions?

- Drug dealing and usage.
- Gang-banging.
- Criminal behavior.
- Acting as dead-beat dads.
- Killing our own kind.
- Unemployment as a life-style.
- Ignorance and having no appreciation for education.
- Not taking control of one's community.
- Disrespect of our women (so endemic that it was happening long before Aretha Franklin sang that all she wanted was R.E.S.P.E.C.T., and it hasn't changed since).

The Honorable Elijah Muhammad taught his followers that, "no nation can rise higher than it's women." The standard of respect, according to Muhammad, was how men treated their women. Not their hood, their body count, or wallet size. The highest standard of nationhood is womanhood.

In his autobiography, the infamous pimp Iceberg Slim relayed a story where an old head - an O.G. pimp - taught him about how pimping came about shortly after slavery. During times of slavery, myths about a Black womans sexuality were so prevalent that even the White slave masters would enter the slave pens to sleep with them. This mystique survived abolition, creating a market that Black men were all too willing to profit from (slavery: the "gift" that keeps giving, right?).

Of course, their favorite customers were the people that still largely held all the wealth: White men. So, at the same time that Black men were demanding their own respect after slavery, they offered very little to their own women. Adding insult to injury, to this day, after Black women carried their men's Black asses through slavery, Black men are falling all over themselves for the White man's trophy: White women.

Over 20 years ago an assistant minister to the Nation of Islam told me: "You're never gonna walk away from gang-banging because that is where you believe you get your respect from." Ouch! Charles Muhammad further elaborated: "Why would Kobe, a basketball superstar, leave the sport he's most respected in to go play soccer?" He was trying to expand my viewpoint on respect. That the respect I thought I was achieving was rooted in false beliefs and an unwillingness to change because I was benefitting from my gang status.

This came from a man who grew up in the same community as I had, but didn't succumb to drug dealing, gang-banging, or criminal activity. He worked, took care of his family, and sought to be a pillar in the community. That was, to him, what was worthy of respect. Not the lifestyle I was living that conveyed a measure of respect while requiring no true responsibility. Vic Blends - a 22-year old barber - said it this way: "Give up what's good, for what's great."

Here I was, destroying poor people like myself, and then demanding that they fear and/or respect me like a Machiavellian. By the age of thirty, I had been charged and prosecuted for killing two Black men. The jails and prisons are full of men like myself.

Around the U.S. (and - sadly - in Africa), Black life seems to be the cheapest commodity. Black lives don't matter to too many Black men! We have filled up cemetaries with potential leaders, teachers, doctors, lawyers, fathers, and even presidents. More importantly, we have killed off the very people who, if well informed and organized, could free us from White domination and oppression.

In the book "Malcolm X Speaks", the brother talked about how Black men were willing to shed blood and fight wars for every White man's cause, but how we had no blood to give for the liberation of our own people. That is as true today as it was 57 years ago when he said it. George Jackson, in "Soledad Brothers", wrote about the fear he found in Blacks when he first arrived to prison. A state-of-mind he worked, and died, to transform into one of pride and courage. He didn't give his life for prisoners' rights so you all could just lay down!

This same fear (to fight something other than one's own) was witnessed, and recorded, in Stanley "Tookie" Williams book "Blue Rage, Black Redemption". In it, he revealed an incident when he was left for dead to fight a group of latino gang members on his own while in Juvenile Hall. Abandoned by the very same Blacks that were all too willing to be violent when it was time for Black-on-Black violence.

One of the saddest parts in the book "Roots" (by Alex Haley) was when the big house slave named Sambo was used to hunt down, capture, and return Kunta Kinte to the slave master's plantation every time he made away to escape to freedom. Something similar has happened in almost every planned slave revolt and revolutionary movement in history. One good example of this was written about by Nelson Mandela in his book "A Long Walk to Freedom". In it, he revealed how the gangsters in his South African prison with him, mimicking what they saw on television about Black gangsters in America, sought to intimidate the very revolutionaries (Mandela included) who were in prison seeking to liberate them. Other similar examples include:

Check List

- Gabriel Prosser
- Denmark Vessey
- Nat Turner
- Toussaint Louverture
- Patrice Lummumba
- Jesus
- Malcolm X
- Elijah Muhammad
- Martin Luther King Jr.
- Leonard Peltier
- John Brown
- Geronimo
- Sitting Bull
- Huey P. Newton
- Fred Hampton (See the movie "Judas and the Black Messiah" about brother Hampton's life)
- Geronimo Pratt (different from the above Geronimo)
- So many more....

All sold out by a Judas, the antagonist, of the real heroes and sheroes. The "Sets" of the game (yeah, and your gang set too!). According to F.B.I. reports, there were thousands of informants placed within Black communities during the Civil Rights Movement. Black men and women trained, and sent by, the government to infiltrate, disrupt, and destroy Black organizations. The same organizations working on their behalf. It is a crime to begin with to betray those fighting for a worthy cause. It's the height of betrayal and crime to do it to those working for your benefit.

I have struggled to get older Black men to commit their lives, as they once did for negativity and genocide, to educating young Black men and being an instrument in their transformation. Basically, commit to revolutionary service! Unfortunately, this task doesn't seem to resonate with nearly as many as I would like as much as hurting their own people does.

If I try to kick G.A.M.E. to them, they become downcast or defensive, and say, "oh, there he goes!" Basically, me trying to exhort them to be real men instead of gangsters is too much for them to contemplate. They don't see that they could still be gangsters. Ones that have real power, authority, and run shit!

A lot of these men have life sentences for killing a Black person, and are the most well-behaved individuals when it comes to "obeying the system" (slave syndrome). That is, until it's some conflict that allows them to showcase their self-hatred and glamourize some violence committed against another brother. In contrast, you would think they were "good Christians" in their demeanor towards other races and the authorities.

They have no idea how entrenched this form of complacency and submission is in the psychology of Black people. They are all teeth with others, and frowns against their own. They have, to our disadvantage, no time, no knowledge, and no blood for a worthy cause. They are lames in the game. Buck 'em!

By: James Wilson

"There is another level in the Lakers."

- Kobe Bryant

Chapter 7
The G.A.M.E. Goes On

I am so glad that, every time my mother thought that I did something out of pocket, would tell me, "boy, I didn't raise you like that!" A stand up woman who would fight a bear to defend her children (there were seven of us). We were all unbearable, so she ended up in a lot of "bear" fights!

Growing up in Pasadena (The Valley*) presented some status problems for those of us who became gang members. We weren't Watts, we weren't Compton, and we weren't L.A. property. They called us "Valley Bloods" in order to "other" us as being from the "soft side" of the gangster spectrum. So, when I met and learned stories about those first generation Pasadena Bloods (like Big Lunchmeat, Big Herc, and others) who paved the way for our hood to be respected in the system (jail and prison), I recognized men of their stature as "hood heroes". I knew that I would follow in their footsteps if I ever took up the mantle. This is precisely the burden that fell on my shoulders at 13-years of age in Juvenile Hall. We carry the weight of others because that is what leaders do (sounds like Superman to me!).

Like the Jews, who had Superman and other heroes in the comic universe, we had gangsters in my youth. That were the thought leaders, warriors, revolutionaries, and entrepreneurs of my community. While it was just about inevitable in the early stages of my development that I'd emulate them in the negative sense, now that I'm older, I am able to distinguish the positive principles they represented rather than simply copying and glorifying the harmful practices. It is the same as historians do when they talk about those like George Washington, Andrew Jackson, and Robert Lee. They say that despite their flaws these were "great men".

Growing up in the system, older homies taught us that whatever makes us a good gangster can also make us a good leader. A good father. A good man. The principles like courage, loyalty, and discipline, that is. So, don't knock me for honoring these men (and women).

---

*Pasadena is in Los Angeles County, but is a part of the San Gabriel Valley.

I am proud of who I have become. That I came of age in an era not so far removed from the Civil Rights and Black Liberation era that we still had strong representations of Black men and women in our community, even if they were gang members. They were stand up people who had backbone, and weren't simply about violence. They were diplomats and ambassadors of the hood who kept at bay much of the self-hatred that American culture (racism) had engineered within us.

Unfortunately, the enemy wasn't satisfied with any version of Black strength, so in came more powerful drugs and military style weapons as well as prison and other forms of kryptonite! Let me kick you a story real quick that illustrates my point:

There was once a king who, after succeeding his father, his family ruled their country for over a hundred years. The king decided to celebrate his family's successful reign by throwing a great party. He invited all of his friends and supporters to join in this celebration, but amongst his friends were some of his enemies. They came to kill the king.

They offered him liquor, but he turned it down. He was not a man given to wine. They offered him drugs, but again he refused. His enemies (being wise and undeterred) decided to offer him some beautiful women, which he gratefully accepted.

He went into his chambers with them, and some offered him liquor, which he took. He drank to his heart's content. Others offered him the same drugs he had first rejected, and he gladly took them. Before you knew it, his Highness was high. At his lowest point, his enemies besieged him and his country, and it looked like he did it all to himself!

Remember: we are only as strong as our weaknesses. The enemy will attack where we lack! This is why we can't allow ourselves to be compromised or have interests that can easily be exploited. I see too much of that in the men I mentioned in chapter 6. They are afraid to stand up, thus they will fall for anything less. This is because:

1. They don't want their cells searched (they fear retaliation from staff).
2. They don't want to be labeled as a "Black leader" (it's perfectly acceptable to be a gang leader though).
3. They smoke, or deal, illegal (and unhealthy) drugs or tobacco. This

means they feel obligated to not piss off correction officers by
standing for what is right, as it could jeopardize their ill-gotten
gains.

4. They don't want a disciplinary write-up (if they are targetted).

5. They don't want other races to target them as "Black leaders" (we've
got to shake that post-traumatic slave syndrome!).

6. They are trying to get home to their own kids. All of a sudden finding
the priority after taking other Black men away from their own.

7. They are so deeply in love with some woman (mainly so they can feed
their bellies and put shoes on their feet with canteen and packages)
that they have lost their balls.

8. They have life-sentences and are afraid that they'll lose their opportunity
to prove to the "White man" that they are now good ol' boys. Basically,
afraid to upset the status quo and piss off "da' massa".

They are fully compromised. Weak. Selfish. Cowardly. Like Martin Luther
King Jr. said: "A man can't ride you, unless your back is bent." These men
are bent all over!

I have seen men responsible for killing a small village worth of people
take the stand and testify against their co-defendants. You see them in the
jail clutching their Bibles, talking about family, being good, and going to
church when they get out. No sooner do they get out though, or get a reduced
sentence, that they show up somewhere back in the mix, committing crimes and
gang-banging again.

I am so glad, since I chose that path at one time, that I saw the originals
(original gangsters). It allows me to spot a fake easily. They are trying
to win today's game off of yesterday's score. I was introduced to Black literature
when I was 17 and already in the system. Lessons that promoted pride in my
ancestry, and love of myself and kind. We were asked in one lesson, "who is
the original man?" The answer: "The Black man, the maker, owner, cream of the
planet, god of the universe."

I now had this new image and idea in my head competing with everything
I'd learned up to that point. All my life, I'd been happy being a "real nigga".
Now, someone was telling me:

> "Brother, that ain't who you really are. You
> are really the original man, God's first choice."

Even though I was still, at this time, a rising leader in my gang, I had something else growing inside of me. Getting to the top of the mountain, from the valley, always meant that I had to work harder.

During this period, i "met" (via books):

- Malcolm X
- Dick Gregory
- Elijah Muhammad
- Minister Farrakhan
- Master "J" Man
- Naim Akbar
- John Henrik Clark
- George and Jonathan Jackson
- John G. Jackson
- Cheik Anta Diop
- Huey P. Newton
- Marcus Garvey
- Clarence 13X ("The Father")
- Cesar Chavez
- God (yes, the lady upstairs!)

And, this is just a partial list of the strong, intelligent, and powerful Black men I would learn about that school never introduced me to. We instead learned about all of "their" leaders, and a co-opted version of Dr. King, never receiving any knowledge of other - "alternative" - leaders (at that time they hadn't polished Malcolm X up to make him palatable for public consumption). I had no idea of the existence of any of these men, nor their works and literature.

Having always wanted to be a "Top Dog" (at the top of my game), I now had more role models, and pathways, to choose from. These men were unbought, unbossed, and unbowed. Just the way I conceived of the leadership as a gang member. I now had something positive to look forward to. It was a game-changer for me.

I developed a passion for reading, and teaching, at an early age. It is the reason why, over 20 years later, my G.A.M.E. has become so tight and I got a second chance at life. It is the reason why my G.A.M.E. is still ongoing.

I'm now retired as a gang member. My life didn't end with that script. Honestly, it only recently began when I finally put on the <u>new man</u> (the original man). I'm now working on turning a negative heritage into a positive legacy: going from zero to hero! I have finally discovered my true <u>purpose</u>! It took:

1. <u>Knowledge</u> of self.
2. <u>Skills</u> of mastery.
3. <u>Time</u> and experience.
4. <u>Rules</u> of rulership.
5. <u>Purpose</u> out of pain and passion.

Don't Hate the Player, Change the Game!

Who would've thought, following the George Floyd murder by police, that so many athletes would follow the examples of Muhammad Ali, Colin Kaepernik, and Jim Brown. Leveraging their celebrity, and platform, to become real-life heroes both on and off of the court / field. They boycotted games, repeated the names of victims of police violence (during post-game interviews, rather than discuss their performance), attended protest rallies, donated money to Black Lives Matter (and other) movements, wrote books on social change, took a knee, raised the fist, created new organizations to assist peer communities, developed funds to assist Black businesses, helped at food banks, joined prison reform causes, talked about their own experiences with racism and police harassment, wore apparel with socially significant values and names of victims on them, pushed the athletic industrial complex to do more for poor communities and social justice causes, and the list (like the G.A.M.E.) goes on! They went from playing the game, to changing it!

As Angela Davis said: "You never know when conditions will give rise to circumstances that call for radical change." This speaks greatly to my own journey. I fell on my ass in the street G.A.M.E. It's not how you fall however, it's how you get up!

When talking about America once, James Baldwin said, "it has always been easier to murder than to change." There have been far too many George Floyds, Afghanistans, and electric chairs! America, like any criminal, can change if she wants to.

Take a page from this book. You can be more than just a gangster. You can be a G.A.M.E. changer.

By: James Wilson

Don't put down the gun, just turn it on the right people."

- Naim Akbar

Chapter 8
The Right to Bear A.R.M.S.

During the time that slavery ended, a White abolitionist asked Frederick Douglass (an escaped former slave himself) if the other slaves left behind needed Bibles. His response is classic. Frederick Douglass said:

"No. What they need are guns and compasses!"

Basically, tools to escape to freedom! The gun to get free, the compass to locate a place of freedom (the northern states).

We know that the second amendment of the U.S. constitution was largely established (one of America's best-kept secrets) to:

1. Keep guns out of Black people's hands
2. Give power to local "free citizens" to keep down slave rebellions.

The right to bear arms meant that it was only right for White people to own guns! The gun, no doubt, was a key instrument in gaining America it's freedom from the British monarch (1776), giving the U.S. it's independence. A war also fought by slaves, who were "enlisted" to assist their own oppressors with fighting their enemies.

One of the first people to die in the build up to the war (Crispus Attucks) was a Black man. Yeah, it's true, and Uncle Sam wants you too! (A partial Cee-Lo Green lyric on a Goodie Mob song from 1995: "Fighting for Our Spirit and Minds").

A gun in the hands of Black Panthers for Self-Defense members was much too frightening for the average American. This is the backdrop to the book "Niggas With Guns", written by Robert Williams. A man who had to flee to Cuba because, as an N.A.A.C.P. leader in Mississippi in the 1960's, he wasn't about to "turn the other cheek" (a Biblical philosophy co-opted by the non-violent Civil Rights movement).

He took up a gun and fought against the K.K.K. (Ku Klux Klan), eventually fleeing to Cuba to save his life and his freedom (he had his gun and his compass!). In writing his book, Mr. Williams was just following the advice of Frederick Douglass when he said that we should always tell the narrative of the slave because there are always those to tell the one for the slave master.

Growing up in the Nation of Islam, it's members weren't permitted to carry carnal weapons. The Honorable Elijah Muhammad taught that the greatest weapon we had was our unity. According to him, power didn't grow out of the barrel of a gun (as was taught by the Panters - from Mao Zedong's "Red Book"), but strength in numbers. Numbers and knowledge, to be exact.

One of Elijah Muhammad's students, Clarence 13X, started what is now called "The Nation of Gods and Earth" (also called "Five Percenters"). Clarence came up with a numerological system called "The Supreme Alphabets and Mathematics". In it, each number and letter of the alphabet has an attribute (quality) or character (idea, thing, person, etc.) that it represents. The numbers are as follows:

Supreme Mathematics

0 = Cipher

1 = Knowledge

2 = Wisdom

3 = Understanding

4 = Culture

5 = Power and Refinement

6 = Equality

7 = God

8 = Build or Destroy

9 = Born

And, as they are the focus of the G.A.M.E. I want to impart (and part with in chapter 8), here is the alphabet:

Supreme Alphabet

A = Allah	N = Now or End
B = Be or Born	O = Cipher
C = See	P = Power
D = Divine	Q = Queen
E = Equality	R = Rule or Ruler
F = Father	S = Self or Savior
G = God	T = Truth or Square
H = He or Her	U = You or Universe
I = I or Islam	V = Victory

J = Justice	W = Wisdom
K = King or Kingdom	X = Unknown
L = Love, Hell, or Right	Y = Why
M = Master	Z = Zig, Zag, Zig (Understanding)

Think of it as similar to how some Christians interpret the Bible as an acronym:

[B]asic [I]nstruction [B]efore [L]eaving [E]arth

In the science of life, the G.A.M.E. of the Five Percenters, it would be:

[B]e [I]slam [B]e [L]ove [E]quality
(Basically: peace, love, and equality. "Islam" means "peace")

So, don't ask me if I read my Bible. I live it! In the science of the Five, life is now, including Heaven. We make our Heaven, or Hell (two conditions) with our minds (our knowledge).

Using the alphabet, G.U.N. would be:

[G]od [U](you) [N]ow
(you've probably heard this in a rap song)

So, God (is) you (right) now! God is within you. Not in a book, or up in space (the universe).

You've probably heard Lil' Wayne play on the science in a song when he said:

"I'll shoot you in your [A]rm, [L]eg, [L]eg, [A]rm, [H]ead."

The first letter from each word spells ALLAH: "God" in Arabic and Islam. In the "science of the Five" Allah is the Black man, the God Body, united. In short, our unity and knowledge is more powerful than man-made weapons because it is the power of Allah. The power of God!

America's G.O.D. has been [G]uns, [O]il, and [D]rugs. This is a battle of the G.O.D.'s for sure!

During the American Civil War (1863-65), when Black people were again called to fight in a White man's war and permitted to use guns, one general asked, "can a slave fight?" The response was perfect: "No, but a Black man can!" The difference between the slave and the Black man was knowledge (self-knowledge). Knowledge empowers you. A slave is a tool for someone else. A slave is powerless because he lacks agency.

The slave masters understood that if you taught someone their value -

that they are men with inherent goodness, virtue, and significance - that they would stand up for themselves. They would fight and become the heroes (and sheroes) of their own cause and destiny. They would step up and be the original man / woman of a new dispensation! They would have a G.U.N. (Divine empowerment, now, on earth; not after leaving it) and a compass.

They would be able to use the power in their heads to build with their A.R.M.S. The knowledge of self would free them to do for themselves. They have the right to bear A.R.M.S.!

Break Down

[A]llah [R]uler [M]aster [S]elf

Only after we have truly mastered ourselves can we rule like gods here on Earth! You can bring your Bible, but don't forget your G.U.N. and compass! You have the right to bear A.R.M.S.!

By: James Wilson

Late Note

A compass is composed of North, East, West, and South. Basically, the entire Earth belongs to the righteous, right? The G.A.M.E. is world-wide! It is time to build a better world and destroy the one that is not working for us: poor White, poor Brown, and poor Black people. Don't miss this news (G.A.M.E.)!

THE 9TH CHAPTER

DROPPING G.A.M.E.

"The next level of the
G.A.M.E. is helping others
find their position in it."
                    - James

"I may not rule the world,
but I can teach the mind
        that will."
                    - Tupac Shakur

"You gotta believe something, why not believe in me?"

Part I
Brown Jesus - Pro-Testament

I am sure you have already heard of "White Jesus" or "Black Jesus" in our culture. What you probably have not heard of yet is who I want to talk about: "Brown Jesus". Let's use his Spanish name - Jesus (pronounced 'hey-zeus'). If the real Jesus wasn't Black, then he had to at least be Brown. After all, he was born in the Middle East! Here are some of the things Jesus of the Bible would have in common with Jesus (hey-zeus):

1. They were both born in a manger, below stars (mangled conditions with hope).

2. They both have a long and rich history.

3. They were both born poor, but were descended from royalty. The sons of kings!

4. Both were born with a purpose (promise).

5. Their ancestors had some ties, or interactions with, Africa (Egypt, etc.). Like the Olmecs of ancient Mexico did.

6. They both grew up in their homeland, which was occupied by foreign powers (like Rome over Jerusalem or the United States over California; once a part of Mexico).

7. They both grew up without a father (born of a woman with no present father).

8. Like in Nazareth, he grew up in the hood. No one believed that any good could come out of such a place.

9. Much of his life (around age 12 to 30) was shrouded in mystery because God was working out His plan of salvation for him (This also happens to be the most dangerous age group for Mexican males).

10. They stayed "on the lamb" (the run) from secular authorities, as well as the Creators plan for them. The system and the spirit were both after them.

11. They both were involved in the Ghetto Gospel, also called "The Social Gospel" (social justice). Helping people in need regardless of race, religion, class, or gender. Something like the "Liberation Theology" co-founded by his latino brothers in Latin America.

12. They had many homies (disciples), but only a few "kept it real"

while some were fake (like Judas). Some ran off when it got tough. Some even tried to sell Jesus (hey-zeus) out. They tried to "cross" him up so the authorities could "nail" him. Putting him away for good.

13. God had a plan for them both. He would bring them back anew and transform them so as to be an example for others. They would rise again! They are heroes; saviors! They gave up their old lives to help others find freedom.

G.A.M.E.

The letter 'M' is the 13th letter of the alphabet. It is the number of mastery (or you can say, Mexican!). I grew up representing the "big 13" in the streets. Now I know (for me, anyway) that it has a higher meaning.

Jesus was one man who had 12 disciples (12 + 1 = 13). Jesus was a master teacher who wanted to tranform lives to raise men towards the Godly. Like the ancient Toltecs and Aztecs taught at Teotihuacan (the place where men become gods). The 13 is about self-mastery and cultivating one's lower potential (the earthly man) to reach the highest potential (the heavenly man). It is about elevation and transformation (and one of the reasons that elevators in buildings go from the 12th to 14th floor, skipping 13). It is the number of spiritual mystery. The high science of transcendence.

This is what I think about when I contemplate a Brown Jesus. Making him accessible and a great teacher to those Black and Brown youth who need inspiration for elevation. Find that Jesus within you! Follow in Jesus' footsteps. Sacrifice your life by giving up your old life. Become new and lead others to community and personal fatherhood (we need fathers in the hood!). Pick up your "cross" (responsibility of struggle), and lead others to freedom!

Part II
A Little About Me

I grew up in Orange County, California. My father left when I was around five-years old, so my mother had to raise me and my five siblings (three brothers, two sisters) alone. It is no secret that I was raised in a barrio, or the hood - as it's commonly called.

Prior to joining a gang at age 14 I belonged to a street crew; a pre- 'set' experience that usually preps youngsters before they take the leap into a hardcore 'set'. Less than a year later I got into a hardcore barrio called Los Wickeds Trece (or thirteen), a Sureno gang. It didn't take long before I started getting into trouble and found myself inside the juvenile system. In the "blink of an eye" I transitioned from a kid into a young street warrior. At least, that's what I thought.

My home life was tough. I felt lonely at home because my mom was working all the time, and my brothers and I didn't get along. So, it was easier to go into the streets to find "love", or act out at school to get attention. My soul was starving for what it needed: love, appreciation, and acceptance. Without this nourishment I became aggressive, even taking my lack out on my girlfriend, who I tried to use as a replacement for my mother. Eventually, the relationship became so toxic that it imploded without hope for repair. I regret the damage I caused in retrospect, but I didn't change my behavior at the time.

Eventually, I found my way to the "big leagues". I started by going "in and out" of the county jail until my chances finally ran out and I was sent to prison. Prior to this inevitability, on one of my jail terms, I began re-thinking my tenure in the gang. I didn't like being "taxed" by gang members or being sent on missions to do other people's dirty work. The seed was planted already for my next transition.

Ultimately though, I found myself in prison. Leading up that, I was still acting up and doing wrong out of poor judgement and bad habits. I knew that I needed to fully change. I opened myself up for a new message: The Bible. Of course, I didn't change in an instant. It took time, like all trans- formations do.

This is a part of what God's grace is about: unearned time. While we don't deserve it, He grants it to us, with the hope that we have truly accepted His mercy and we're ready to walk a new path. Complete with a new mindset and practices.

Unlike some Christians, I took God's "second chance" as an opportunity
to take on a radical new educational endeavor. I started reading, not just
my Bible, but history books about my ancestors and the stories of other oppressed
peoples (Jews, African Americans, etc.). This made the Biblical lesson of
redemption for undeserved suffering all the more relevant for my time.

Now I just wanted to help build that world that the Apostle Paul envisioned.
One where there was no Jew or Gentile (racism), no rich or poor (classism)
and no male or female (sexism). A world where everyone could live in peace
and experience equality, in the Kingdom of God, on Earth, as Jesus promoted
during his life and service over 2,000 years ago.

I had not made it to the "big leagues" as an amateur player. However,
I have my "bat" (my calling) now, and am ready to take a swing. The G.A.M.E.
has just begun. I am stepping up to the plate.

By: Gary Figueroa
#BI6643

"Stepping up my game, one step at a time."

Born Again
Part I

I was born on December 29, 1995 in Tucson, Arizona, into a broken home and an unfair system. I was abused by my mother for the hate and anger she carried for my father. I was beaten, tied up, and neglected by the woman who had just given birth to me less than two years prior.

At just one and-a-half years old, a lot took place in my life. My father was sent to prison with a sentence of 36-years-to-life, and my mother lost me and my brother to Child Protective Services over the abuse I had suffered. After being in the foster-care system for a few months my grandfather (mother's father) adopted us so we wouldn't be separated or lost to the system. My brother and I would live with my grandfather until we turned 16- and 17-years old (respectively), but our lives were far from normal. This is my story.

Growing up in my grandfather's house in the late '90s and early 2000's was a challenge, to say the least. My grandfather had about ten other kids besides me and my brother, and we all lived under one roof. Throughout his lifetime Leo B. Thomas (my grandfather) would father 26 children.

Some time in 1998, my grandfather took a trip to New York City. About two weeks later his wife received a phone call. My grandfather had been stopped coming through the airport with over $100,000 in his possession and needed to prove where it had come from. I remember his wife getting all these receipts and ledgers together and taking them downtown. A few hours later, my grandfather was home with a suitcase of money.

At that point in my life, my grandfather was the only successful person I had to look up to. He was a leader in our community. I watched him help people, and give people chances to improve their lives. Shortly after this incident at the airport, my grandfather had a dream that he was living on a big ranch somewhere with his daughters.

All throughout history, some of the strongest community leaders had dreams, visions, or strong thoughts. These thoughts were so powerful that they would make history. People like Martin Luther King Jr. who had a dream to end segregation, Harriet Tubman who dreamed of getting people to freedom, or Genghis Khan who dreamed of united his people into a single tribe. All humans have the ability to form revolutionary thoughts. It is those who imprison that thought upon formless substance that can cause this thought to become reality. In order to achieve this for yourself you must form a clear mental picture of the things you want, then act with faith and purpose every day; transmuting those thoughts into their physical counterpart.

One day, my grandfather went out and bought that big ranch house, along with about 15 acres of land, to live out his dream. When he moved us from the city to the country we all thought he had lost it, but his ranch was another life lesson for me. He bought every farm animal known to man, and then some. He built cages, corrals, and everything else these animals needed to live, by hand. All while teaching my brother and I along the way.

We had to learn quickly, and we did. We now had responsibilities, and the skills to take care of our responsibilities. A few years in, my grandfather started running a slaughter house. People came, bought an animal, and we would kill it, carve it up, and package it for them to take home.

Eventually I started school, and I was one of the smartest kids in my grade. I was placed into the G.A.T. program, which stands for Gifted And Talented. I made the honor roll list every year, always earning straight A's, but I had a problem. I was mad at the world, and I loved to fight.

I got suspended from school every other week for fighting. Soon enough, the principal came up with a solution. He took away my recess privileges, which was where I caused most of my trouble, and made me spend this time in the school library. This went on until I went to middle school.

Since I was suspended so often, I would spend much of that time coming up with all kinds of get-rich quick schemes. I was the kid who, at just eight-years old, convinced our neighbor to pay me $10 per-hour to ride and train his horses. Riding horses was a love of mine from a very young age. It was one of those few things that kept me calm.

I also spent a lot of time with my grandfather's daughters (my aunties), who were younger than me. They were the only other kids I had to play with every day. One day, my auntie Leona got sick, so they took her to the hospital. The doctor prescribed her some medicine, but there was a mix up at the pharmacy. The medication she was given was for a 50-year old man named Leon who had heart problems. She passed away due to a drug overdose.

This loss tore my family apart. Everything following this tragedy was a spiralling plunge into greater turmoil. My grandfather spent a lot of money on her funeral. With 400 people in attendance that day, they held a parade with horses, carriages, and buggies. It was beautiful. After the funeral though, when everything falls back into it's "normal" routines, my grandfather started to have mental breakdowns.

His wife soon began to cheat on him with his own brother. When my grandfather finally learned of this his wife would decide to take their other daughter Anna, drain his bank account, and run off to Texas. This left me, my brother, and grandfather with bills still to pay and no money to pay them.

Although she had taken "everything" from him, it didn't seem to phase my grandfather. He just made a few phone calls, and the next week took another trip to New York City. He stayed up there for almost a month, but when he returned he came with bikes and all kinds of new toys for me and my brother. A few months later, my brother and I would return home from school to a surprise. His wife was back like nothing had happened.

I couldn't believe it. He let her come back after she had run off with $350,000 and his daughter. Even though I was just a kid, I knew that this woman did not mean my grandfather well.

Towards the end of the school year my grandfather and his wife got into a big fight. I remember going to the store with my grandfather that night and attempting to reason with him. I asked him, "Papa, what if she takes all your money and runs off again?" He tore my butt up when we got home for being in "grown-ups business". The next day though, when my brother and I came home from school, he was sitting on the porch with his head down. He simply said, "she's gone again, y'all." All I could think was: "I told your ass."

She got him for over $200,000 this time, but that wasn't the worst part. She had also taken a loan out on his house. This time we weren't just broke. We were about to lose our home.

At the end of the month we were forced to move. The worst part was that instead of selling all of the animals, my grandfather decided to keep them when we had to move to this broken down house. The house was terrible. There was trash piled up inside the house waist high, the ceiling was caving in, and there were roaches everywhere. He told us it was temporary, but that is not what happened.

Once we got settled in and everything cleaned up it didn't seem all that bad. The thing that stood out to me was that my grandfather slept outside in his R.V. It was when we started middle school that I realized that life wouldn't be the same. We didn't have any school clothes or shoes. We couldn't afford anything because all of his money was going to bills and the animals.

We were officially on our own.

I realized all of this pretty quickly, and began enacting my get-rich quick plans. My brother, on the other hand, went to live with my mom. He was her favorite. She wouldn't do anything for me, and I was the youngest. I stayed with my grandfather, helping however I could.

While my brother and I attended the same school, we were living separately. He used to come to school in brand new clothes everyday, while I was always busted up. Luckily, nobody said anything to me because I was known for fighting.

A few years past, and our living conditions only got worse. The roaches took over the house. There were so many that you couldn't go in any other part of the house except the living room, which doubled as my bedroom. We also had a rat problem. These rats were the size of pitbull puppies. They would actually fight with the cats and dogs we had. Their real home was a big tree that was in the front of our house that allowed them onto the roof. My grandfather ended up buying us a BB gun and a cat to take care of the problem.

I could tell that my grandfather felt defeated. He hadn't bounced back like before. In the middle of our school year though, he hooked up with this young white lady. He was around 50 while she was just 24. It seemed like things were taking a turn for the better. He was getting money and making improvements.

One day, out of nowhere, the city showed up and told us that no one was supposed to be living in the house. It had been condemned six-years prior, and was scheduled to be torn down in two-weeks. It turned out that the people who we rented the house from were scamming us for our money. We got all our belongings together, packed them up, and moved them to the empty lot next to our house. We would live in our R.V.'s for about two-years. I was so embarrassed about my living conditions that I would ride the school bus to this abandoned house I had removed the real estate sign from, pretending that I lived there. I would get off the bus, jump the gate, and walk through the front door of the house only to go out the back door and run to the trailers we lived in. I remember bathing in these horse troughs. Cars would be going by as I was inside taking a bath. We had a water hose that stretched from our house to the neighbors. We paid $100 per-month for the use of their water.

Eventually, I began living with my friends. I would ask to stay the night and end up staying for a month. I bounced around from house to house like this for about a year. My grandfather seemed to have lost track of me, not being concerned where I was. He had become hooked on drugs trying to keep up with his young wife.

After not seeing me for a while, they picked me up from school one day, telling me that they had moved. When I went to check it out I noticed that it was better than how we had lived for a while. It was one of those trailer homes like the ones you see on the freeway split in-half, only this one was already missing the other half. The missing side had been boarded up with plywood. I had to admit that the inside was nice, though it did have it's problems. There was no bathroom or water, and with all three of the rooms you had to walk through one to get to the next.

I started at a new school that year, and things started to improve, but we were still broke so I started looking for ways to make money. This new school didn't tolerate truancy and had a sheriff that would come to your house if you didn't show up. So, to make money I had to find a way around this. I eventually found a hustle, but it was far from "the right way".

Whatever may be said in praise of poverty, the fact remains that it is not possible to live a really complete, or successful, life without adequate funds. Every man should have access to all that contributes to the power, elegance, beauty, and richness of life. To be content with less is sinful. The desire for riches is really the desire for a richer, fuller, and more abundant life. that desire is praiseworthy. The man who does not desire to live more abundantly is abnormal, and so the man who does not desire to have enough money to buy all he wants is abnormal. "The science of getting rich."

Part II

Growing up, I was always a leader. Whenever I got into trouble my teachers would tell my grandfather, "Mr. Thomas, your grandson is very smart and all the other kids follow him, but he just has to change his attitude." I never followed their advice, but the words always stuck with me.

I never wanted to be in a gang. I never even really thought about it. All I cared about was getting paid enough that I could get some new kicks and clothes for school. When I was in the 7th grade however, I had had enough of poverty. I wore some of the worst clothes you could imagine, and shoes far too big for my feet. One day, I decided to start breaking into houses. Not for jewels, guns, or any of that stuff. I did it to steal the clothes of kids that I knew had all of the fly clothes my size.

After a few break-ins I was feeling fly, until one kid at school put me on blast. I was wearing his shirt that even had his initials on the tag. After this incident I threw all of the clothes away, but I did keep the shoes. I also broke in a few more houses, but would only steal the piggy banks and any actual money I found. After a while I came up on enough money to get new clothes for myself.

One day, I was talking to this kid that went to my school who was in a gang. He told me that he wanted to break into his neighbor's house to steal some of the guns they had. I ended up telling him about my own expertise in this area, and that I would go with him. That weekend we broke in and grabbed my usual while my new friend was taking guns, jewelry, and a laptop, placing it all into backpacks.

When I asked him what he was going to do with his stuff, he told me that his "big homies" would buy it from us. This was good enough for me, so I did the same thing. Once we sold everything, we had profited nearly a thousand dollars. After this, it was all down hill for me. I would break into a house, get everything of value, and take it to my friend who would walk to his homies' to sell it.

Eventually, after one break-in, my friend wasn't home. So, I walked down to his big homies' by myself to sell my stuff. One of the guys tried to take my stuff and tell me to leave, but I told him that he could either pay me, or me and him were gonna fight until I got paid. I was young, but he saw that I was serious and respected it. It wasn't that he was afraid of me. He could have easily whooped my ass, but the way I presented myself made him respect me.

I ran around breaking into houses until I was 14. One day, I was scoping out this older cat's house when I saw him leave. Being in my line of work, I quickly decided to break into his house. He lived so close to me that I took trips back and forth from his house to mine. I was cleaning up! On my last trip, I ended up running into my homie from school. He asked what I was doing, so I told him I was just passing.

Two days later the O.G. Sticcs came to my house while I was outside trimming the weed I stole from his house. I was about to run into the house, but it was too late. He confronted me and said his little homie told him that I broke into his house. He told me that if I didn't have all of his stuff he was going to mess me up. Now, I had all of his stuff, but I damn sure wasn't going to give it back. So, I rushed him.

I was 12 years-old fighting a 40 year-old man, and he was tearing my butt up. The next day, I went to school like nothing happened. I had a black eye, a busted lip, and bruises everywhere. After school I was walking home when a car pulled up on me. It was Sticcs and about four young guys about three years older than me. They all were about to jump me, but Sticcs told them to fight me one-on-one. We went around the corner, and that's what we did. After it was over, he told me that he wanted his stuff back. I just walked home.

the next day after school there they were again, waiting on me. Sticcs made me fight every day on my home from school. One day, I beat the breaks off of one of the guys. The next day that guy came to my school with a gun. When we saw each other on my way home that day, I thought that he just wanted to fight. He pulled out the gun instead and pointed it at me. My heart skipped a beat.

This incident seemed to have flipped a switch in my mind. I started looking for guns in the houses that I broke into. I collected as many as I could and carried them to school in my backpack, all while waiting to see this dude again (as it turned out, I wouldn't see him again until high school). When I told my grandfather what happened he just said, "you don't need them guns," and walked out. I took this as a sign that I was on my own.

At school I had a clique of friends that became really tight. We weren't a gang, but close enough to it. Whenever I spotted anyone waiting after school we would all go and fight them.

One day I had an issue with a young hispanic kid at school. I beat him up real bad and got suspended. The next day, the hispanic kid's homies jumped one of my friends at the community center. A week later, I saw the guys who jumped my friend, so I approached them. There were about eight or nine of them, and I told them to follow me down the street. When we got their I punched the closest person to me. I had my little cousin with me, so he hit another one. For some reason the other guys didn't want to fight, so we jumped the guy I had punched while everybody else watched. When we started kicking him he pulled out a knife and stabbed me in the stomach.

My shirt just started gushing. I remember leaking blood everywhere. I had a 3-inch cut into my stomach pouring blood, and I thought that I was about to die. I walked around the corner to my homey's house and laid down in his front yard. Everyone ran outside and started screaming. I could hear his sister saying, "Lil' Wino, don't close your eyes." I told her, "I'm alive. I'll tell y'all when I'm dead." The last thing I remember was my homey Big Ace holding my stomach, trying to keep the blood from coming out, then I passed out.

I woke up in the hospital with tubes everywhere. When my friends snuck in to see me I pulled all of the tubes out, and we left. When I got home, my grandfather had all of my stuff packed. He told me that I was going to live with my uncle in Hemet, California. It was the biggest mistake he made with me.

When I got to Hemet I would learn quickly that my uncle didn't care what I did. I already smoked weed, so he smoked with me. I started bringing my friends out there, and the next thing I knew we were tearing the city apart. We broke into everything with a lock. By age 14 I had my own car, I had guns, and I had a large chip on my shoulder. Going from living with my grandfather, killing animals, and fighting to survive, the city life was like a video game to me. There was nothing I wouldn't do.

One day, I went to the mall with my homeboy, and when we were walking out a car pulled up. It was two hispanic dudes calling us niggers and yelling. I had a 9-shot .22 on me. I pulled it out and started shooting into their car. When they pulled off, I ran. I hit a few gates, but I got caught by Hemet P.D. They took me to juvenile hall, and I did four years because they coulnd't find who I was shooting at.

I got lucky, but juvenile hall was a whole new ball game. While I was there I ran into some of Sticcs' young homies. Everytime I did, I would beat them up. I served my time and built a reputation for myself. By the time I got out my clique of friends had become a gang.

We had a little get together with all of my old and new friends the day I got out. While we were sitting in front of my apartment, some of the guys I had beat up in juvenile hall walked up with the same guy who had pulled the gun on me a few years back, but now he was huge and I knew I wasn't going to be able to whoop him anymore. He called me out, but when he did all of my friends told him, "you know we don't give heads up." He backed down from the rumble, but told us that it wasn't over.

When I started school that year I had to go to the continuation school because I had been in juvenile hall. Luckily, all of my friends also went there, as well as a few dudes I did time with. My first day at school I got into trouble. I slapped this kid for staring at me. Of course, he didn't like it, but I wanted to get suspended.

After school he and his friends were following me and mine to the bus stop. I remember that we hid our gun in the bushes down the street from the school, so I grabbed it. My homey Lil' Ghost asked to hold it, so I gave it to him. When we were walking by Carl's Jr., Ghost ran over to the hispanic kid I had slapped and shot him in the head. We all went to jail, but Ghost got charged with murder. He's currently awaiting execution on death row for the crime. Two days later my homey Lil' Chopper shot another kid's dad in the head right in the parking lot of our school. He's also currently awaiting execution.

I stopped going to school after these incidents and started hanging on my block with my homies. One night, we went to a party where we ran into some of O.G. Sticcs young homies and the guy who pulled the gun on me. After the party, me and a few of my homies went to my house. When we started walking to the door a few guys jumped out of the neighbor's bushes across the street, shooting at us. This started a ten minute shoot out between us. When the smoke cleared I had been shot three times by two different guns, and two of their guys lay dead. We were literally ten feet apart. My friends took all the guns and ran.

After I got out of the hospital my life became nothing but gang activity and revenge until I could pull my mind out of the ignorance. Even while I was in the life I still used to read books. I would wonder, "what's the point

of all this?", but it didn't stop me. I just justified it to myself as me
simply being "different", or "weird", but certain books interested me. I read
this book called "The Art of War" about Alexander the Great. In it, his father
doubted him, but he went on to head one of histories most successful war expeditions.
I always related to him because I felt that the world similarly doubted me.

Part III

When I was 17-years old I would often be at my grandfather's house, helping him harvest his plants. Back then, my grandfather and a few of his friends had bought a six-acre property with three houses on it and a water well so they could grow weed. At this time, my grandfather was growing marijuana legally. He had over 1500 plants that were over 15 feet tall and produced about two-pounds of bud each.

I watched my grandfather and the other two gentlemen, which were his business partners, make moves that were always carefully calculated and precise. None of these men had ever been arrested or incarcerated in the 30-plus years they had been in the game. I was helping out my grandfather one day when his business partners pulled up to join us. One of them told me not to leave when I got done as he wanted to talk to me, so I waited for them by his car.

When he came out, he told me to take a ride with him to his house. The whole time we were in the car we were talking about me stepping up to help my grandfather in the business more. When we got to his crib and he told me, "I got something for you," I was thinking he was about to give me some money, drugs, or something like that. When he came back though, he had a book and a tablet in his hands. The book was 'Think and Grow Rich', and the tablet had a Youtube channel called 'Found Treasure' on it that was all Bob Proctor, Napolean Hill, and some other like-minded people giving seminars and other videos of people reading then explaining one of their books.

At first, I thought, "What the hell; this is some bullshit," but he told me that if I learned what these men were teaching that I'd be unstoppable. It took about three months for me to even start reading that book and watching the videos, but when I did everything made sense to me. Unfortunately, I was using all this newfound powerful knowledge to perfect my gang life instead of using it to truly prosper.

The purpose of nature is the advancement and development of life, and every man should have all that can contribute to the fulfillment of his life. When I was young, I not only watched the cycle of life in my community, but was a part of it. I remember a family that, when I was 18, lived on my block and comprised four generations living in a single apartment. I didn't understand this because I had lived on my own, in my own house, since age 17. What stood out the most to me was how the great grandmother had lived in the county all of her life, bouncing from one apartment to the next, getting evicted apartment after apartment until it was time for the next generation. I noticed how they all did this, and how it continued with the kids that were my own age. I realized that life was too short to be in such a constant - unchanging - cycle.

If you take a look around at your community, and the people in it, you will inevitably find this cycle. If you find that this cycle is in your own family, destroy it. These cycles occur because people in our communities are content with what the state offers us for free, which is survival at it's lowest level: food stamps, section 8, SSI, etc. We all live in these common neighborhoods that we call our sets, blocks, or hoods not because we choose to, but because we're being manipulated and coerced into these cages called apartments and these corrals called projects, complexes, and ghettos.

These cages and corrals are no better than the slave quarters our ancestors had to endure for hundreds of years. The only difference is that we take pride in being in bondage while our ancestors fought, and gave their lives, to escape poverty, injustice, and torment. Our ancestors fought for us to survive so that we could focus on living. Cages, Corrals, and pens aren't living. It's time to stop being content with less and push to only accept the best.

The problem is that we lack knowledge. Our knowledge determines our position in this world. Our knowledge, and how we apply it.

After playing in the streets for a few more years, not being content but being stubborn, I found myself serving my first prison term. I could have easily avoided it, but my heart and love for my homies got in the way. Being imprisoned made me realize what was truly important to me: family, kids, and my success. I needed to achieve something I could pass on to my kids and family. I wouldn't ever want my family to be a part of the gang life. The criminal life I lived.

I started to change slowly, I gained certificates for skills I need to start my life on the right track. My biggest problem was not having the knowledge to combat my obstacles and adversities properly. When I hit a brick wall I jumped out of the car and went into survival mode when I should have backed up and repaired my car. The consequence was another prison term.

This one has been the wake up call I needed. I've sat in prison
reading and gaining knowledge, perfecting plan after plan until I had my
nuclear weapon to take my family to the promise land. The first step was
to test it out. To do this, I used my already gained (and now growing) skills
to gain legal money in prison, monopolizing the game to help me and my family,
all while continuing to gain knowledge. I've perfected the things I've learned
until I could take my skills to a bigger and better field, with more opportunity.

I knew that before I got released, I needed to make some money to
parole with. I had to start my life over from scratch. I knew a couple ways
to get paid fast, but I wasn't willing to accept the consequences of those
actions, so I stuck to what I knew was legal: taffy. I could make some money
if I made enough, but it's a hard process. One day, my brother told me about
this hustle he does selling candy bars and bags of food. Once he explained
it to me, I was instantly intrigued.

The next day I tried my luck, and it worked! Now, all I needed was
some candy bars. Once I ordered my candy I went to work. I sold as much as
I could to acquire thousands of dollars for my release. I didn't want to
get released and be a burden on anyone. I'm a man, and it was time that I
started acting like one.

Once the money started rolling in I was able to do so much more.
I would send my kids birthday presents. I would help with bills. I felt wonderful
stepping up like a real man is supposed to. I paroled with $11,129.27 in
my account.

The greatest lesson I've learned is that I had to grow up and act
like a man should, not be a burden to my family. One has to want to step
up and take care of their responsibilities to succeed in this world. That
$200 in food stamps the government provides for us is not living, it's just
bondage. Understand that this $200 is the same amount an inmate in prison
is allotted to live off of from canteen each month.

It's time to wake up. Can't you see that they're killing our communities?
They make sure that we barely survive because they don't want us to truly
live.

Some of our lives are like receiving a puzzle without a box. If
you have no image to build from, you start with the edges until you piece
together the right image. In my life, I've struggled. I started my life on

the edge committing crimes, being a gang member, and going in and out of jail until I finally found what kind of image I wanted for myself. It took me 14 years of my life to realize what was important.

I remember when I used to sit on the block with my homies and it still seemed like I was alone because what mattered to them didn't matter to me. the things I liked were weird to them. It took this (final) trip to prison to meet James Wilson to receive this lesson: "You can be in a room full of people and still feel alone."

Part IV

After what felt like decades of violence, incarceration, hustling, and committing crime, I finally did the hardest thing in my life. I left the gang that I had given everything to. Enough was enough. I didn't see the light in my lifestyle. All I saw was the destruction and pain we caused everywhere we went.

During my 10-year sentence I did a lot of thinking. I thought about my five kids, and how they needed me. I thought about the two strikes I got, and how one slip up, even in prison, could get me a life sentence. I also thought about all of the lives lost in the chaos. When I summed it all up, I began to wonder how things could be if I lived a normal life instead.

I knew what I had to do, but my heart didn't outweigh my old loyalties, so I kept participating in nonsense on the yard. The worst part was that I started much of the nonsense myself. Eventually, my own people turned on me after all I did. They turned on me, and it hurt. Not the physical part, but the betrayal by people I felt I had paved the way for in the streets.

After going to the hole with a broken nose, two black eyes, busted lips, and a few stitches, I knew it was the end. I knew I had to let go of my old lifestyle. You always see in the movies, or read in urban books, wild endings to these things. But, reality often doesn't play out that way. I had a choice. Give it up or die, and I had too much to live for.

Once I finally gave it up I cried, but I told myself that I would put all of my old energy into being a man that my family could really be proud of instead. Making the necessary changes became one of the hardest times in my life. I had a lot of work to do.

The first thing I did was drop my gang ties. This meant the language, the signs, and the way of thinking. It was hard for me, but once I got my mind settled in I started praying.

When I was a child my father taught me how to pray, so I started trying to get back to what I knew was right. I started going to religious services. As I learned more and more about Islam, I even comitted myself to a study course. I slowly did the work that should have been done long ago. Of course, I ran into some hurdles along the way.

My biggest obstacle was school. I never finished high school, so I signed up for the High School Diploma program at High Desert State Prison (H.D.S.P.). I got in after about two months, and that's when my first conflict arose.

I had two assignments that overlapped: a Re-entry program and school. When I asked the Re-entry program director if I could leave early on Wednesdays to go and test at school, she was totally fine with it. Unfortunately, when a man named Robinson found out, he told me that the Re-entry program was more important than school and had me removed from school. My only option was to wait until I completed the Re-entry program and re-sign up for school, but the High School Diploma program had been cut by that time. The only program that was offered now was for a G.E.D., so I signed up for that. I was just 20 credits away from my diploma, and with the G.E.D. program I would have to start from the beginning. It sucked.

I signed up anyway, but I found out that the wait list was long. There were guys who had been waiting for years to get into the program. As I waited to get into the G.E.D. program, I knew that I had to find another way to get out of prison faster (earning a G.E.D. also takes six-months off of your sentence). I knew that if I kept my nose clean I could get a behavioral override to a lower-level yard and get my time out, so I stayed out of trouble.

After I got to the lower-level yard I immediately wrote to education to get into the G.E.D. program. To my surprise, these lower-level yards didn't offer any education except for college, so I was screwed.

Eventually, after gaining everything I could from the lower levels, I knew I had to make a move that would get me back to a yard with the G.E.D. program. Once I got back, I started pushing hard for the education program to get me assigned. I hit a few brick walls, then I found out about this volunteer program that was supposed to get people ready for the G.E.D. test, so I got into that program just to have a way to take the test quickly after I got into the G.E.D. program itself again.

I hit more walls. There were people taking the test, but I was at the back of the line because I was new. Eventually, I came up with the idea to get the counselor involved. I asked and pleaded with her to get me assigned to education. Two weeks later, I was assigned.

Once I got in, I did all I could to prove to the teachers and tutors that I was more than ready. Every test I took I blew out of the water. Once they saw my test scores they put me on the list to take the G.E.D. The only problem I had now was that the G.E.D. testing wasn't going to take place fast enough as I was to be released. This just gave me another task. I needed to convince the testing coordinator to let me test before I left.

One day, he brought me in for the pre-G.E.D. test. I let him know my situation, and he told me, "let's see how you do first with this test." I took all four G.E.D. pre-tests and got some very high scores. I stayed back to wait for everyone else to leave and spoke to the test coordinator again. I asked him how he thought I would do on the real test, and he told me that he didn't see any reason that I wouldn't pass. He brought me back the next day for the real test, and I knocked it out with some high scores.

I could tell that he was surprised. After we got done talking, he told me that we would take the last two tests the following week. I passed these as well just two weeks away from my release. I finally had my G.E.D. It took me almost eight months of jumping through hoops to get it, but finally I was going home with it to start my new life.

A phoenix is a mythological bird that consumed itself by fire and rose renewed from it's own ashes. I destroyed my life with ignorance and games. I burned my life to the ground. I was tried by fire, yet I rose from the ashes of my self-defeat.

Having run into men like James Wilson and Donel Poston; men who I was raised listening to these crazy stories about, changed me. They changed me as I saw them change. I watched them make amends for the evil they have done in their own lives and help young men like me change my own. It's my hope that I can do the same for others.

By: Anthony Thomas

Step Your Game Up

My idea of game is having knowledge. Not only having it, but applying it with the appropriate force, or finesse, needed to achieve an intended result. You can only be successful if you know what is necessary to achieve your goals and how much is necessary to situate yourself, not saturate yourself. Power can be both brutal and gentle, solely dependant upon the circumstances. So, when I think of game, I think of versatility and a person who can turn his/her process towards success from brutal to gentle as easily as a pendulum swings.

It's sometimes difficult to describe who I am as a person and what has led to my accumulation of game. I have come to realize that I'm not the gold that comprises the ring, but more the diamond that it encases. I don't say that to say that I am valuable. Quite the opposite.

It's my belief that I am invaluable to society in the same way that we all are. Each person has something that only they can bring to the table; their perspective. Our perspectives are unique, creating a view of this world that, if seen collectively, would be a beautiful amalgamation full of understanding. The reason I define perspective as relative to a diamond is because a diamond's brilliance - it's colors and clarity - are not revealed in it's natural state. The beauty of a dimaond only comes to light after it has undergone many cuts, generally a human process. Our every experience has cut (diversified) us in much the same way. Just like each diamond is unique, so is each person. A great stone can shine in the dark with even the slightest luminance, and bring it beauty.

Personally, my experiences (both good and bad) have shaped my game. My knowledge has earned me many titles. Some not so endearing. I've been called an opportunist and manipulative. It is terms like these that have stunted and destroyed the dreams of countless youths when applied incorrectly. The human psyche loves labels - to categorize people and things.

In order to have game you must also have confidence in yourself and your actions. Along with confidnce you must have self-esteem, respect, and trust, just to name a few. Your perspective shapes your personality, making you who you are. If you don't have the aforementioned qualities, how can you apply your potential? Without self-respect, how can you trust yourself? If you don't trust yourself, how can you believe in yourself? These are things we must instill in ourselves before we can be successful. What we in the culture call "game tight".

Everything you do must be conducive to your ultimate goal. If that's not true for you today, you need to change your daily habits. You will always have those who don't share your vision, and that's fine, but if you are not hyper-focused nearly to the point of tunnel-vision, you will be derailed. So, if you lack, get on track.

Build up your trust in yourself with small victories. You can cultivate self-respect by taking care of your body with diet and exercise. Your self-esteem could be boosted simply by reading self-help books, or having insightful conversations. You have to test yourself and challenge your values. You have to know why it is you do what you do. You have to have purpose. In this life, you will lose many more times than you will win. You have to know that when you lose you didn't lose your chance, you lost your turn. The table keeps turning, however. It will be yours again.

It has been said that, "you miss every shot that you don't take." In other words, we can't succeed if we don't try. Having game is about being prepared. Oprah Winfrey once said, "success happens when opportunity meets preparation." Everything we do in this life leads to the next thing in it.

With the exception of those elements outside of our control like sickness, accidents, tragedy, etc., we are in control of our own lives. With game, you can minimize those uncontrollable elements and eliminate those self-imposed derailments. Stay prepared. Turn losses into lessons. Turn wins into wisdom. Don't allow life to push you around. It's only okay to go with the flow if that flow is headed towards greatness. If not, it may be time to make waves. Your life is your story. Who could write it better than you?

The more game you have, the more you'll be able to see through those things that truly do not matter. Let your knowledge guide you. Let it be your compass. Never allow yourself to believe you know enough so you continue to learn from everything.

It wasn't until I was nearly 30 that I learned to be gentle and use that as a form of power. My wife taught me this at a point when I wasn't sure what would work to further our communication. You can even learn invaluable lessons from a baby. Too many times I thought that I had it figured out only to have to pivot on a dime in order to avoid a collision.

Practice humility and accept advice, and in the end you will be wise. You gotta learn before you can earn. It's not accumulation, it's appropriation. Slow feet are better than no feet. After all, it's not a race, it's a marathon.

A recurring theme of life is that if you knew better, you'd do better. So, accumulate that knowledge. Step your game up!

By: Darnell "Deezy" Dorsey

Embracing A New Game

I grew up in Pasadena, California. I was raised in the projects, a low-income housing unit, where most residents were poor families living in strife, many torn by violence. I am the youngest child of my parents, my family affectionately calling me Fatts. I'd later be called Lil-D Fatts in the same streets that eventually claimed my young life.

When you are young - especially when living in a challenging environment - events seem to happen fast, and your understanding of these events are typically severely lacking. Somewhat like a jig-saw puzzle, a kid has to put things together slowly, and in piece-meal sessions. For me, the picture that began to emerge consisted of many puzzle pieces of various strange white men that would frequent my mother's room and her many suspicious transactions with people who'd show up at our home at all hours. These activities, though criminal in nature, were (and are) every day methods of survival for many single Black mothers in the projects. They did whatever it took to make ends meet and help their families survive unemployment and poverty.

My family didn't have much. New clothes and shoes were scarce, so my brother and I had to go for prolonged periods with the same old clothing and footwear. This meant that our poverty was on public display. The embarrassment pushed me to engage in criminal acts before I was even a teenager to assist my mother with providing for us; a move that deeply upset her. The day I handed her $600 she scolded me. "Where'd you get this from?!," she yelled. "Don't start doing this type of shit, Chris."

Without question, she knew that I had offered her ill-gotten gains, and despite her own poverty demanded that I return the money. At the time, I was confused because I thought that I was helping the situation. Looking back now, I know that it was like holding up a mirror to my mom and reflecting both her own wrongdoings and our utter deprivation back at her. Poverty engulfed all of us; man, woman, and child. It does not discriminate.

With my youthful confusion and ignorance, by the age of 13 I had already stepped past the realm of my mother's authority and control, falling into the streets with a vengeance. I started indulging in gang violence and gun-play. I soon found myself going in and out of Juvenile Detention centers. Before it was over I would spend many of my teen years in state custody.

Miraculously, I did attend school during the time I did spend out on the streets. There were teachers and other mentor figures who took an interest in me and wanted to see me succeed. Though I listened with my ears, my eyes were always to the streets. Being a leader, I leveraged this position and skill to my advantage. I had other youngsters following me and looking up to me for all the wrong reasons.

Besides school, the streets, and my misdirected following, I turned my anger into a passion for music. My secondary weapons became my pen and a composition book. I learned to vent my frustrations on heads and paper. My talents for music and mayhem honed my reputation among my peers, and just as the song: "We did it out way."

My mother grew increasingly concerned with my life-style through my teen years. She repeatedly asked me, "why did you go down this path?" At the time, I had no solid answer for her. I didn't want her to feel like my choices were her fault. That her inability to provide for me the way I desired forced me to go out and get what I wanted for myself. Basically, I had chosen the easy way out.

While at school I played sports, just like so many young, angry, Black kids. Sports were another outlet for my rage, and I was good. The street life would compromise my scholarship to Clemson though, sealing my fate. I ended up in prison with a 12-year sentence and two strikes.

Looking back, I realize that I have never been to a beach or an amusement park in my life. My childhood was lost to the streets, along with my football scholarship. While in prison there have been no letters or pictures sent in from my homeboys. I, like many other incarcerated gang members, am out of sight and out of mind. I have learned that the street's "cons" far outweigh it's "pros". I made an investment into a lifestyle that yielded nothing in return.

I've lost family members and friends to the street - to the hood - only to be virtually forgotten. I realized early in my prison sentence that I couldn't, in good faith, repeat this process upon release. I've seen how it would inevitably end if I did, so I've decided to save my own life and love myself while there is still time. This pushed me to start hitting the books, expand my knowledge, and begin perfecting my craft (music). If I had another shot at life, I'd bet it all on myself. At least I know I'd show up for me!

Instead of putting in work on (so-called) enemies, I've decided to work on myself. I've learned along the way that, instead of being a thug or gangster, I was a Black king. I've begun to see other Black men and women as kings and queens as well, rather than all the negative images I'd been fed about my own people. I now see our value and our worth as human beings.

My new education and thought-patterns has given me an opportunity to use my leadership and gifts in a positive manner. Today I try to lead people towards what is good; what is right. It has all come full circle for me, and I encourage you to give yourself a similar chance to come-anew. I'm finally back in the game and moving the ball (my goals) forward. Can't stop, won't stop!

By: Christian Smith
BF7444

Religion-Outside-The-Box
Portland, Oregon 97212

June 2022

In religious communities we use the word *redemption*.
We use it lightly.
We don't speak about it often.

Redemption happens only seldom.
Very few regain possessions or clear their debt.

Unlikely successes.

The authors on this book are unlikely successes.

How blessed the world is that they not only have been redeemed, but that
they have shared their accomplishments with us in this book.
So that we can be inspired, lifted up.
Redeemed.

I am a better person in this world having read this book.

-Rabbi Brian
rotb.org

Why We Must Initiate Justice Paperback – March 31, 2021

by James Wilson (Author), Kenneth Washington (Author)

Initial Justice was become one of the more prominent criminal justice reform advocacy groups in California, claiming among its members incarcerated persons as inside organizers.

This book is inspired by their groundbreaking work, containing essays on advocacy, education, and freedom by those most affected by systemic racism, poverty, and mass incarceration. This work proves that unjust laws and prisons may stifle bodies, but they cannot suppress voices of freedom.

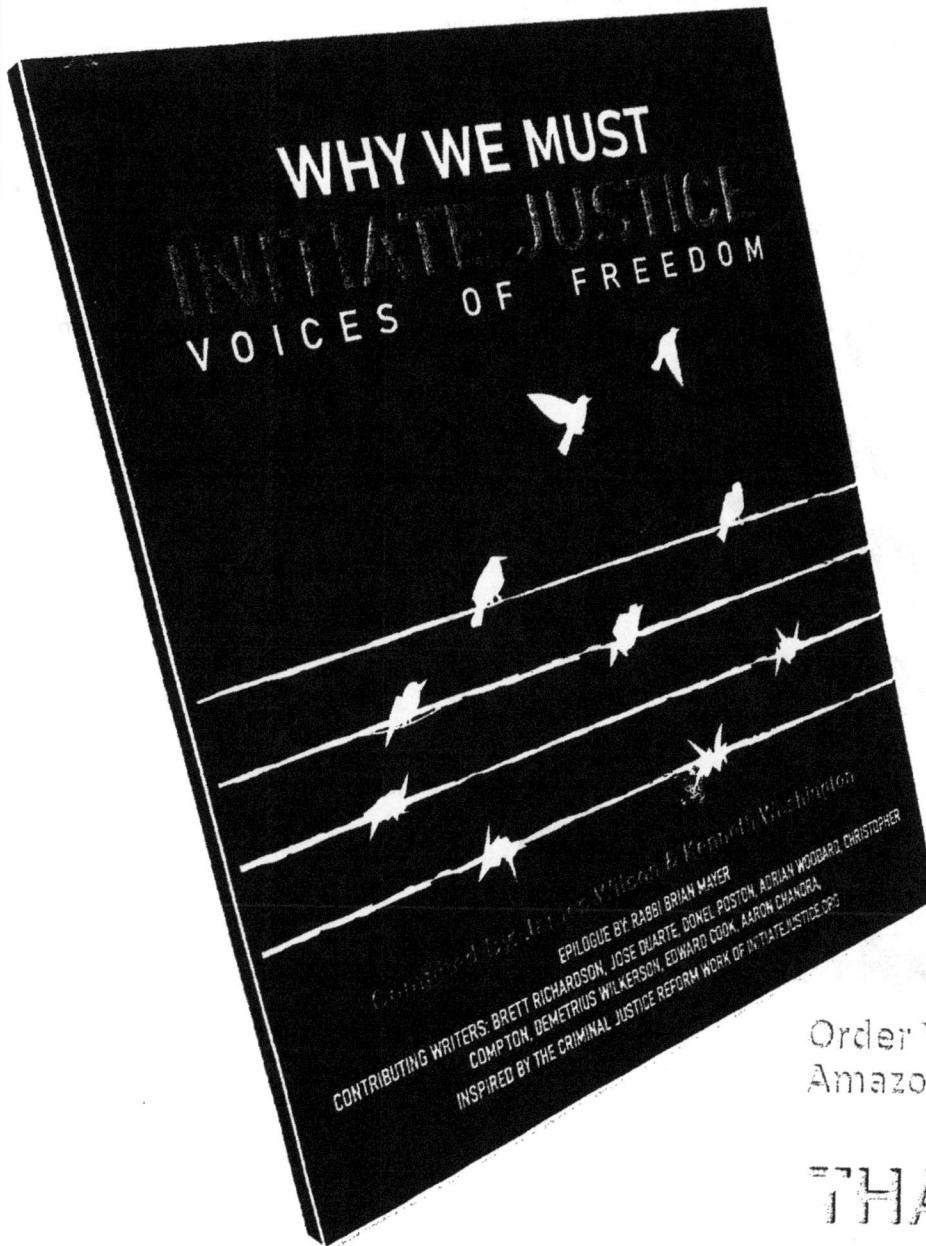

Paperback $20.00

Other sellers & formats   >

Buy new: $20.00
Get Fast, Free Shipping with Amazon Prime

FREE delivery. **Friday, June 18** on orders over $25.00 shipped by Amazon. Details

Fastest delivery: **June 16 - 17**

◎ Select delivery location

Available to ship in 1-2 days.

Qty 1 ▾

🛒 Add to Cart

▶ Buy Now

We Must Initiate Justice!

Order Your Book Today on Amazon and Help Support Our Project!

THANK YOU!

amazon Hello
⊙ Select your address

All ▾   write our wrongs   🔍

Write Our Wrongs: Letters to Victims, poems, and short stories Paperback – August 15, 2020

by Donel Poston (Creator), James Wilson (Creator)

Share ✉ 📘 🐦 📌

⊙ **Buy new:** $20.00

FREE Shipping   on orders over $25.00 shipped by Amazon or get **Fast, Free Shipping** with Amazon Prime

Arrives: **Dec 1 - 3** Details

Fastest delivery: **Nov 25 - 29**

Usually ships within 2 to 3 days.

Qty: 1 ⌄

🛒   Add to Cart

> See all formats and editions

Paperback
$20.00

1 Used from $15.79
6 New from $14.95

THIS BOOK IS A GENUINE ATTEMPT AT REDEMTION.

With the increased attention on prison reform and rehabilitation, the message of transformation has reached deep into one of California's most rigid and violent prisons. This work is a **true** testimony that change is possible, even for the worst offenders. *Write Our Wrongs* gives each of us an opportunity to express our remorse for criminal activity and find a pathway to atonement.

Copyrighted Material

Write Our Wrongs

LETTERS TO VICTIMS, POEMS & SHORT STORIES

A WRITING PROJECT FROM PRISONERS IN HIGH DESERT STATE PRISON CA
CREATED BY DONEL POSTON & JAMES WILSON
INSPIRED BY SHAKA SENGHOR'S WRITING MY WRONGS
Copyrighted Material

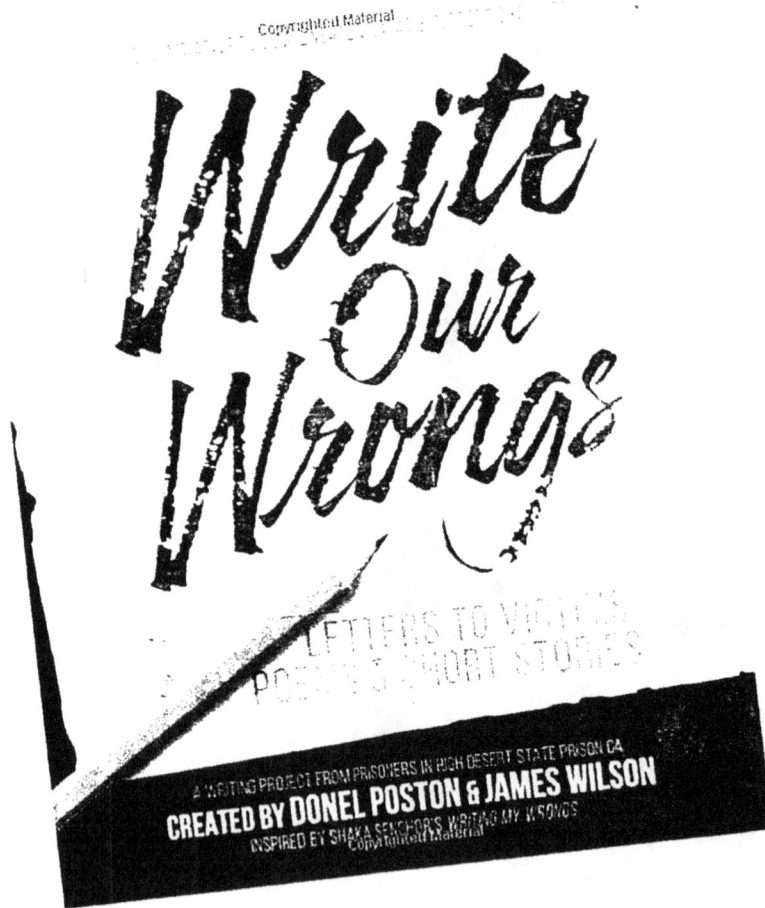

There are some people who belong in Prison and I am one of them. The Streets wanted me dead; the cops and my victims families wanted me on Death Row, hoping the State would kill me via lethal injection some day.

During 15 years of incarceration I have sought to redeem my soul and justify my reason for being, fully embracing the mercy - the undeserved kindness - God has granted me.

James Wilson

**Cofounder of
"Write Our Wrongs" Project**

Order Your Book Today on Amazon and Help Support Our Project!

THANK YOU!

www.ingramcontent.com/pod-product-compliance
Lightning Source LLC
Chambersburg PA
CBHW080618030426
42336CB00018B/3012